Best wishes

Bill Cunningham

CASTLE

The Story of a Kentucky Prison

by

BILL CUNNINGHAM

McClanahan
Publishing House

Cover design and book layout by James Asher Graphics
Senior Editor, Gloria Stewart
Cover illustration from postcard photograph
published by Walter Martin, Eddyville, KY

All book correspondence should be addressed to:
McClanahan Publishing House, Inc.
P. O. Box 100
Kuttawa, KY 42055

(502) 388-9388
1-800-544-6959

McClanahan
Publishing House

Dedication

This book is dedicated
to prison guards everywhere,
especially in Kentucky.

There is a castle on a hill.
In my dreams it comes and goes—
Light in dark, dark in light;
What it means, I do not know.

Chapter 1

⬚⬚⬚

Eighty-year-old Mitch Cunningham made his way up the steps in front of the Kentucky State Penitentiary in Eddyville, Kentucky. It was January 21, 1993—clear and cold.

It had been almost seventy years since, as a ten-year-old lad, he had made the same long trek up the massive stairs which led into the mouth of Kentucky's only maximum security prison.

On that morning of October 3, 1923, Mitch was at home with his mother in their small frame house just outside of the prison wall. He was running late, "slacking off," as he would later put it. His older brother Perry had already left for school.

There was a knock at the door, and a prison guard informed him and his mother that his Dad had been shot in a prison disturbance. No definite word was given on his father's condition. His mother could not face up to the situation. Little Mitch was sent to check on his father

Seven decades later, the old man now made his way up the steps, his white hair twitching in the winter breeze sweeping across Barkley Lake. He was possessed of an energy and agility which belied his years. His warm and gracious personality was endearing. He was hard of hearing and spoke loudly.

At the front gate, he was greeted warmly by Warden Bill Seabold. The massive metal door slid open, operated electronically from the control center located inside the lower hallway. Mitch and his two relatives stepped inside.

As the four moved down the corridor toward the second gate, he turned and pointed to a room off to the right. He matter-of-factly related what he found there on that frightful autumn morning seven decades ago.

Amidst chaos and confusion, little Mitch had been led to a stretcher on which lay a body, covered by a sheet. They pulled it back so he could see his dead father, shot four times in the chest and once in the leg.

Slowly he had been led out of the prison. He was still only ten years of age, but now much older.

⌗ ⌗ ⌗

It was shortly before 11 p.m. on October 2, 1923.

Hodge Gregston Cunningham was only minutes away from his forty-third birthday. He quietly closed the door behind his sleeping wife and two young sons, and headed out into the clear and mild autumn night. The temperature hovered around sixty degrees.

The slumbering village of Eddyville was dark, with the exception of intermittent street lights which cast pale circles upon the pavement. Calvin Coolidge had become President of the United States upon the death of Warren Harding in August; and the people of Oklahoma were trying to impeach Governor J. C. Walton.

In Berlin, political upheaval and confusion reigned in the Reichstag as Chancellor Stressman came under fire from both socialists and communists—planting seeds for the eventual rise of the little paper hanger from Vienna.

Most people were whistling and patting their feet to the popular tunes "Tea for Two," and "Yes, We Have No Bananas." Vincent Youmans' highly successful musical "No! No! Nanette!" was taking New York by storm. The movie to see was "Covered Wagon."

In nearby Paducah, the people of that town were enthralled in the trial of insanely jealous Henrietta Wagner, charged with the dynamite murder of Rosetta Warren, the wife of the object of her affection.

Baseball season was winding down. The New York Giants, led by a young hard-hitting Casey Stengel, were on their way to capturing the National League pennant. They would face the cross-town Yankees, led by Babe Ruth, in the fall classic. The Bronx Bombers were finishing out their first year in Yankee Stadium.

Just below the hill where Hodge strolled, the scenic Cumberland River slid silently by. The newly constructed lock and dam built by the U. S. Corps of Engineers, at a cost of over one million dollars—a gargantuan sum in those days—was just a few weeks from being placed in operation.

Whether any of this came to the mind of Hodge Cunningham that evening is unknown. He was on his way to work the graveyard shift as a guard at the Kentucky State Penitentiary.

While the little burgh of 900 residents snoozed in the darkness, the monolithic form on top of the hill sat brooding over the town. Lights from within its massive stone walls filtered out into the night through the long and narrow apertures.

From the medieval-like fortress came the midnight sounds of captivity—the clanging of a metal door, the short yell of a prisoner, the hum of electric lights—the low growling of a monster at rest.

On this fateful night of Hodge Cunningham's last shift, the prison was already over thirty years old. Its existence had arisen out of Kentucky's dark and bloody past.

※ ※ ※

In the untamed days of old, when pathfinders were leading early settlers into the vast and rugged western portion of what was then Virginia, law and order was a personal concern.

The area that became Kentucky was governed by the criminal code of the Old Dominion. As a matter of practice, the code had limited influence. Whether a malefactor was hanged most times depended upon the character of the accused and the temper of the crowd, rather than the formalities of law.

With Kentucky statehood in 1792, came a more meaningful attempt at establishing and enforcing some kind of uniform criminal sanctions. Jail houses and stockades sprang up throughout the wilderness—but no prisons.

Without a penitentiary in which to incarcerate the more serious offenders, the Commonwealth adopted a very practical if draconian approach. The state simply made the death penalty the punishment for most felonies.

This changed in 1797, when Kentucky revamped its criminal penalties and all but did away with the death penalty, reserving it for only one crime—murder. Immediately there was a need for a prison.

In 1799 it was constructed in a low swamp area near what was then the governor's mansion in Frankfort. From then, for about 80 years, the state's penal system was largely ignored. Due to this neglect, by 1875 the Frankfort prison was a disgrace.

The walls encompassed about five acres of poorly drained and ill-kept grounds. The facility consisted of a chapel, hospital building, workshop, infamous hemp houses for making rope, a five-tier cellhouse for men and a smaller one for approximately thirty women, and a variety of ugly shacks used as smokehouses, bathhouses, and latrines. Almost one thousand men lived in the poorly-ventilated, inadequately-heated and filthy quarters.

The unheated bathhouses contained only two large tubs in which several inmates bathed at the same time. Almost a dozen would wash—if that is the right term—in the same dirty water.

Their diet consisted primarily of rancid meat, clammy corn-bread, and scorched and unsweetened coffee made from chicory. A local farmer insisted that he witnessed the skinning of a cow carcass, which had been lying in the field for two days, and the meat taken to the prison kitchen. Scurvy ran rampant, due to the lack of vegetables.

Inmates were required to stand for roll call each evening out in the uncovered prison yard. Their rain-soaked clothing would often freeze in the cold and unheated cellhouses during the winter nights. The following morning their garments would be stiff. The hapless criminals slept on ticking mattresses filled with straw, and were given a couple of cotton blankets.

The authorized punishment was the whipping of inmates and bones were sometimes broken.

Working conditions were deplorable. The most despised assignment was to the hemp houses to beat out fabric from the weed. This awful place of choking dust irritated the eyes and throats, and caused a variety of pulmonary and respiratory disorders.

Within a two-year period, a prison physician reported that three men chopped off their hands with hatchets, five cut off one or more fingers, and two slashed their arms—all to escape the hemp house. A former inmate poignantly proclaimed, "God wither the arms that built that room."

The prison was operated by a private keeper, or lessee, who simply rented the institution and its residents from the state. It was a system ladened with corruption and abuse.

First of all, the lessee or "keeper" was appointed by the legislature. This led to all kinds of political feather bedding and influence peddling.

The keeper had complete control over the prisoners—feeding, clothing, and housing them. He also hired guards and maintained order. The inmates worked at varied jobs to include production and bagging of hemp rope, construction of chairs, tables and other household items.

The profits, after covering the costs of the prison operation, went into the keeper's pocket. Naturally, the lessee increased his profits by cutting corners. The facilities and inmate welfare suffered.

It was a lucrative business, up for contract renewal every four years. And it was a tidy little way for the politicians to keep prisoners out of sight and out of mind.

In 1879 Jeremiah South began his fourth consecutive term as lessee of the Frankfort prison. There was probably not a more popular man in Frankfort than this 68-year-old native eastern Kentuckian.

A member of the politically potent Democratic Central Committee, he lavishly courted the legislators with cheap board, free laundry and drinks. He even presented them with gifts of walking sticks, cedar chests, and other inmate crafts.

Needless to say, he had a tight hold on the lawmakers. The legislature had repeatedly rejected any proposals for change in the penal system that did not meet with South's approval.

Then upon the scene came Luke Pryor Blackburn, destined to upset everyone's apple cart.

Blackburn was a Woodford County native, receiving his medical degree from Transylvania University in 1835. Nine years later, he entered politics and served in Kentucky's House of Representatives for two years. He then abandoned politics—and Kentucky—and moved to Natchez, Mississippi in 1846. He became particularly interested in yellow fever and established successful quarantines throughout that state.

The Kentuckian served the Confederacy during the Civil War, which included an unsuccessful effort from the Magnolia state to infect Northern cities with yellow fever. He was charged by the Union authorities for conspiracy to commit murder, but was never brought to trial.

The indictment only served to endear him to the hearts of most pro-Confederacy Kentuckians. He returned to his native state in 1872, a legendary figure. His reputation was enhanced even more by his subsequent battles against yellow fever in Memphis, Florida, and Hickman, Kentucky. By 1879, Luke Blackburn was a 63-year-old Southern hero.

It was a time for Confederate veterans to shine. Throughout the Commonwealth, at camp meetings and political picnics, the old men of the Gray were first in the hearts of Kentuckians. They gathered at reunions, wearing tattered old uniforms, and proudly exhibiting stumps for a leg or an arm—speaking tearfully of Shiloh, Vicksburg and Chickamauga. Politically, their time had come. So, in 1879, they picked their man.

After many years on the front lines with disease, sickness and death, Luke P. Blackburn was persuaded by his many Confederate friends to run for governor. He easily won the Democratic nomination and rolled over Republican Walter Evans in the general election.

Blackburn came to the office of chief executive as a doctor first, and politician second. Thus, when he saw the wretched condition of the state's prison, located virtually across the street from the governor's mansion, he took action.

First, he began to issue pardons generously to help alleviate the overcrowding. By the time the legislature met in December, he had pardoned fifty-two men and boys confined to prison. This was met with loud and bitter criticism from the public.

The dedicated physician was impervious to the blasts of the disgruntled public. In response to one scathing editorial which chastised his liberal pardoning policy he retorted, "no little eight-by-ten backwoods newspaper would deter him from doing what was right."

In his message to the 1880 General Assembly, he challenged the lawmakers to take arms against the "great college and university of crime."

His proposals were bold and simple. He called for the abolition of the leasing system of the prison; ole Colonel South and his friends threw up a wall of protest.

Next, he asked the legislature to employ a full-time physician for the penitentiary.

In what would be a standard and recurring plea from Corrections until this very day, he asked that the monetary limit for felony theft be raised, so that more offenders could do their time in workhouses and county jails instead of the state prison.

Last, but certainly not least, he called for the appropriation of money to construct a new "branch penitentiary."

"Let us abandon," he eloquently pleaded, "a policy which is based on abasement and cruelty, and whose only marks are degradation from the moment the wretched convict dons his striped zebra suit, until he emerges from the prison with hope forever blasted and manhood forever crushed."

Maybe to simply put things off, or perhaps out of genuine response to the governor's leadership, the legislature appointed a committee to investigate the prison and report its findings.

Whatever its intended purpose, the committee's report had an enlightening and sobering effect on the General Assembly. It told of convicts confined to the hospital who would be dead by spring. In the grim report was news of over 200 inmates unfit to work, poorly drained and malaria-infested grounds, accumulated filth, overcrowded cellhouses and unwholesome food.

Shocked by what they heard, other investigations followed. The sordid facts, known to a few earlier, soon became common knowledge and pained the conscience of even the most hardened lawmaker. Public sentiment began to shift in favor of Blackburn and his humane efforts at prison reform.

What followed next was an interesting and ultimately fatalistic development of political intrigue. It had become clear that drastic change was needed. At the same time, politics would not go away.

The governor and his growing number of supporters wanted the leasing system abolished and the beloved Colonel Jeremiah South out of a job. A warden system of governing the prison was being advanced and most agreed it was an idea whose time had come.

But Colonel South had to be protected. Too many people owed him. Besides—leading legislators argued—his contract would not expire until 1883. It could not be broken.

But, the reformers urged, he could be impeached and removed by the Senate—an unlikely possibility, given the popular lessee's political leverage.

So the battle grew fierce and by March the state's leading newspapers had joined the fray in favor of Governor Blackburn.

The influential *Courier Journal* said that the state should feel proud "on having an executive who knows his duty and dares to do it."

Then an incredible twist of fate took place and which could only happen in Kentucky where "politics is the damndest."

Under growing and devastating fire from his detractors, the supporters of South decided that he should appear in person before the legislature and defend himself.

This he did on the morning of April 14, 1880, to an overwhelming and enthusiastic crowd of legislators and onlookers. In the midst of the splendid reception, he gasped and fell over dead.

The capital was frozen in shock. Both houses of the General Assembly adjourned until after South's funeral. For five days flags flew at half-mast and adulating eulogies were given. Finally, at one of the largest funerals ever held in Frankfort, the old prison man was laid to rest. For all practical purposes, the political crisis surrounding prison reform was over.

When Colonel South's body hit the marble flagging of the historic old capitol building that spring morning, down went the last stumbling block to eliminating the private keeper system for corrections. The issue of privatization of prisons would not surface again for a hundred years.

Only days after the death of South, the General Assembly passed and sent to the governor the centerpiece of his prison reform agenda—the abolition of the lessee system and a long-range plan for relieving prison overcrowding.

The new laws provided for a salaried warden to run the prison. They also authorized the appointment by the governor of a committee of three to study other prison systems in the United States and select a site for a new branch penitentiary.

To serve as a short-range stop-gap relief of prison overcrowding until a new facility could be built, Governor Blackburn reluctantly agreed to the contracting of inmate labor to private industry.

The "contract system," howbeit under a state warden, replaced the lease system. It sounded good in theory.

A contractor, such as the railroad or some other public work, would pay the state a flat fee of twenty-five thousand dollars a year. In return, the employer would receive the services of five to six hundred convicts and the responsibility of housing and feeding the felons.

The departure of the criminals from within the walls of the prison would help alleviate the overcrowding. And, to the liking of the general public, the state would be making a profit from their labor.

Some contractors, such as manufacturing concerns, were allowed the use of state facilities. They came into the prison and ran the workshops.

In practice, the idea was a disaster. Inmates were exposed to more inhumane conditions than they had experienced in Colonel South's confinement. It was under this arrangement that inmate abuse reached its worst, including self-mutilation in order to avoid the unbearable "living hell." Convicts sent outside the walls begged to be brought back into the prison—now known as the "Black Hole of Calcutta."

What was worse, the contractor of the outside work wielded all the power. Private employers did as they pleased, threatening to renege on their agreement if pressured, and dump the hapless pawns back into the overcrowded prison, already filled to the brim.

Kentucky's first and only physician governor was left with two weapons to fight the unacceptable situation. He continued—to the chagrin of the general public—his lenient pardoning practice. And he moved on with his plans for a branch penitentiary.

※ ※ ※

The committee to locate a suitable site for such a facility consisted of three highly respected and influential citizens representing a geographical cross section of the state. They were former Congressman R. H. Stanton of Maysville, editor and Judge William M. Beckner of

Clark County, and former Confederate General H. B. Lyon, of Eddyville.

Unquestionably the dominating member of this group, by reputation and personality, was General Lyon. He came from a distinguished lineage. His grandfather, Matthew Lyon, had been a personal friend of Thomas Jefferson and James Monroe and had fought in the Revolutionary War. His public service included serving in the U. S. Congress both from Vermont and later Kentucky, after he settled in Eddyville.

The General's uncle, Chittenden, had served for eight years in Congress as a Jacksonian Democrat. In 1854 Lyon County—with Eddyville its county seat—was formed and named in his honor.

Hylan Benton Lyon was born in Eddyville on February 22, 1836. Orphaned at an early age, he attended Masonic University in LaGrange, Kentucky, when he was fourteen.

In 1852, Hylan received an appointment to West Point, where he graduated 19th in his class in 1856. He was commissioned a second lieutenant and stationed in California and the Washington Territory. On April 30, 1861, he resigned his commission and joined the Confederate army.

During the Battle of Fort Donelson, just a few miles down river from his hometown of Eddyville, he was captured by the Union forces. In September of that same year he was released.

Lyon made brigadier general in 1864 and took part in many well-known battles including Vicksburg, Battle of Chattanooga, and Battle of Brice's Crossroads. He was engaged in the Franklin and Nashville campaign during the latter part of 1864.

It was during the latter stages of the war that he became famous as a daring and swashbuckling commander by burning several west Kentucky courthouses to keep them from falling into Yankee hands. He spared the one in Eddyville, reportedly because he had a close relative sick and confined to bed in the house next door.

After the war, fearing Reconstruction retribution, he spent a year in Mexico. He then returned to Lyon County to farm and share in the resurgence of political power enjoyed by Confederate veterans. His appointment to the prison commission by Governor Blackburn was just another example of the "good ole Confederate boy" practice of the day.

If the appointment of the trio was primarily political, its work was certainly a matter of substance. The charge of this panel was not merely to find a location for a new prison—although that was its primary mission. But Blackburn envisioned the commission as an agent for change.

As a visionary, many years ahead of his constituents, the governor not only wanted another home for convicted felons, but he also wanted to usher in a new and enlightened concept of penology.

The cornerstone of his prison philosophy was the "Irish System"—so known for its place of origin. It was based on the idea of graduating imprisoned criminals through different levels of treatment.

The first level would consist of hard labor and solitary confinement. Through good conduct, obedience to prison rules, and repentance, the convict could earn admittance to the second level.

At this plateau, he would labor on public works outside the walls, receiving religious training and schooling. As he continued to behave and reform, the felon would receive expanded privileges and rewards.

Finally, the prisoner would progress to the third and last level. Here he would be released under supervision, or—if he did not have a home or employment—to special boardinghouses for newly-freed convicts who needed shelter and guidance.

Of course, all of this today is standard fare in American penology—classification, parole, and halfway houses. At the time of Blackburn, it was science fiction to the mostly rough and unschooled people of Kentucky.

The commission was no band of fools or buffoons, but an educated and enlightened group of men for their day. Inspired by their leader, they enthusiastically responded to the challenge.

They traveled extensively. Their first trip was in June, 1880, to visit the Ohio State Penitentiary and they ironically concluded that it was controlled too much by " the fluctuation of Ohio politics."

At the Conference of Charities and Correction in Cleveland, they heard of the latest concepts in penology.

Then the commission toured institutions in Massachusetts, New York, Indiana, Illinois, and Tennessee. In the state of New York, they observed firsthand an adaptation of the "Irish System" of prisons. The commission agreed with their governor. The three-level progressive classification of prisoners made sense.

It was their recommendation that such a system be adopted by Kentucky. But to do so required an additional prison.

So, they turned to the second responsibility of their charge: find the appropriate place for a new branch penitentiary. To find the right spot, they had to understand what type of facility would be built.

It was decided that a massive stone edifice, like the one at the new reformatory at Joliet, Illinois, would be their model. Availability of building stone thus became one of the top considerations in searching for the right site.

After much thought, the commission hired a Louisville architectural firm, H. P. McDonald and Brothers, to assist them. It was the job of this consultant to evaluate various locations in the state, prepare plans, and give estimates of the cost for the construction of a new prison.

By 1880, the little village of Eddyville, Kentucky, was home to about 600 people. It already had an impressive past, and was one of the oldest settlements in the Commonwealth.

The town was settled by David Walker, a Revolutionary War veteran in 1798. One year later it was designated as the county seat of Livingston County—which at that time encompassed a large chunk of west Kentucky.

Lying on the north bank of the Cumberland River, the town received its name from the large eddies that swirled in the passing stream. It was a beautiful site, nestled in a fertile valley and in the protective lap of high ridges which overlooked the town. The hills in the area were abundant with timber and iron ore and plenty of limestone rock for building stones.

One of the first settlers of Eddyville had been Hylan Lyon's illustrious grandfather, Matthew. In addition to his political prowess, he also became the leading businessman of the town, to include the operation of a shipbuilding yard during the War of 1812.

When the Civil War broke out, Eddyville sided heavily with the Confederate cause. In addition to General Lyon, the community produced Cobb's Battery, a Confederate artillery unit named for Robert Cobb of Eddyville. It gained recognition for its exploits at the battle of Chickamauga.

During the War Between the States, Willis B. Matchen of Eddyville served as Kentucky's representative to the Confederate Congress in Richmond, Virginia. So avid were the southern sympathies, that the few who had been Union supporters had to take refuge after the war in a new settlement being established two miles down river, called Kuttawa.

Needless to say, when the commission went prison hunting in 1880, ex-Confederate General Hylan B. Lyon was king in this far western Kentucky community.

Eddyville wanted the prison.

The iron industry, which had flourished in the county during the earlier part of the century, was now all but dead. The devastation of the Civil War had not only obliterated many iron buyers in the south, but it also eliminated the much needed slave labor. Finally, cheap Pennsylvania steel sounded the death knell for iron.

Although river trade was still booming at that time, it basically just kept the town alive. The promise of Eddyville becoming a major trading center had passed upstream to Nashville, and downstream to Paducah.

The railroad did not bring prosperity. And it took away as many passengers as it brought. A new prison would bring jobs, and families, and a necessary economic boost to the sleepy, little burgh.

Not hurting the cause at all was State Senator William Stone of Lyon County. He was a Confederate veteran who gave up a leg in the lost cause. Needless to say, he put his political shoulder to the wheel as well.

The urban centers of Kentucky—Covington, Louisville, and Lexington—showed little interest in the new prison. The battle was waged on the western front.

Approximately 125 miles east of Eddyville, but still in back country of west Kentucky, the promising and much larger town of Bowling Green made its bid. The proposed prison site in the Warren County seat was on a bluff overlooking the Barren River, three-fourths of a mile from the center of town.

Served by both the river and the busy Louisville and Nashville Railroad, this area was blessed with an abundance of brick clay, limestone, and other supplies needed for the construction of the prison. Since the town was larger, and not as remote as Eddyville, there would be a much greater supply of skilled craftsmen and mechanics. More supplies and special machinery were available in the town.

The costs of constructing a prison at Bowling Green would be much less than at Eddyville.

In spite of these factors, and incredibly, the Louisville consulting firm gave its nod to Eddyville. It cited the shortage of coal near Bowling Green as a critical disadvantage, since this fuel would be the source for heating the new facility. The engineers also stated that the heavier-populated town would be more disrupted by the "sojourning of released prisoners within its borders."

There were a couple of much weaker reasons given. One was that a prison vegetable garden at Bowling Green would be impossible.

Lastly, it was reported to the commission that Bowling Green was farther from the markets for prison-manufactured goods than Eddyville. This simply wasn't true. Bowling Green was closer to both Louisville and Nashville. In fact, one of the advantages which they rung up on the Eddyville side of the ledger was that it was sufficiently remote from a town of any size and therefore ideal for a prison.

In its case for Eddyville, H. P. McDonald and Brothers liked the location of the 80-acre proposed tract, 116 feet above the Cumberland River's low water mark. Its mild and healthy climate was also noted. In fact, it could not possibly have been more radically different from Bowling Green, just over a hundred miles to the east.

Lyon County, they reported, was conducive to agricultural endeavors and held great stores of coal, iron, lumber, brick clay, and building stone.

These were professional comparisons. Studied closely, one could see their coloring by other less-tangible considerations. But they would serve to cover the commission's recommendation to the General Assembly.

Undoubtedly, the choice by the commission of Eddyville was purely political. Citizens of Eddyville had lobbied heavily for the prison and had pledged money to help the state purchase the land.

Between Eddyville and Bowling Green, commission members William Beckner of Clark County, and R. H. Stanton of Maysville, didn't give a hoot.

Hylan B. Lyon called the shot: Eddyville would be the site of the new Branch Penitentiary.

❖ ❖ ❖

The original plans drawn by McDonald called for a structure of brick and stone. In the main building would be offices for the warden, assistant warden, physician, and guards. For the convicts there would be a laundry, chapel, hospital, storerooms and even cells for women.

The drawings included two cellhouses, each containing a schoolroom, bathroom, and 320 cells. Twelve solitary cells were also in the plans. Estimated costs of the project—just over half a million dollars. Use of inmate labor could substantially reduce the expense. To Blackburn's great disappointment, the 1882 General Assembly refused to appropriate the funds for the new prison.

The contracting of inmates to work on railroads had greatly reduced the population of the Frankfort prison. Legislators' interest in prison reform had cooled. They bewailed the prospects of spending over half a million dollars on criminals. So, in spite of the pleading of their governor, the measure was passed over.

Governor Blackburn continued to fight the inhumanity of the Frankfort prison by issuing a continuous stream of pardons. During his four years in office "Lenient Luke," as he became known by a disparaging electorate, handed out more than one thousand pardons.

Because of his support for the unpopular cause of prison reform, and his liberal pardons, Luke Blackburn left office a very beleaguered and unpopular man. His true worth would be left to history.

Finally, in 1884, and after his term was over, the General Assembly appropriated funds for the the construction of a branch penitentiary at Eddyville.

Chapter 2

H odge Cunningham had reason to be concerned as he headed up the long stairway to the front entrance of the prison. If the weather on this soft autumn night was perfect, things at the penitentiary were not.

He had been a prison guard for three years. Two years before he had been on a wall stand when he had been struck by lightning. One minute he was peering out over the yard—the next minute he was laid out on the floor of the wooden pill box, unconscious and given up for dead.

They lowered his limp body off the prison wall with a rope, and took him to his house, which was only a short distance away. For five days he could not speak. Finally he came around and stared up into the face of an angel, who happened to be his wife, Emma. He had survived, with hardly as much as a headache.

Gnawing at him almost continuously from that day on, how-ever, was the belief that his close brush with death was a premonition—some kind of warning. Maybe the good Lord wanted him to do some-thing else.

He had been happy to get the job three years earlier. But it was dangerous work. The Kentucky State Penitentiary housed some of the most ruthless criminals in the country. Murderers, rapists and kidnap-pers were thrown together with forgers and chicken thieves. The vast number were there because of circumstances—too much booze, financial problems, a cheating woman, being in the wrong place, with the wrong crowd, at the wrong time.

Warden Henry Smith, in his report to the prison commissioners in 1901, gave a very perceptive insight as to the causes of crime at that time. It remains a timely piece of wisdom.

> "Drunkenness is the cause of grave crimes, and a large percentage of inmates of prisons can date their downfall from the time they became intemperate. It stimulates to deeds of violence, and sends to prison men who—had they remained sober—might have escaped reproach. When it becomes a habit it is attended by loss of power of application to work, and perhaps followed by poverty which leads to temptation and theft. The inability to resist drink, and the inability to resist other temptations may be, and probably are, indications of a disposition which is not created by alcohol, though an excessive consumption of alcohol may, and I think does, increase the weakness."

But there were some who were there because they were simply cold and of a psychopathic personality. Or to use street parlance, just plain mean, through and through. Such a person lacked a conscience and would cut the throat of a guard if it served a purpose. Especially if that purpose was to escape.

Often times it was hard to separate the copperheads from the garden snakes. One could be lulled into a sense of complacency and false security by the daily tedium of the prison routine and the apparent good will of most of the inmates. It was easy to let one's guard down. And then disaster could strike.

The life of a prison guard is ninety-five percent boredom, and five percent sheer terror. So it was constant pressure for the prison guards to stay on their toes; to keep a keen watch for the slightly unusual, peculiar movements, changes in demeanor.

Hodge Cunningham was a good guard. That is precisely why, on this evening, his mind was cluttered with worry.

The prison grapevine is an amazing thing to behold. A guest can visit the yard, being escorted by the warden. Before he exits the front gate, the segregated convict in the hole will know his name. The personal background of the new guard on five stand will be better known by the inmate population at the end of his first shift than by his own supervisor. No inmate killing, no disturbance, no escape ever comes as a surprise to the cell dwellers. They know in advance—by the grapevine.

This unsophisticated, but highly efficient, system is not restricted to inmates. Prison guards, if they are smart, tap into it as well.

The informer network is as old as our penal system. A guard treats the inmates well—nothing illegal or on the take. He talks to them in a nice way or looks the other way when cigarettes are passed as currency. Maybe he overlooks an extra blanket.

In return, he gets information—given in full confidence and most times by way of a hint, subtle suggestion, or a nod–a sticker hidden in the laundry, some yeast stored away in the mess hall, somebody going out of two cellhouse tonight.

And, of course, there is another compelling motivation behind the informant. An overwhelming majority of inmates in most any prison are not troublemakers. They have resigned themselves to their fate and simply wish to serve their time as securely and painlessly as possible. They resent any activity by other convicts which puts their contentment and security at risk. If they can thwart these disruptive prospects by disclosure, they will inform.

Hodge knew from his informant and by the grapevine that something was afoot on the yard—and it wasn't good. He felt uneasy.

Cunningham was a native of adjoining Trigg County, where his ancestors had multiplied in droves. The family name was so pervasive in that community that there was hardly a person who could not point to a Cunningham in their pedigree. As a Union captain said about the Cunningham clan during the Civil War, "The woods are full of 'em. And every one of them a damn Rebel."

To whom Hodge was not related directly, he was by marriage.

Sam Galloway was a prisoner, serving time out of Graves County. Galloway had run for sheriff and was promised a deputy's position if he would pull out of the race. He pulled out of the race, but the winning candidate refused to carry out his end of the bargain. So Sam killed him with a shotgun—right in the sheriff's office.

Sam Galloway's sister was married to the deputy sheriff of Trigg County, Jim Humphries. Not surprisingly, Humphries was closely related to Hodge. Neither is it surprising to learn that Sam Galloway and Hodge Cunningham—guard and prisoner—had a special relationship. Sam was his informant.

Galloway had advised Cunningham that a breakout was being planned and a gun was to be smuggled into the prison to a convicted murderer, Monte "Tex" Walters. He further told the guard that the weapon would be brought in by black inmate Andrew Hawkins.

Hawkins, serving a life term for murder, was a trusty who worked at the water pumping station outside the wall in front of the prison. He lived inside the prison but went in and out of the front gate almost at will.

Prison trusties were a special breed of inmate. The operation of the giant correctional facility was an expensive endeavor. In order to cut costs, the state authorized a number of convicts to work at critical jobs outside the prison walls.

They were screened as good security risks and assigned to such important positions as groundskeepers, cooks and housekeepers for the warden, barbers for the officers' canteen, and even clerks in the administration building. Some even helped at keeping the count for the cellhouse clerks.

The responsibility of running the water pumping station was one which required special training and skill. Hawkins, who was amiable and well liked, was an expert mechanic and a valuable trusty. Consequently, he was afforded liberal privileges to include going outside when he wanted, cooking and eating special food on the job site, and even fishing from time to time in the river.

Most importantly, and most troublesome as far as Hodge Cunningham was concerned, the guards paid him little mind. They routinely turnkeyed him through the huge metal barriers from the outside world to the bowels of maximum security, totally unmolested. He could have carried in an artillery piece.

Beware the daily tedium of prison routine. It had been that way since the first stone was laid.

On October 18, 1884, construction began on Kentucky's new penitentiary. Fifty-one convicts arrived from Frankfort on October 21 to begin their labor. At 4:30 p.m. on October 30, the first blast was set off by prison contractors at the nearby rock quarry in pursuit of building stone. The Branch Penitentiary was at last underway.

The state had paid four thousand dollars for 87 acres, fourteen hundred of which was donated by the citizens of Eddyville. Only 10.5 acres would be encompassed by the prison walls, with the remaining ground to be used for farming and garden plots for prisoners.

Eventually, about 114 convicts from Frankfort arrived to make up the bulk of the labor force. They were quartered in log houses built inside the intended walls and under the charge of 18 guards.

They were assisted by thirty Italian stonemasons, who hewed the large stones from limestone slabs dug from a quarry within three hundred yards of the construction site and transported over a small gauge railway, built for the purpose.

Slowly, the massive limestone structure began to rise upon the hilltop, dominating the horizon and posing like a giant sphinx against the sky. It took on the appearance of a large medieval fortress.

The "Castle on the Cumberland" officially received its first prisoners for confinement on Christmas Eve, 1889. The prison had been built at a cost of only two hundred and seventy-five thousand dollars. This Gothic cathedral of corrections, sitting high overlooking the Cumberland River valley was an impressive site. The stone walls of the structure enclosed ten and a half acres and, with the coping on top, were twenty feet high.

When facing the prison from the front, one was confronted with the administration building, which rose four floors into the sky. It housed the administrative offices, an arsenal, an institutional infirmary, and living quarters for the warden.

To the left were the three cellhouses connected one to the other. They were four stories high, with narrow wooden catwalks leading to the cells. Much of the cavernous environs was left to open space.

Due to the shortage of funds, the cellhouse wing planned for the right of the administration was not built. It, along with others, was added later.

Sizes of the cells varied but averaged about seven feet in length, six and one-half feet in height, and four and one-half feet in width. The different sizes reflected, in a relatively small way, the Blackburn philosophy of penology. It was intended that the better behaved prisoners would have the larger cells, thus affording accommodations in accordance to their conduct.

The buildings were massive masterpieces in stone, with sweeping arches and turrets. A huge self-supporting arch graced one cellhouse. The bearded and fun-loving stonemasons of Italy had left a lasting legacy.

One building sat high upon the hill overlooking the magnificent vista of the Cumberland River. It was on site before the construction began and the prison was simply built around it. This was the stately mansion of Robert Louis Cobb—grandfather of the renowned humorist, Irvin Cobb.

The two-story, brick structure was painted white and was appropriately named White Hall. The wandering rose garden of the estate was located where the death house and electric chair would eventually be placed. The building itself would become the prison hospital for almost seventy-five years. Cobb fell on hard times and the home eventually was sold at the court house door. Ex-Confederate

Congressman Willis Matchen bought the land. He then sold it to the state for the prison project.

Once again, evidence of the Confederate syndication.

In the middle of the yard at its highest elevation was constructed a water tank or "stand pipe." The water was pumped through pipes from a large spring 300 yards outside the walls.

There was a lot of room for additional buildings to be added. The wall enclosed the summit, so that when walking on the yard, the formidable stone barrier would often slip below one's line of sight.

Before the mortar had hardly dried and inmates began filling up its cavernous confines, a large sign was placed above the front entrance: "Abandon Hope, All Ye That Enter Here."

Even with the new building, Luke Blackburn's dream of prison reform had fallen on hard times. Conditions at Eddyville were pretty grim from the outset.

At first there were women prisoners at the new facility. They apparently were "imported" early in its occupation to do the cooking. These female recalcitrants lived outside the walls of the main prison near a "cook shack" where the meals for the inside population of men were prepared.

Early on, twelve-year-old boys were being incarcerated at Eddyville. Corporal punishment, including lashings at the post, was inflicted regularly. Often permanent injury, such as broken bones, was sustained.

The mortality rate was shocking. In 1896, there were 33 deaths—including two sixteen-year-olds—from "natural causes."

A year later, 27 prisoners died. Most were buried in unmarked graves at Vinegar Hill, the convict cemetery located on the ridge behind the penitentiary. They were planted in shallow graves and there were complaints by some citizens of a bad odor hovering over the grounds. Many were embalmed by the prison physician and sold to the college of medicine in Louisville for four dollars a cadaver. The doctor pocketed the money—a neat little arrangement.

Malaria hit hard in the summer of '97, killing five within two weeks.

The main cause of their demise, overall, was the sewer gas which languished in the damp and squalid basements of the cellhouses. Long term prisoners were confined there without proper ventilation or exercise.

Each inmate was given a wooden bucket—a "night bucket"— to keep in his cell for his own excrement. In the morning he would carry it out to a common dumping area which was covered with lime and dirt. He would hang his bucket on a peg to air out through the day. The stench in the cells, especially in the summer, was sickening.

Other fatal maladies included diarrhea, typhoid fever, malaria, syphilis and pneumonia. Surprisingly, suicides were relatively rare given the awful and hopeless conditions.

On May 11, 1891, Francis Pace from Harlan County became the first inmate of what would begin an endless and gruesome procession of those killed by acts of violence. He was stabbed in self-defense by a guard.

There was a tunnel constructed which connects all the original cellhouses and the administration building. It is now sealed off but carries much of the steam piping and heavy wiring for the institution's utilities. Branching from this underground corridor beneath two cellhouse's are three or four dungeon-like niches. Heavy iron rings are sunk into the stone walls and flooring. There, in solitary darkness, unruly prisoners were chained to the walls for days, on a diet of bread and water, while they contemplated their wrongs.

The warden of the Branch Penitentiary during those first forbidding days was Louis Curry. He was a hard taskmaster. His journal entries over a two-week period in the fall of 1888 give vivid testimony to what life was like for a convict at Eddyville.

Entry 4th Sept.

Prisoner Watkins, #123, was reported for smoking by the one-block Day Keeper. His cell was searched and a small quantity of tobacco was discovered secreted within his night bucket. The tobacco was neatly tied in a fold of moisture-proof oil cloth. The lengths these prisoners will go to hide ill-gotten contraband never ceases to amaze me. I ordered Watkins confined to his cell for an indefinite period since this is his second offense for smoking.

Entry 9th Sept.

Prisoner Seth Barton, #328, was delivered into my keeping by the High Sheriff of Cumberland County. This is a villainous felon charged with murder, rape and selling whiskey to Indians, and is to be hanged in four months. It will be good riddance to the likes of him! I ordered him confined to a basement cell in two-block and a death watch is being kept lest he make any attempt to escape his just punishment.

Entry 15th Sept.

Matron Helen reported a disturbance between two of the women prisoners. They were caught fighting near the cook shack, which is presently located outside the prison. We have a total of nine women prisoners, and they are all a slatternly lot! I ordered the two women prisoners confined to their quarters for three days. No quarreling will be tolerated among them.

Entry 17th Sept.

Prisoner Phillips, #186, was released today after serving a six month sentence for chicken thievery. His attitude, upon departing, was quite distasteful and I was sorely tempted, despite his legal release, to order him chained and whipped. The horse given to him, he loudly claimed, was worm-eaten, and he demanded another one. He also found quarrel with the blanket roll that was issued to him. I had him run off the reservation, horse and all. I fear he will be back, within the fortnight, with a more serious charge. Then we will see if he cannot be taught a bit more serious discipline. Worm-eaten horse, indeed!

Entry 19th Sept.

The prison's 205 charges, including nine women inmates, has been quiet. But a report has reached me that a Keeper has been seriously injured at the Frankfort prison. The full details are still unclear, but it appears the Keeper was attacked by a prisoner with a sharpen-down piece of metal during the noon meal hour. We would not allow such an occurrence to happen here! I venture to predict that no such assault will ever occur at this prison.

Entry 23rd Sept.

The weather has turned foul for the past two nights, and the prisoners have complained that the closed windows have increased the smoke that emits from the cell oil lamps. I have ordered the upper windows to be left open. Now I fear that the Night Keepers will complain of the chill when they make their rounds. This is but a few of the many petty whines I must put up with! If the complaints persist, I will order the lamps removed from the prisoners' cells.

Entry 25th Sept.

Prisoner Berry, #289, was put on report for refusing to haul stone through the sallyport gate. He said he was not a beast of burden and does not care if the prison wall ever gets finished. Beast of burden, indeed! I ordered him confined and chained to the dungeon cell beneath two-block. Eventually, I predict, Berry will learn to march to my tune. There is yet one-third of the wall to be built. And, every able-bodied prisoner will be expected to do his share.

Entry 29th Sept.

Keeper Simmons has failed to report for the second day. He is rather young and I fear he finds the work at the prison distasteful. But, I have serious doubts whether he can find a job that pays more than the $38.00 per month he receives here. If he does not report back to work by tomorrow, I will be forced to discharge him.

Entry 2nd Oct.

Prisoner Shaffer, #149, died in his cell. This is the fifth prisoner death during my tenure. As with the other four, this death was of a natural cause. It has been reported to me by our prison physician, Dr. Harper, that Shaffer had numerously complained of chest pains and, consequently, was assigned to light duty. Since Shaffer is without funds, friends or relatives, he will be buried at Cherry Hill, located a short distance outside the prison. His few personal effects will be distributed among the prisoners.

Entry 5th Oct.

Prisoner Burton, #152, caused a disturbance in the three-block dining area at the evening meal hour. He loudly claimed his beans were unfit to eat and splattered the contents of his bowl against the wall. He was in the process of doing further harm when he was overpowered by several alert Keepers and dragged away. He is presently chained up in the dungeon where I am sure he will cause very little mischief. I am glad to report no other prisoner was involved.

Entry 7th Oct.

Prisoner Wheeler, #169, requested an audience with me. Wheeler, even by prison standards, is an odious creature who is presently serving a 20-year sentence for incest. I also suspect him of strange behavior within the prison, but thus far, has escaped detection. Upon granting him an interview, it was his request to obtain a Bible. The very idea that such a vile creature should hold God's Word was quite repugnant to me. I ordered him back to work, without further ado, and requested the Keepers to retain a close scrutiny at his doings. One false step and Wheeler will know the true meaning of prison. A Bible, indeed!

Entry 9th Oct.

Prisoner Penrod, #147, was released from the dungeon after seven months' confinement. An incorrigible conniver, Penrod was reported attempting to subvert a newly-hired Keeper to bring loose tobacco into the prison. I will not tolerate any prisoner to misuse my Keepers for such nefarious deeds. As an added reminder, I have ordered Penrod's right ankle to be shackled with a ten-pound ball weight. This will perhaps go far in correcting his evil ways.

Entry 10th Oct.

Colonel Clarence C. Harlan appeared to hold his

annual Parole and Commendation Review. A kindly gentleman, Colonel Harlan granted an early morning audience to eighty felons, including three women prisoners. He completed his onerous chore by granting another forty interviews during the afternoon hour. From among the numerous prisoners proclaiming repentance, Colonel Harlan was gracious in granting the female prisoner, Joyce Kimberly, #325, an early release from her 6-month sentence for immoral soliciting. She will be released in the morning, but I fear she is fringing repentance and will no doubt return upon her evil path. We can be thankful that these paroles will be but a passing fancy concocted, no doubt, in the addled mind of some liberal-thinking Yankee. Paroles, indeed!

Entry 15th Oct.

Upon my word, a Black Freeman appeared at the prison gate and requested employment as a Keeper. It is widely known that I bear no malice towards any of the numerous races that comprise humanities total. But this is a bit too much. I fear Constable Aaron or Princeton may have been the source of this outrageous maneuver since he is burden with a prankious twist of mind. Be that as it may, I sent word to the Freeman that our employment list is full for the remaining part of the century.

Entry 16th Oct.

Physician Harper appeared for his monthly visit to the prison. I thereupon had Prisoner Berry, #239, brought to the mid-yard post and shackled. After assembling the prison population, I supervised the administration of twenty-five lashes. Keeper Gray wielded the braided whip. Upon completion of this punishment, I inquired of Berry whether he was now ready to resume hauling stone. He cursed me vilely. For this unwarranted affront, I would have personally administered another twenty-five lashes had not the good Physician staved my hand. Still, I was sorely tempted to ignore the Physician's warning and have the whip again laid to the villainous creature's back. With a great deal of effort, I managed to temper my outrage and await the Physician's next monthly visit to administer the added twenty-five lashes, which are the maximum number allowed. Prisoner Burton, #152, received twenty-five lashes for the recent disturbance he caused in the dining area. Both prisoners were then placed under guard in the prison infirmary. When their wounds have finished festering, they will be returned back to the dungeon.

Entry 22nd Oct.

Prisoner Sully Martin, #329, was delivered into my keeping by two constables from Paducah. An obvious troublesome character, Martin received a five-year sentence for rustling and assault. Upon receipt of this felonious person he loudly voiced his alleged contempt for the two Constables who had accompanied him and their lice-infested jail. I was sorely tempted to strike this odious creature in his tracks but was able to control my pending outburst. Martin was removed at once to the dungeon where he will remain until he learns to use a civil tongue!

It must have been a terribly bitter pill for Warden Curry to swallow when his lovely daughter Topsy met, fell in love with, and married an Eddyville convict.

※ ※ ※

In 1895, William O'Connell Bradley was elected the first Republican Governor of Kentucky. On April 26, 1896, W. H. Happy of nearby Mayfield replaced Curry as warden at Eddyville.

The position as head of the prison was, up until recently, a political job and subject to change, depending on the political winds in Frankfort. So Happy was in, and Curry was out.

But the new warden would have his problems—most of them inherited from his predecessor. Within a year of taking over, a full scale legislative investigation was underway as to the conditions at his prison.

The legislature had grown tired of picking on the dismal correctional facility in Frankfort. Eddyville gave them a new target. The new prison had old problems.

Less than a month after Happy arrived on the job the work shops burned. This created havoc from the beginning.

Most of the inmates at Eddyville were contracted out to the private firm of Mason and Foard & Company. This outfit ran the work shops inside the prison and manufactured various wares to include shoes, pants, and brooms. There was even a wagon factory.

When the workshops caught fire and burned because of broom shavings being too close to the boiler, a substantial number of prisoners were suddenly idle. Foard & Company even hired out some convicts—as many as fifty at a time—to work a farm across the river where they were billeted in rough dorm buildings.

In addition to these prisoners outside the walls, some were leased out to individual citizens who would work them, feed them, and send them back inside to sleep. Prison officials took trusties of their own—indentured servants if you will—to work in their homes. These felons were fed and boarded by their caretakers as payment to the state for their labors. All of this led to a great number of prisoners running around the little village of Eddyville.

They were, on the whole, well behaved and generally tolerated by the populace. However, there were some strident citizen complaints which came to the ears of the local politicians.

Their complaints also made it into the Senate Report of the investigation:

> Convicts have been permitted to run at large in the city of Eddyville and community by the present chief official of the prison to the annoyance and disgust of the citizens. The convict, Ed Settle, was permitted to go to the depot, nearly a mile from the prison, procure the keys of the office, and build fires in the depot. The convict, "Andy," was allowed to go at large and finally turned up in the post office in a drunken condition in the presence of Miss Martin, the post-mistress of Eddyville, and other good citizens. The convict, "High Ball," was permitted to go at large, and annoy the family of Dr. James, until Town Marshall Opie had to and did interfere in his official character to protect the family, and after that he still roamed at large until he, in disregard of all decency, in open day time, in the suburbs of the city of Eddyville, and almost under the shadow of the prison building, in view of the dwelling of one of the good citizens of the vicini-

ty, was guilty of cohabitation with a Negro woman in the presence of numerous children, several of whom, white and black, have testified to this sickening debauchery. But the question was asked at the instance of Warden Happy if he was to blame for "Andy's" drunkenness or "High Ball's" indecency. Common sense vehemently responds that had Warden Happy been at home, and performed his duty by keeping these outlaws incarcerated in the penitentiary where they had been consigned, and where the Constitution requires they should be kept, then "Andy" would not have been drunk and annoying people at the Eddyville post office, nor would "High Ball" had an opportunity to outrage civilization in public places.

The burning of the inside shops took care of one problem but created another one. As a result of the working places going up in smoke, Mason and Foard gave up their contract with the state. Consequently, the wandering tribe of convicts, complained of by the citizenry, was returned to within the prison walls. They joined the others who were now without work, to comprise a prison full of idle prisoners.

The Senate commission had an idea for that problem:

"There is a space of ground immediately in front of the prison, and lying between it and the street, sufficient in area to make a handsome front lawn to the premises, and thereby add beauty to the property of the Commonwealth, but this frontage is permitted to remain in gullies, covered with chips of rock which fell from the chisel when the structure was being built, and with coal cinders and other unsightly rubbish, while scores and even hundreds of idle convicts loiter inside the walls without work sufficient for healthy exercise , and the same is true of the large unoccupied area inside the walls, much of it being rough and rugged, covered with rocks and rubbish, while the unemployed convicts seek the level and smooth places in this space to rest and idle on. . . . The State has to feed, clothe, shelter, guard and furnish the idle convicts with medical attention when needed. Now, why should they not be put to work, and required to grade, cleanse and beautify these grounds, when it would not cost the State an additional penny, and at the same time furnish them needed and wholesome exercise?"

These 1897 Senators expressed a sentiment which would continue to be applauded one hundred years later.

And Warden Happy had other problems, as the investigators were quick to point out.

The guards were accused of ripping off prime beef and pigs' feet which were intended for inmate consumption. There were serious personnel problems—backbiting and acrimony between staff and guards. One employee was paid by Warden Happy to eavesdrop on another. Guards sometimes slept on duty and a few could not hold their liquor. Early releases were given to some prisoners and payoffs were suspected.

One of the main complaints by the Senate panel was that Warden Happy spent to much time away from the prison. Apparently he went back to Mayfield frequently and also traveled around the area on political jaunts.

The inhumane conditions of the cellhouses and deplorable death rate were noted. There was concern of abuse in the infliction of corporal punishment to the convicts, especially in violation of the "twelve hour law."

By statute, inmates were not supposed to be punished within twelve hours of the infraction. Supposedly that was to allow cooler heads to prevail, and afford time for proper investigation and the accused a chance to respond to the allegation. The whippings were not only being inflicted within the twelve hours, but in the estimation of the Senate tribunal, applied with excessive force and severity.

The inmate would be held face down over the "whipping stone" and lashes applied to his bare back and bottom with a leather strap. It was alleged that in some instances the large belt would be dragged through water and sand before its use, supposedly to make the ordeal more painful. As many as fifteen blows would sometimes be applied.

There was one bright spot however, if the legislative group believed Chaplain Kerr. "I have not heard a prisoner swear in ten months," he boasted to the undoubtedly skeptical inquisitors.

In the end, this special committee appointed by the General Assembly to inquire into the management and lack of discipline of the Branch Penitentiary at Eddyville lamented the situation but did nothing.

In spite of his warts and gashes, they decided that Warden

Happy was probably an improvement upon his predecessor and compared well with his counterpart at the Frankfort prison. In what has to be considered a lukewarm endorsement, the committee recommended that the prison "be continued and perpetuated as a penitentiary."

Then Chairman Sims and his colleagues closed their notebooks, packed their bags and returned to the blessed Bluegrass; they were grateful, no doubt, to be free and clear of the wilds of west Kentucky.

Chapter 3

H odge Cunningham moved up the long steps, under the huge stone arch, and through the front gate of the prison. He greeted the familiar turnkey, who let him through the first portal. The brightness of the lights hanging from the high, vaulted ceiling caused him to squint momentarily until his eyes adjusted from coming in out of the dark.

Armed with his massive ring of hand-sized keys, the gatekeeper and Hodge exchanged pleasantries as they moved down the marble-floored corridor toward the second gate. Ceiling fans turned slowly high above them, barely stirring the stale air.

As with every prison guard on every prison shift, a slight knot in his stomach reminded Hodge Cunningham that uncertainty lurked behind the clanging doors. They passed darkened administrative offices on both sides of the hallway. During the day they were teeming with activity. Now, in the middle of the night, they were dead.

And then to the second gate, beyond which only the brave and desperate dared to tread. Opened and closed. He was now in the belly of the beast. He turned left toward one cell house.

The crucial information given to him by Sam Galloway had been passed on to Warden John Chilton.

While the weapons were expected to be brought into the prison by trusty Andrew Hawkins, a woman was also involved. Inmate

Galloway reported that the wife of inmate Tex Walters was to be part of the conspiracy for the gun smuggling.

Lillian Walters was a slender, twenty-one-year-old beauty with a bewitching personality. She was born in Sellsburg, Indiana on December 19, 1901. Her father, Louis Manger, a native of Kentucky, was a roofer—or "tinner"—as they were called in those days. Shortly after Lillian's birth, he moved his wife, Lena, and his two daughters and son to New Castle, Indiana. There her father worked at his trade and her parents took in boarders to supplement their income.

When Lillian was only sixteen she fell in love with a charming young boarder by the name of Monte "Tex" Walters. She was captivated by the mysterious mechanic who would reveal to her very little of his past. They ran off and got married, landed in Louisville, Kentucky, and lived with her older sister.

By this time she had become aware of the criminal ways of her new husband but was too smitten to really care. Walters became the leader of a bandit gang in Louisville responsible for several robberies. Lillian went with him on a few of his criminal expeditions. She was driving the car for Tex and two others on a robbery mission one night in December, 1921. They jumped out of their car on Rammers Avenue in Louisville to rob a milkman by the name of Alex Ehrler. When their victim resisted, they killed him. Walters later confessed to his involvement in the murder, only after being promised that the charges against Lillian would be dropped.

In May of 1922, Walters was convicted of murder in the Jefferson County Circuit Court and sentenced to life in the penitentiary. He first went to the Frankfort prison but was transferred to Eddyville on August 17, 1922.

Lillian remained totally devoted to her man. Some say she was even mesmerized by the handsome looks, and "tough guy" ways of the 32-year-old outlaw. As a faithful wife, she corresponded with Tex regularly. She also got a job in Paducah and moved there in order to visit with him more frequently.

After receiving the warning from his prison guard, Warden Chilton began to personally read the letters between the two lovers, looking for any clues of their plan. They revealed nothing.

Chilton suspected that the enchanting wife, not the water plant trusty, would be the means for the guns to be slipped into the hands of Tex Walters.

It was now Tuesday night, October 2, a few minutes before 11 o'clock as guard Cunningham headed for his duty station. He was beginning the third shift, after coming off of days on Monday.

Two unsettling developments had occurred within the last 48

hours which had made him ill at ease. First, on Monday morning, Lillian Walters had paid a visit at the penitentiary. Nothing unusual about that. But she had met with Warden Chilton and asked that she be allowed more than the customary time for conversation with her husband.

"I am going away and will be gone a long, long time," she told him.

Chilton was not the first, nor would he be the last, to be duped by the beguiling beauty. He granted her request.

Although the experienced prison keeper may have fallen for her wiles, he had not lost his senses. He stipulated that two guards, as opposed to the customary one, would be present during the visit. Hodge Cunningham and V. B. Mattingly were the two officers assigned to the task.

So the two silent sentinels stood and watched as Tex and Lillian consorted closely for two hours. The watchful guards made sure nothing was passed between them. But it was impossible to pick up all the conversation. Innocent as it appeared, Hodge found the meeting suspicious.

The second occurrence was even more bothersome. Trusty Andrew Hawkins had disappeared that day. He had escaped.

At that very hour, guards had been drawn away from the prison to search the surrounding hills and hollows for the errant water plant operator. On his trail they would find an empty cartridge carton.

A dark sense of foreboding pressed down upon guard Cunningham as he moved through yet another prison gate.

▨ ▨ ▨

Foreboding is the nature of the beast. A brooding grimness hovers over the cold stone edifice. The sounds of laughter and merriment are rare and bounce off the metallic gates and ancient rock like pieces of glass.

No one knows how long the "Abandon Hope" banner remained over the front gate but its meaning is pervasive through every cell and crevice of the "Castle on the Cumberland."

If one could miraculously compile the thousands, perhaps millions, of letters written from the residents of this palace of woe, the reading would make the biblical Lamentations sound like a cheery post card from the beach.

A Camp Meeting flyer for the "season" of 1899 was left for over ninety years in a book in the prison library. On its face, handwritten in pencil, is the haunting refrain from the dusty past, "Oh how sad for me to know we may never meet again. What care I for this world since. . . ." The message and the messenger fade away.

It has to be a tribute to the resiliency of the human spirit that most have endured and survived.

The suicide rate of those bleak, early years was incredibly low. In fact, not until the prison was over ten years old did Steve Copenhauer of Wayne County Kentucky, do himself in on July 25, 1901. That was the last suicide for over twenty-four years—right through the early grim conditions of this institution.

In over a hundred years, forty-three inmates have killed themselves in various ways including the more common methods of hanging, poison, and self-inflicted knife wounds.

Out of the legions of wretched souls who have passed under the hopeless arch, almost one thousand have died in this prison.

Among that hapless number was 18-year-old James Buckner. This diminutive youth was led up the front steps of the castle on the sunny, spring day of May 20, 1911, shackled in cuffs and leg irons. He was fated to become the first man executed at the Kentucky State Penitentiary.

Since the early days of statehood, the execution of condemned prisoners had been by hanging. Most times justice was swift and sure. Always it was local—the defendant apprehended, jailed, tried, and convicted at the county seat. And it was there, behind the court house, where the scaffold would be hammered together in full view and hearing of the condemned, who stared forlornly through the jail house bars.

The executions were public spectacles, played out to large clamoring crowds who would travel great distances to witness the morbid drama. In some instances, in these small Kentucky towns where life was tedious and hard, a hanging became almost festive in mood—for everyone except the star of the show, of course.

Good entertainment that it was, it was also expensive and a logistical nightmare for local government—especially law enforcement and jailers. Often public sentiment ran at a fever pitch, seething with anger and threatening to tear the little matchbox jail apart and cheat the hangman.

After the turn of the century, a better way of carrying out legal executions was being explored. A wave of enlightenment swept across penology, with two main thoughts prevailing.

First, more and more people were becoming appalled at the carnival-like atmosphere of public executions. Secondly, botched executions from the gallows shocked the senses—necks which did not break, bodies dangling and kicking, even some who had to be dropped through the trap more than once.

At this same time also came the magic of electricity. It moved machinery, lit our nights, and performed other noteworthy feats. It could also kill—and some believed humanely.

In 1890, New York became the first state in the United States to electrocute a criminal. Twenty years later, the Kentucky General Assembly enacted a law which provided that all death sentences would thereafter be implemented by electrocution.

With the assistance of a French engineer, the electric chair was installed at Eddyville. A one floor annex was added on to the end of three cellhouse to house the lethal equipment and a few cells for those under sentence of death. Quite naturally it became known simply as the "death house." It would not be long before the number of candidates for "ole sparky" caused death row to be expanded.

The new procedure for executions in Kentucky worked well for ten years. Then, in 1920, a black man raped a nine-year-old white girl in Lexington. Public outrage stampeded the Kentucky General Assembly to handle rape cases differently.

The death penalty statute which authorized execution by the electric chair was amended to read as follows:

> "Except in cases where the accused has been adjudge to suffer a death sentence for the crime of rape or attempted rape, in which event sentence shall be executed by hanging the condemned in the county in which the crime was committed."

So, for the next 18 years, the public hangings came back to the Kentucky county seats for the crime of rape. During that time, nine men were hung for the crime of rape—eight of whom were black men who had raped white women.

By 1938, once again the public had become fed up with the spectacle of public hangings. Also, black leaders had attacked the law as simply a way for racism to vent its venom by "legalized lynching."

That year the legislature repealed the requirement that death sentences for the crime of rape be conducted by hanging in the county seat where the crime was committed. The execution for all crimes was to take place at Eddyville.

During the 18-year hiatus on electrocutions for rape, some of those assigned to hanging were nevertheless housed at the Kentucky State Penitentiary for safe keeping. They would be transported back to the county of their demise for the final *coup de grace*.

But, in 1911, that was all in the future, and on a steamy summer night James Buckner was destined to make history.

The repentant youth had murdered a police officer in Lebanon, Kentucky, by stabbing him thirteen times. He was black, as would be over half of the future victims of the chair.

Forty-five people including prison officials, ministers, and newspapermen crowded into the death chamber to watch Buckner take his final walk.

Calmly, at 4:05 a.m. on July 8, 1911, he left his cell on death row. The mournful sounds of the electric dynamos filled the cellhouse. Without any support or touching he walked into the room between a prison chaplain and a guard.

While awaiting his fate on death row, he had been baptized. He had spent his last night reading the Bible. His only request was to "tell mother I hope to meet her in heaven."

Near the bulky and ominous-looking wooden chair, Buckner slowly turned and casually glanced at the onlookers. Then, as if he was sitting down in a barber's chair, he seated himself.

He slid his feet together, and laid his forearms and hands upon the wide arms of the chair. The electrodes were attached to his ankles and his head. His lower legs and a wide round spot on the crown of his head were shaved. What looked like an old football helmet with a copper plate attached on the inside was placed on his head. The metal rod protruding out the top was connected. Large leather straps were used to fasten his arms to the chair.

His lips were seen to mutter a prayer just as the black hood was gently pushed down over his head. Then he courageously and serenely waited, while the spectators stared breathlessly.

Prayers were said by the prison chaplains. At 4:13 a.m. a nod was given, the lever in the adjoining control room was pulled and 1,500 volts of electricity surged through the being of James Buckner. His entire body leaped forward, pulling against the restraints, and his hands were doubled into fists.

After what seemed like an eternity, but was only a few seconds, the charge ended. Only a moment later, a second surge of 2,300 volts was applied. After a few seconds, the body was left to rest.

The dynamos wound down and the death house grew eerily quiet. A physician stepped forward and checked the limp frame of Buckner. At first he detected a pulse. He stepped back and waited for a few moments while the gathering looked on in dreadful silence.

Once again he checked the heart and felt for a pulse. At 4:21 a.m., James Buckner was pronounced dead. The first legal electrocution at the Kentucky State Penitentiary had been carried out.

Chapter 4

By 1923 the Kentucky State Penitentiary had lost the look of new-
ness. Cellhouse four was added as the south wing in 1904. It
was of identical architecture and gray stone material as the original, and provided esthetic balance.

In 1912 the prison in Frankfort was renamed the Kentucky
State Reformatory. Eddyville lost its "branch" status and became simply the Kentucky State Penitentiary.

The fresh stone chippings and barren wasteland, both in front
of the prison and inside, had long disappeared. Now the grounds were
well landscaped and manicured by inmate labor. The prison yard was
a smorgasbord of buildings—most of them constructed of brick.

The "hill"—as the broad summit within the walls was now
called by the residents—was immaculately groomed and maintained.
A macadamized road—an early rendition of asphalt—twelve feet wide
and over three thousand feet long, made an oval around the prison
yard. Like a country lane, it moved past brightly whitewashed curbs, a
lawn of neatly cropped grass and blooming cannas, well-kept hedges,
and full-bodied shade trees. The prison yard almost had the look of a
college campus. There was even a greenhouse.

It brought to life Longfellow's refrain, "No tears dim the sweet
look that nature wears."

Pastoral as it may appeared, it was still a rough and brutal university of criminals.

Since 1909 inmates were no longer required to wear stripes, except for disciplinary cases. The ball and chain would still be used as punishment for certain offenders until as late as 1940. Convicts were dressed in baggy denim pants and jackets, cloth hats, and cotton shirts. Numbers were stenciled on their backs.

Most convicts under 18 were gone, having been shipped out to the new reformatory. Juveniles, one way or another, would still land there—some as young as fifteen.

The guard force consisted of less than fifty men, their individual pay ranging from 90 to 100 dollars a month. Unlike their counterparts at the Frankfort prison, they were still armed while patrolling the yard and cellhouses.

While the new state constitution of 1891 prohibited leasing convict labor outside the prison walls, the contract system was still very much in use. Private contractors maintained operations inside the walls at Eddyville with prisoners manufacturing shoes, shirts, brooms, and leather goods. The state was paid one dollar a day per man. Not until 1929 would the U. S. Congress—in response to pressure from organized labor—pass the Hawes-Cooper Act which allowed states to prohibit interstate shipment of prison-made products. That measure would effectively run the private contractors out of the prison business, as they anticipated the loss of their markets.

But in 1923 the manufacturing shops at Eddyville were still operating at full steam.

In 1913, whipping as a means of punishment had been abolished by Warden John Chilton.

A new settling basin and water filtering system had been built in front of the prison to provide "perfectly clear water" for the inmates. The cellhouses were not supplied with running water, but the cells were now lit by electricity.

Night schools had been inaugurated so that prisoners had a chance to secure at least a secondary education.

The diet of the prisoners had improved dramatically since the days of Warden Curry. This was due primarily to the cultivation, by convicts, of 15 acres of farm land outside the institution which provided fruits and vegetables for inmate consumption.

Prisoners were allowed to play baseball and other "legitimate" games on Sunday after Chapel services during the summer months, and a picture show was provided for them during the winter.

By 1923 the most subtle, but meaningful change within the prison walls was the demographic makeup of the convicts.

During the first thirty years of the penitentiary's existence,

America had moved from a horse-and-buggy society to the age of the automobile. The motor vehicle increased our mobility to an astounding degree. There were more automobiles manufactured in 1923 than all the previous years put together.

More and more, crime took on an interstate flavor as miscreants moved easily and often across state boundaries. No longer did the penitentiary population consist only of native Kentuckians—mountain lads from the east, or river boys from the west.

There began to appear upon the criminal blotters and docket sheets across Kentucky more and more bad actors who were not home grown. Needless to say, there were many craggy-faced convicts showing up on the yard who didn't become misty eyed upon hearing the strands of "My Old Kentucky Home."

Monte "Tex" Walters was the quintessential interstate criminal. His very identity was shrouded in mystery.

Prison records reflected that Walters grew up in San Antonio, Texas, and he listed both of his parents as dead. This information was incorrect and apparently was an effort to protect his family from the knowledge of his criminal ways.

A thin paper trail of public documents provide a hazy outline of Tex Walters' past. He was the son of a railroad man from Ohio who met Tex's mother, Eleanor Buck, in Guthrie Center, Iowa—a small town just west of Des Moines. The couple married when Eleanor was barely seventeen years of age.

His father's job moved his parents around the plains states and Tex was born in Nebraska sometime in March, 1890. He was named Chester Monte Walters and did not pick up the label "Tex" until his later, wayward years. While Tex was still a baby, his father was killed in a railroad accident in Denver. The young widow and her infant son moved back to Guthrie Center. There, on September 4, 1893, when Tex was only three years old, his mother married William Grandstaff, a respectable and hard working painter and paper hanger. The quick and energetic little boy grew up thinking of Grandstaff as his real father.

His parents were good people and did their best to raise Tex right. They took him to church and Sunday School and made sure he obtained a high school education. But he fell in with the wrong crowd, left home and soon became an outlaw. From that time on, Tex consciously tried to cast a shadow over his past.

The choirboy good looks were irresistible to the women and disguised a cold and ruthless killer.

His first prison term was for burglary. As soon as he got out, he stabbed a man on the streets of Boone, Iowa. Tex served out a five-year sentence for that crime.

He headed to Texas. Not long after arriving there he got into more serious trouble. He murdered a Texan and was sentenced to the penitentiary. While in prison he was shot trying to escape. Later, after being paroled, he returned to Iowa and was married.

Moving on to Colorado, he and his wife were suspected of murdering a rancher there. There was not enough proof to convict them. What happened to his wife from Des Moines is not known.

In between prison stints and criminal acts Tex would work at various places. He even worked at one time as foreman in an International Harvester plant in Akron, Ohio—at least that is what he said.

Nebraska, Texas, Iowa, Colorado, Ohio, Indiana, and finally he brought his criminal ways to Kentucky.

He was 32 years old when he arrived at the Kentucky State Penitentiary in August of 1922 to begin serving his life sentence.

In October of that same year, he was shot and wounded by a guard when, in broad daylight, he placed a crudely crafted ladder against the prison wall and tried to escape.

Tex Walters was a complex and charismatic individual. He appeared much larger than his deceptive five feet nine and 138-pound frame. His personality and character teemed with contradictions.

His dark black hair was always neatly groomed and he possessed soft and seductive chestnut colored eyes. But underneath the clean-cut handsome face was a person who could kill without the least compunction. While on the run with his companions in the Ehler murder, one of them asked him how many men he had killed. Without the least bit of feeling he casually began counting on his fingers, "One, two, three. Counting this one, I have killed four."

Although he professed to have religious conviction, his life of sin and crime belied any evidence of it. His language was filled with vulgarities and profanity, except when around his wife or other women. Then he became a perfect gentleman.

Tex was a natural leader. His way was not to talk tough, but to be tough, as he moved within the inmate circles with a quiet but manly confidence. He had that indefinable quality—perhaps it was the power of his intellect—which caused convicts to hang on his words and want to be counted among his friends.

Although he tried to escape from every prison where he served time, and was an extreme security risk, he was otherwise considered a good prisoner and the guards liked him. He obeyed the rules, worked hard, and got along well with guards and inmates alike. Tex had served enough time behind bars to know that it was a lot tougher to escape from the hole or with a ball and chain than from the prison yard. So—except for his escape attempts—he behaved himself. In fact, the correctional officers were somewhat fascinated by his charming personality.

This wanderer with the mysterious background was not the regular rough-hewn prisoner. He was intelligent, articulate and a ferocious reader.

Since most of his fellow convicts lacked the capacity to engage in much conversation of the intellectual or philosophical bent, he would often seek out such a dialogue with his keepers.

The meager prison library was no match for his literary appetite. Walters was particularly interested in books on religion and psychology. He was fascinated by the study of psychic powers and hypnotism.

Tex reached outside the institution for intellectual succor through regular correspondence with educated people interested in sharing with him their thoughts. One of these was Reverend J. R. Crawford, pastor of the Kentucky Avenue Presbyterian Church in Paducah, Kentucky.

In a letter to Crawford dated January 17, 1923, Tex Walters, the convicted killer, reveals the depth of his intellect. He relates his love for his wife Lillian and his appreciation to the minister and his wife for their friendship to her.

Then the insightful prisoner observed:

> "It is a characteristic trait of those who are confined in prison to feel that the hand of society is against them, but I believe that most all things that we term as hardships really happen for the best. . . ."

He wrote extensively about theological matters, concluding:

> "My dear friend, you are right when you say 'that we can only take the world's condition as we find it.' Jesus said 'we are not to judge,' but are to look in spirit and in truth. My interpretation of that is not to hate the individual but to hate the sin that is within him. I would like to ask from what authority we separate and classify sin? If from no authority, is it because as a rule the moral philosophy of man is: this pet sin of man is not as bad as the other man's sin, that he would not do what the other man did, and the other man would not do what he done, etc.? There is

a great many things in Christianity that I do not understand. I will appreciate and value your opinions and advice. The rule of this institution is that there shall be only two sheets to each letter, consequently I am forced to bring this letter to a close. Wishing you success in your great work, I am your sincere friend. (signed) Monte Walters"

Tex and Lillian had been married over four years when he was sent to Eddyville. By all accounts the outlaw was totally devoted and loyal to his young bride. She was a bright ray of sunlight in his violent way of life. She lightened his darkened soul.

A baby was born to the couple in Iowa, but died shortly thereafter. Lillian had an especially hard time grieving over the infant's death, and Tex did all that he could to console her. According to her, these efforts included his placing her under hypnosis several times. On one dramatic occasion she saw her baby, apparently healthy and well, in the afterlife. This moving episode gave her great solace.

Lillian idolized her husband to the point of virtually being possessed. No sooner had Tex checked into the castle than she got a job at the Friedman Settlement House in Paducah. There she taught life skills to underprivileged children—most of them orphans. She rode the train to Eddyville two and three times a week to visit. Not a day went by that she didn't write him a long and loving letter. The forlorn wife lost one job for taking too many Sundays off to go to Eddyville.

Their relationship was so intense that it immediately caught the eyes of the prison administration. Wives and girl friends were always suspect anyway and prime agents for smuggling. Lillian's fanatical devotion to her prisoner husband placed her in a special category.

When Walters was shot trying to escape in the fall of 1922, he almost died. The wound was through the side, and he hovered between life and death for many days. She visited him almost daily in the prison hospital. On one occasion he sadly and lovingly suggested that her life with him was no good and she should forget about him.

"You see that tape over there?" she responded, pointing to a roll of surgical adhesive on the hospital shelf. "I'm going to stick to you just like that tape."

Slowly he recovered in the prison hospital. Without rancor or bitterness, he matter-of-factly told the guard who shot him, "You will have to do it again."

It was most likely during those crisp days of autumn, as he recuperated in the old, two-story brick prison infirmary, that Tex began to lay his plans for another attempted breakout.

In those days all of the guards were armed—the watchmen in the towers with high powered rifles and the ones patrolling the cellhouses and yard, pistols on their hips. The bullet through his gut, while attempting to scale the formidable stone wall, may have convinced Tex that the next time he would need to be armed.

And he considered bringing others along in order to even up the odds—more fire power was needed than one solitary man could provide. Otherwise it was pure suicide.

By Christmas of 1922, Tex had recovered from his wound enough to leave the hospital. He then had to serve out his time in solitary confinement for his attempted escape. It was early spring by the time he returned to his regular job at the shirt factory.

Lawrence Griffith was a twenty-two-year-old inmate from Dresden, Tennessee. He arrived at Eddyville on May 24, 1922, to begin serving a life sentence for murder out of Graves County. He had shot and killed his uncle.

Griffith was a much different hombre than Tex. He was big, burly and defiant. His hair was cropped close to his head, convict style, and he looked the part. Griffith was constantly in trouble with the administration, violating one rule or another, and generally making himself a problem. In the summer of 1923, he stabbed and killed another convict. Across his arm was tattooed, "Death Before Dishonor."

Walters and Griffith worked together in the shirt factory. They became friends and discussed ways to escape from the Kentucky State Penitentiary.

They needed weapons. To obtain them they needed outside help. Tex assured his confederate that Lillian would do the job.

"She'll do anything I ask her to do," he bragged not only to Griffith but to other inmates.

Two things soon became apparent to Walters. First, there was no way that his wife could smuggle anything into the penitentiary, let alone weapons. She was watched closely by the prison authorities and all their visits were observed by a prison guard who stood nearby. They could hardly carry on a confidential conversation, let alone have her slip him contraband. The guns would have to be either pitched over the wall, or brought in by a prison trusty. Either way, it was a risky business.

Secondly, he realized that the scheme had to be financed. They had to have money to purchase the weapons and ammunition. Other costs would also be incurred in carrying out the conspiracy.

Lillian's meager income would not be sufficient. She was spending all she made for her own upkeep and for expenses of her frequent train trips to Eddyville. Much of the money she had made had also been spent on books for Tex. Besides, she would quit her job in July because of sickness. Lillian had to sell some of her clothes for her own support. Several friends, including the Crawfords, were providing her financial as well as moral support.

Clever and conniving Tex found an answer to the money problem. Working with him and Griffith in the shirt factory was a petty thief whose real name was Cellond Henry Knudson. It is little wonder that with a label like that, he had taken on the simple tag of Jim Sparks.

Sparks was a twenty-two-year-old youngster from Litchfield, Kentucky, who was serving a two year sentence for horse stealing. His only prior offense was stealing a bicycle.

It is telling evidence of the total lack of any meaningful classification of inmates within the prison system of Kentucky in 1923 that young Sparks—hardly a dangerous or seasoned criminal—was serving time and working side-by-side with murderers Tex Walters and Lawrence Griffith.

Sparks was a shiftless worker and was repeatedly reported for goofing off in the shirt factory. He was also a very weak and easily intimidated prisoner. This made him an easy mark for the likes of Walters and Griffith.

Most significantly, Jim Sparks was a disabled veteran of the World War. In July of 1923, he received upon his inmate account a lump sum pension payment from the U. S. Veterans Bureau of $741.78. It was a whopping amount for those days and the talk of the yard.

Tex had found his money tree. What promises were made to Jim Sparks, or how he was persuaded to put up his fortune and become a part of the plot of Tex and Lillian Walters is not known for sure.

The most likely explanation for the conversion of Sparks to the cause is two-fold. First, he no doubt fell victim to the charismatic charm and colorful personality of the notorious Tex Walters. Secondly, being a weak and young inmate made him a prime target of being preyed upon sexually by some of the older, tougher inmates.

Tex and Lawrence Griffith would give him protection. At that time, walking the hill at Eddyville with those two was better insurance than Lloyd's of London. Of course he may have simply been threatened by Walters and Griffith to fall in line or else. Most likely it was a combination of all three.

By the end of the summer, Sparks was already dancing to the tune of Tex Walters. Records reflected that he drew large amounts from his account for cigarettes, candy and the like—no doubt much of it for his hero, Tex. On August 27, he sent a check in the amount of

$35 to a Minnie Sweeney in Paducah. Sweeney was the landlord of Lillian Walters.

Jim Sparks was to serve out his term and get out of prison on September 14. The plan was for him to take his money with him, hook up with Lillian, and purchase the weapons for Tex and Griffith. Lillian would then bring them to the prison and arrange for them to be thrown over the wall at a predetermined location.

Tex knew that it would not be easy. Pitching guns and ammo over a twenty-foot wall would be quite a feat. To do it without detection by the guards in the wall towers, even at night, would be extremely difficult. For his lovely wife Lillian to be assigned to the task was unthinkable.

Sparks would have to do the job, even though there was a high risk of the ex-convict being detected as soon as he hit the city limits. To avoid recognition or suspicion, Sparks would have to get off of the train in neighboring Kuttawa, two miles away, and cover the rest of the distance on foot and under cover of darkness.

Even if the guns made it over the wall, picking them up from inside would be about as treacherous as snatching an egg from the nest of a sitting condor. But it was the best they could do. Tex was a high roller and he was ready to throw the dice.

Early on the morning of September 14, 1923, Jim Sparks packed his bag, said his goodbyes, and processed out of the Kentucky State Penitentiary. He cleaned out his inmate account and the prison clerk gave him a check for $400, as well as $115.52 in cash. He was loaded—and free.

Even though Sparks was liberated, he did not head eastward toward his home in Litchfield. Instead he took the train westward toward Paducah.

One can only wonder what went through the mind of Cellond Henry Knudson, a/k/a Jim Sparks, as he rode along on the train that September morn. As he sat peering out of the window at the passing landscape of fields, woods, and rivers, he must have felt the exhilaration of an animal uncaged. Yet, the unseen strings of captivity controlled him still. He was on a mission for Tex Walters.

Safely out of the shadows of the Castle on the Cumberland, and no longer in need of strong arm protection from other prisoners nor under direct threats from Tex, he inexplicably carried on the plan.

His train arrived in Paducah at 8:30 a.m., where Lillian Walters was waiting at the station. She took him to the Citizens National Bank of Paducah and they cashed the $400 check.

The couple then took a train to Metropolis, Illinois, and registered as brother and sister at the Julian Hotel. Sparks spent the next few days looking for guns to purchase which would not be easily traced.

He was unsuccessful, and they took a train down river to Cairo. There they bought two revolvers: one, a .38 caliber, and the other a 32-20 police special, and four boxes of ammunition with 100 rounds in each. They wrapped the weapons separately in cloth and returned to Paducah on Saturday, September 22.

The next day, Lillian made her Sunday pilgrimage to Eddyville. Sparks remained in Paducah with the guns.

During her visit with Tex, plans were made to heave the pistols over the wall that night. They talked about where the guns would be thrown. He told her that he and Griffith planned to climb up the rain spout coming off the death house and go over the wall. He assured her there would be no shooting. But if there was, this time he would be on the sending end. In parting, he told her he would communicate with her some way after he had made good his escape.

Upon release from their cell house for breakfast on Monday morning, Walters and Griffith scoured the grounds for the guns. They were not there. The pieces had not come over. Not until Wednesday, when Lillian returned to the prison, did Tex learn what happened.

Sparks took a train from Paducah to Kuttawa at 1:30 a.m. Monday morning. However, he was apparently recognized by someone at the depot, and he was trailed all the way to Eddyville. In short, he was spooked, and did not get the guns over the wall.

Tex was not surprised. Sparks was a weak sister. They could not depend on him—except for his money. They would have to find another way to get them inside. He gave his wife careful instruction.

Before daylight on Thursday morning, September 27, Lillian and Sparks arrived by train at the Eddyville depot. They brought with them—still wrapped in cloth—the two pistols, as well as the boxes of ammunition.

The train station was located almost a mile north of Eddyville and out of sight of the prison. Nearby, on the road to town, was a long narrow bridge which crossed Lick Creek. During various times of the year the stream would run deep and wide. In late summer and fall it was reduced to a trickle. At that time, the bridge spanned nothing but dry ground and horse weeds.

This odd couple—the weak-kneed ex-con and the pretty young lady—made their way down the road in darkness to the depot bridge. Underneath it they buried the guns and the ammunition with their hands. A stick was stuck into the soft earth to mark the spot. By 8:30 a.m. that morning they were back in Paducah.

Walters never had much faith in Sparks being able to get the guns in over the walls. At some time he began to think of an alternative. By the time Lillian visited him on Wednesday to explain Sparks' failure to get the job done, another plan was in effect.

Inmate Harry Ferland was from California. At age 23, he was serving time in Eddyville for robbery. Ferland had been a problem convict from the time he was first sentenced and received at the prison in Frankfort. There he escaped, but was captured, and was constantly serving time in solitary confinement for making trouble. Finally, he was sent to Eddyville, where the Californian continued to misbehave. In July of l922, he was put back into solitary confinement for trying to escape. In short, Harry Ferland was continually in trouble and difficult to handle.

By September of 1923, this trouble maker was working in the prison laundry which was located in the first floor of the mess hall on the same level with the kitchen. Ferland was a friend of Lawrence Griffith and Tex Walters.

Almost every prisoner in the penitentiary made trips to the laundry regularly. Trusty Andrew Hawkins dirtied up a lot of shirts doing mechanical work at the water plant out front. He was a frequent visitor to Ferland's shop.

Tex Walters brought both Harry Ferland and Andrew Hawkins into the conspiracy. Both were captivated by the thoughts of flight. Ferland, though a late comer to the Walters' scheme, had a history of escapes. It was right down his alley.

Hawkins, on the other hand, is more of a puzzle. He had a fairly good life for an inmate, and being well liked by the prison administration, the amiable felon was a good candidate for parole.

Perhaps he was promised some of Sparks' money. Maybe he was simply tired of hitching up to a life sentence. For whatever reason, Tex weaved him into his spell.

Sometime between Thursday, September 27, and Monday, October l, Andrew Hawkins recovered at least one of the guns and the ammunition from underneath the depot bridge. Exactly how he did this is not known. It was a pretty good trek from his duty station at the pump house in front of the prison to the bridge. It took the better part of an hour to get there and back on foot. Even though he had liberal range and privileges, it was a risky venture.

On the other hand, it was not uncommon for trusties, including Hawkins, to make trips to the depot by truck to pick up freight for the prison. He may have been assigned such a task unsupervised. That would have made it an easy matter to retrieve the buried treasure.

Hawkins took one of the pistols—a brand new 32-20 police special—and three boxes of shells, and wrapped them in his dirty shirts at the water plant. As casual as one taking a stroll through the park, he sauntered up the front steps of the prison and—as he had done on countless occasions—moved nonchalantly past the turnkey who routinely opened the several gates at his behest. He took the soiled wadding of shirts to the laundry, and handed them to Harry Ferland.

Early on Monday morning, October 1, trusty Hawkins—in pressed convict denims and cloth hat—checked out through the front gate, joking and talking with the guard in his usual manner. He reported to his regular duty station at the water plant. After a short while he told his supervisor, Guthrie Ladd, that he was going to the bathroom. He was never seen again.

Later that same morning Lillian Walters arrived for her two-hour visit with her husband. Tex told her in a low, whispered voice that one of the guns and the ammunition had made it in.

Standing by observing the visitation closely, but unable to hear what was being said, were prison guards Hodge Cunningham and V. B. Mattingly. Little did they know what grave danger was lurking in this cozy conversation between two lovers.

Chapter 5

⊠⊠⊠

One common thread running through all human kind, regard-less of one's station in life, is the yearning to be free. So it was merely a natural progression of things when, as soon as the new doors slammed for the first time at the Kentucky State Penitentiary, that inmates began to plot ways to escape. Tex Walters and his confederates were not the first, nor would they be the last, to seek their freedom by departing unlawfully.

Not all of the inmates assigned to pull time at Eddyville in those early days were security risks. Some were serving as little as one year for chicken theft, for instance, and were so far away from home that they simply dug in to grind it out.

Eddyville has always been maximum security. When con-structed in the late nineteenth century is was considered state of the art. But the massive cellhouses, steel doors, towering stone walls, and glow-ering guards have not proven to be infallible. There have been many to make it over the walls.

Some methods have been ingenious. Artfully created man-nequins, complete with eye lids and hair, have been crafted to look like sleeping convicts—only to be discovered long after the real occupant of the cell had cut his way out of prison through the utility chase running down the middle of the cellhouse. Some have simply used small bits of hacksaw blades to patiently cut their way out, over a period of weeks, camouflaging their work each day with soap which had been colored with shoe polish.

Warden Chuck Thomas was a tall and lanky southern gentleman who dressed the part in seersucker suits, colonel ties, and broad brim hats. He also carried a cane. Reportedly on a routine inspection stroll down the walk of a cell block one day, he casually raked his staff against the bars. At one unfortunate inmate's cell, the blackened soap putty popped out and landed at the warden's feet!

Once out of their cell, escaping prisoners made their way up into the cavernous attic of the cell block and out onto the steep roof. Then they would make the long, perilous descent to the outside world by ropes of bed sheets or other fabric.

And there were other ways. Two convicts escaped by hiding amidst the slop cans and garbage being taken from the kitchen loading dock, out the sally port gate, and to the farm center eight miles away. They jumped out at the first stop. From then on the back of the trucks were carefully checked.

This did not deter the ingenuity of the criminal mind however. One desperate felon sneaked under the truck and latched on to the axle. He was seen by prison Captain Pat Kilgore, who allowed him a free ride—and no doubt high hopes—to the gate. Then, only one swinging door away from freedom, guards advised him that his fun was over. This episode led to the use of a mirror device to check under all outgoing vehicles.

There is a huge cave under the old town of Eddyville. Ever since the prison was built, there have been rumors about an opening from the cavern into the bastille. Of course, no such passageway exists. Nevertheless, in 1975, convict Steve Martin decided he would go underground.

"Jock," as he was called because of his midget-like, five-foot frame, squeezed down through a narrow duct into the grid of steam tunnels crisscrossing the prison grounds. These underground corridors are barely large enough for a person to walk bent over, and are the conduits for the large steam pipes servicing the prison's heating system. They are dark and, as one would imagine, very hot—over one hundred degrees when Jock submerged.

Prison guards gave search for a while, sweating and swearing as they probed with their flashlights. As Jock would report later, once when two officers approached him he slid into the almost imperceptible opening between the large pipe and the floor of the tunnel. When the pair of searchers stopped, one of them was standing only inches from his head.

"Well one thing's for sure," the unsuspecting guard proclaimed, "the little bastard's not down here."

Three days later, Jock staggered through a vent into the basement of one of the buildings, almost dead from heat exhaustion and dehydration.

The crime of escape at that time included the act of hiding in an unauthorized part of the penitentiary. Incredibly, a Lyon County jury acquitted Jock—apparently believing that three days in a Turkish bath was punishment enough.

In the 1920s, the shirt factory ran a night shift of convicts packing shirts in boxes and then large crates to be shipped out by rail the next day. One ingenious convict, who knew the exact weight of the finished canister, secreted himself in one of them, along with some junk hardware to bring it up to the proper weight. He—along with the shirts which covered him—were lugged out the wagon gate on the back of the truck, taken to the railroad and shipped out on a train. He was never heard from again.

Many attempts were much more straight forward.

As tall and intimidating as they may appear, the massive gray stone walls that surround the "hill" have not been completely effective. Their rough and sculptured surface makes them vulnerable. It is certainly not an easy climb—but it can be done. Over the years, some have simply caught the tower guard asleep, or staring another way, and gone over the wall.

Eugene Jennings, in the late 1960s, was an expert wall climber. Jennings would study for weeks the habits and routine of a particular wall stand guard. At the right time, he would make his move and scale the stone barrier. He escaped three times.

For some reason or another, the towering water tank which has always stood at the pinnacle of the hill has been the target of adventuresome prisoners. Obviously, it offered no means of escape. Simply out of boredom, to protest some administrative action, or for some other reason, inmates have from time to time climbed the long ladder to the catwalk which circumvents the tank some 200 feet off the ground. From there they would shout invectives and taunt the guards.

Again Eugene Jennings came into the picture, staying aloft one time for three days.

On another occasion three unruly residents made the climb. They got so caught up in berating their captors that one of them pulled down his pants and shot them a moon. This was too much for veteran guard Stonnie Parker. With the approval of Warden John Wingo, Parker proceeded to sprinkle the unsuspecting convicts with a shot gun blast, whereupon, the three scampered down the ladder like firemen rushing to a fire.

It is not known how many hapless souls have attempted to tunnel under the ancient walls.

In the spring of 1959, inmates Herman Fleming, Ruby Foster, and Melvin Osborne dug a tunnel from the prison cannery to just outside the prison. It took days of strenuous and secret digging as they dumped their dirt into underground sewers. The end of the burrow was concealed by a piece of heavy equipment. Nevertheless, an alert wall guard saw them emerge from the hole and shot at them. Two were slightly wounded, and all were recaptured.

Undoubtedly, the most creative and novel escape was pulled off by con artist James Bell Yager in 1964.

Yager, from Louisville was serving time for some scam and was one of the inmate legal eagles. He was also exceptionally bright. More significantly, Yager was the king of con. Even the prison guards could not keep from liking the bubbly and friendly convict. There wasn't a violent bone in his body, but he couldn't be trusted any farther than the next step on the prison yard.

Since there was no prison optometrist, convicts needing eye examinations were taken to a doctor in Paducah. Yager managed to wrangle the prison administration into setting him up an appointment for May 6. That was the only opportunity the effervescent prison lawyer needed.

He nonchalantly talked a prison guard into making a seemingly innocuous phone call. It was to a woman in Murray whose father was an inmate. James Bell Yager was doing legal work for him. He wanted the guard to tell her to meet the inmate's lawyer in a parking lot in Paducah at a certain time on May 6. The parking lot just happened to be right behind the eye doctor's office. The time just happened to be the same as Yager's eye appointment.

Yager was escorted to his appointment by a prison guard and was allowed to wear his own civilian clothes to Paducah. The two were sitting in the waiting room, thumbing through year-old magazines, when Yager requested to go to the bathroom. Totally taken in by the friendly convict, the guard simply released him from his cuffs and let him go on his own.

Yager went out the bathroom window and met his inmate client's daughter in the parking lot. He had with him a very impressive stack of legal documents including a writ for habeas corpus on her father's behalf. He convinced the woman that he was the lawyer representing her father and she gave him three hundred fifty dollars.

After a courtly thank you and farewell, he possessed the audacity to actually go to the Federal Court House in Paducah and file the writ seeking his inmate friend's relief.

There is honor among thieves—at least as far as Mr. Yager was concerned.

Next, he went to a Paducah store and outfitted himself with a suit of clothes. Looking like a Philadelphia lawyer, Yager proceeded to a funeral home and rented an ambulance to go with him to Nashville to "pick up my wife at the hospital."

When they arrived in Nashville, Yager had the ambulance driver to wait at the hospital entrance while he went in to "check her out." He returned after a short while and apologetically informed the driver that his wife was going to have to stay another day or two. Whereupon he paid the driver for his services, thanked him profusely and sent him on his way.

Yager was picked up later in Chicago and sent back to Eddyville with another five years tacked onto his sentence. Undaunted by his capture, and in his typical fashion, he regaled inmates and guards alike with his humorous account of the adventure.

In 1937, the population of the prison—which was often referred to as West Kentucky State Penitentiary—ballooned to an all-time high of 1,528 residents. Bunks were set up outside the cells in the open cellblocks to accommodate the influx.

The devastating flood of that year had inundated the old penitentiary in Frankfort and the entire prison population was evacuated. They never went back. That old relic was closed down and demolished and a new reformatory at LaGrange was under construction. That same year, the erection of a new cellhouse at the castle was begun.

Economic hardships also contributed substantially to the overcrowding. Still in the throes of the great depression, many people committed crimes out of need. Times were so hard for some that they broke the law in order to survive—to get a bunk and three squares a day. Incredibly there were a few who came to Eddyville to be treated for venereal disease. Their crime—voting twice.

The guards charged with the dangerous task of maintaining and supervising this teeming and seething cauldron of humanity made one hundred dollars a month.

On the steamy evening of August 6, 1937—a Saturday night—part of this oversized kingdom of criminals was chowing down in the mess hall. Forty-nine-year-old Deputy Warden Ben Wilson was moving about the dining hall when convicts Ezra Davenport, Robert Benewitz, and Earl Webb grabbed him from behind. They wrestled him to the floor as the rest of the inmate crowd looked on in disbelief.

Officer Roy Hogan came to Wilson's rescue. Just as he did, Davenport pulled the pistol from the deputy warden's holster and shot Hogan in the leg. As the wounded guard fell, Davenport picked up his revolver and gave it to Benewitz. All three convicts—two of them armed—then marched Wilson out of the mess hall and toward the front gate.

At that time Warden Jesse Buchanan's chief deputy, Porter Lady, and guard Clyde Twisdale came walking across the yard. Davenport shot at the two officers, the bullet barely missing Lady's head. Twisdale calmly leveled his .45 and blew Davenport away. Convict Webb picked up the gun of his fallen comrade.

In the confusion of the firefight, Wilson alertly and bravely broke away and ran for the door of four cellhouse, forty feet away. Benewitz shot once at the fleeing officer but missed. He and Webb quickly ran to the back gate. They pointed their guns at the startled and panic-stricken turnkey and ordered him to open the gate or die. He opened the gate.

Lady ordered Twisdale back to the mess hall to get things under control and he started running toward the truck gate in the south wall. As he passed a wall stand he yelled for the guard to drop him a .358 caliber rifle. He continued to run toward the gate, and the guard on the tower there pushed a button and the double-wide truck entrance opened.

Lady ran through the opening, out of the prison and turned right. Sprinting like a foot soldier with the rifle held tightly in one hand, he headed up the access road to the front of the prison.

As he turned the corner, Lady ran into a startled Sam Litchfield, an off-duty prison guard, who was walking casually along the sidewalk. Litchfield knew at once that something bad was happening and immediately joined his superior officer. Together they ran in a crouch up the sidewalk behind a low wall to just below the front steps of the penitentiary. There, they waited behind the refuge of the waist high barrier for the two armed desperados to come bursting through the front entranceway of the Kentucky State Penitentiary.

The tension was electrifying as this drama unfolded there on the main street in the middle of town.

Meanwhile, Benewitz and Webb easily overpowered the guard on the front gate and charged out the doors.

Sam Litchfield was known as the best rifle shot on the entire guard force. Lady handed him the long gun, and pulled his pistol. They braced themselves.

Then came Benewitz and Webb, bounding down the steps, blasting away at the last line of resistance. Lady and Litchfield opened fire with their pistol and high-powered rifle. A bullet tore through Benewitz's chest and he tumbled down the long flight of steps to the bottom, dead. Webb immediately threw down his gun, raised his hands and surrendered. The murderous prison break was over.

That night, Warden Jesse Buchanan made the lasting decision to take away the firearms from the guards working the yard and cellhouses.

※ ※ ※

Any prisoner at Eddyville is a security risk. After all, it is the state's only maximum security jail. But there's a big difference between a security risk and an escape artist. The same difference as between a surgeon and a butcher.

Any inmate doing a lot of time is likely to bolt if given a good chance to succeed. They may act on impulse, jumping at a fortuitous opportunity. Most are moved simply by the desire to be anywhere but in prison. The escape artist is also motivated by the longing to be free. But he is driven to a greater degree by the gamesmanship: "Lock me if you can."

Don Tate was an escape artist. On May 4, 1978, he was residing in five cellhouse, in a single cell facing the prison yard. His window was about thirty feet above the ground. Underneath him was the prison mess hall, which took up the entire first floor of the cell block. From his cubicle he would make the most spectacular escape in the history of the Kentucky State Penitentiary.

Five cellhouse was no match for Tate. Built by the Works Project Administration of the Roosevelt years, it was completed in 1941 and provided 363 new cells. The huge structure is five stories high, divided into three parallel wings fingering off from the front. Sandy brown in color, this concrete edifice is attached, with a slight inset, to the end of four cellhouse—or to the extreme right, coming in the front gate.

It is an ugly addition, marring the elegant medieval facade of the Castle on the Cumberland. The inside of the building, especially before recent renovation, was even worse. Inferior material, defective design, and poor planning have made it a security nightmare down through the years.

Windows—the outside ones overlooking the yard, and the inside ones overlooking the roof of the kitchen—have no bars, but were covered with metal louvers. These and the frames which encased them were easily sawed out. Death row inmates were located there for a while—until one night they were discovered with their doors and windows all cut out and ready to go.

Inmates have even deplored it, preferring to stay in the much older cellhouses. The narrow halls running down the wings have cells on each side, providing little privacy and much noise and bedlam for their occupants.

Don Tate's rap sheet was as unsightly as the building in which he lived. He was serving a life sentence for armed robbery plus various shorter sentences he had received in prison for escapes and attempts.

In December of 1976, Tate had been taken out on a hospital call to Princeton, about 12 miles away. While at the hospital, he managed to slip the gun out of the holster of one of the two escorting guards and free himself of his restraints. At gunpoint, he forced them to drive out into the country, where he intended to leave them shackled to a tree and flee in the car.

As he walked his captives into the woods, one of the officers panicked and grabbed him. They wrestled to the ground and the gun went off, wounding the guard. Tate proceeded to shackle the two to a tree, assured them he would call in their location and took off in the car.

By this time the law was after him in full force, to include the use of a state police airplane. Tate was soon apprehended, returned to the prison, placed in segregation and charged with his crimes. By the fall of 1977, he had received his extra time for the escape and shooting and was back on the yard, living in the porous five cellhouse.

The administration was careful to locate him on the inside row of cells on the first floor above the dining hall. This way, he was a long way from the roof, and if he came through his window—it would be a thirty-foot drop to the prison yard, and still within the walls.

He was in Cell 1-A-27. The only way out would be through the window, onto the yard, and up over four cellhouse—an impossible feat. But Tate was undaunted and he began at once to plot his escape.

His plan was audacious and would require great physical strength, especially in his upper body. As the leaves began to turn, and the autumn days grew crisp, the 50-year-old prisoner went to work. He began to jog on the asphalt track which crowned the hill and work out at the weight pile located near the school.

Daily, even as winter seized the yard, he trudged along in the cold and rain, jogging and lifting. Slowly, and apparently without raising suspicion of the guards, the flab began to fall off and his stocky body grew muscular.

During those winter months and early spring, he began to collect the wares he would need to carry out his bold plan. Shrewdly, he placed plastic sheeting over his window, ostensibly to keep the cold winter air out of his drafty cell. There was nothing unusual about that. Several prisoners did the same. Slowly, however, he allowed the plastic to billow out bit by bit so that he could use his mirror without being seen. Also, the spotlight shining directly from across the yard would not detect the louvers after they were cut.

Next, he collected rolls of nylon thread from a friend who worked in the shoe shop out back in the vocational area. Each strand had a weight strength of about ten pounds. Slowly, over many weeks, Tate weaved forty strands, one hundred feet long, into a stout rope. He worked on it at night, keeping a constant look out for the officer on the walk who made predictable rounds. To hide his work from day to day, he tied the end of the cord onto a heavy metal washer and flushed the loose end down his commode. The anchor would be carefully pushed just out of sight into the neck of the basin.

When spring came to the Cumberland, inmate Tate was in prime physical condition. He began the final stage of preparation.

There were two guard towers which had his window covered. Number two stand was directly across the yard at the end of three cellhouse. But he noticed that a limb from a tree could be bent, so that in the spring the full foliage would block the view of the guard in that tower from seeing his window. So, daily, he began to chin on the limb, pulling it down and slowly changing its position.

The other tower was four stand, which protruded high off the center of the back wall. With his shaving mirror, he began to observe nightly the changing of the midnight shift on that stand. Each time, the light was turned on inside the tower as the oncoming guard was briefed. During that critical minute, nothing could be seen from inside the guard stand looking out.

As the days grew longer and the nights milder, Tate pulled out a small piece of hacksaw blade he had hidden in a Camel cigarette package. Little by little, he began to work on the steel window rods upon which swung the metal louvers. Finally, on the night of May 4, 1978, he was ready to go.

A broom handle protruded from his improvised knapsack. He coiled the rope around the lower uncut louver of his window and waited. Near midnight, he saw and heard a group of guards moving across the yard. There was the sound of clanging doors in the cellhouse. The shift change was underway.

Quickly, he made a dummy in his bunk with pillow and blankets. Then, leaning close to the window, he held the mirror in the plastic balloon outside his window and angled it toward the back wall stand. The light went on inside the watch tower. Quickly Tate lowered the knapsack on one end of the rope to the ground. Pulling out the severed louver, he then swung his body through the narrow opening. Hanging just outside, he arranged the plastic covering to conceal the damaged window.

Down the doubled rope he went to the concrete walk way thirty feet below. Hitting the ground with a solid thud, he snapped one half of the line from above. It slipped past the bar and fell near his feet. Gathering up his rope and knapsack, he then moved along the base of five cellhouse to a brightly lit doorway leading into the building. Looking back, he could see the spotlight from two stand bouncing off his window which was safely covered with plastic.

Past the door he dashed, to the copper drain pipe which ran the full ninety feet to the roof line of four cellhouse. He climbed it until he reached the ledge of a cellhouse window thirty feet off the ground and about five feet to the right.

Tate then reached over and transversed to the opening by grabbing hold of the bars. As he stood on the window ledge, holding on for dear life to the bars, he stared directly into the cavernous cellblock inside. The tiers of cells rose before him and the corner of one catwalk was only twelve feet away.

Just at that time, a lone guard came whistling along the prison loop behind him. Tate froze. All the guard had to do was look toward the window and the escaping convict would have been plainly seen. The guard continued on toward the back of the yard.

Tate climbed up the vertical rods of the window which are intersected every two feet by horizontal cross bars. Up the long opening he went, some thirty more feet to the top. With the stone arch of the window just above his head, he fastened his homemade safety harness to one of the bars. The former telephone line worker leaned out over sixty feet of nowhere to test his contraption. It held.

Fishing around in his knapsack, he pulled out the broom handle. Frantically, he fastened one line to the middle of it, leaned back and attempted to lodge it between the dragon's teeth along the roof line parapet above. It clanged back down. Once again, with the same result. He abandoned the idea, and ripped the line from the broomstick and tied the pole to the window bars.

Clinging from just below the overhanging stone cornice which ran along the roof line, Tate's hand fashioned a large lasso. Leaning back, he flicked it toward the dragon's tooth. It caught only a few inches of the stone. He whiplashed it back down and tried again and again until his arms began to weaken. Sweat poured down his forehead and into his eyes. Then it caught onto a rough corner and held.

Releasing his harness, he began to climb, hand over hand, upward, over the ridge, toward the stone parapet. The months of body building paid off as he pulled himself past the stone dragon's tooth and onto the roof.

Drained and exhausted, he only paused for a moment.

Gathering his ropes and knapsack, he then moved down the edge of the roof, hidden by the stone cresting. At the end of the cellhouse, a granite wall ran up the slope of the roof where it joined five cellhouse. By bracing himself against this barrier he was able to climb the steep incline to the top.

As the veteran convict peered over the crest of the roof into the world of freedom, he was staring squarely into number one guard stand. It is the concrete tower which straddles the steps leading up to the front entrance of the prison. If the guard staring out of the window toward the front gate had looked up and to his right, he would have seen Don Tate.

But he didn't, and the escape artist dodged the bullet once again by ducking and moving down the roof line to the end of the cellhouse. There he peered over the stone cornice. It was almost one hundred feet straight down to freedom. At this location, there is an offset where five and four cellhouses join. Going off the end of four cellhouse would put him in the corner of the inset, protected from the view of one guard stand.

Tate tied the thin line around a large ornamental chimney eighteen feet around. The hitch used up valuable footage. He threw over the end, and with a quick deep breath, followed it over the side. Down he went, hand under hand, his legs hanging free and pushing off the wall as he went. The thin rope bit into the rough hewn stone.

Then he ran out of rope—a good thirty to forty feet off the ground. Smartly he pushed over to the bottom of the long window at the end of four cellhouse. Grabbing hold of the bars, he climbed once again to the top as he did on the other side a long ten minutes before. Once at the top and his feet safely on the crossbar, he took a razor blade from his pocket, reached high, and cut the rope. With the severed end he scampered back down the bars to the ledge of the window. There he tied the rope to the lowest bar, and let it fall. Seconds later, he was at its end, still several feet off the ground. He dropped onto the soft grass and rolled into the corner.

The beams from the headlights of a pickup truck danced off the stone above his head. It was the roving patrol passing along the utility road just a few feet away. He flattened into the shadows and the vehicle passed.

Peeping around the corner, he saw the guard in the front guard tower. When the watchman's head was turned, Tate broke into the open, down the grassy slope and tumbled in behind the pump station. From there he dashed toward a hedge row near a residential state house. Lights still burned in an upstairs window. Through the back yard, and across the street, Don Tate ran at full speed, through the shadows of a row of houses and into the woods beyond.

Twenty-four hours later prison escapee Don Tate was paddling a metal john boat through the darkness across Barkley Lake. The night before he had made it all the way to the Eddy Creek embayment before daylight had forced him to take cover in the underbrush.

A massive manhunt had ensued once his getaway was discovered. Prison authorities, along with local and state law enforcement, failed to pick up his trail. A five-mile area was mapped out and roadblocks set up. Guards and dogs trampled the hills and hollows. But Tate remained hidden near some unoccupied lake houses throughout the long day.

He carefully studied one home in particular and detected no movement whatsoever. Well after dark and after determining the home belonged to an absentee owner, he cautiously moved out from his cover and broke into the house.

Strong drink being the root of all evil in Don Tate's life, he was quite naturally drawn first to the well-stocked liquor cabinet. He helped himself to some large gulps of Scotch.

Next, he bagged up a hefty supply of booze and food from the refrigerator, and headed out the back door toward the lake. On the rolling lawn, Tate spotted an aluminum john boat turned bottom up with a large paddle underneath. Grateful for his good fortune, he flipped the skiff over, threw in his newly pilfered supplies, as well as the oar, and shoved the vessel across the dew drenched grass and into the water of Barkley Lake.

The night was inky black, perfect for a runaway convict.

Eddy Creek embayment is one of the major arteries which leads into the Cumberland River and the open lake. From where Tate embarked, it was roughly two miles down the widening bay to the main channel. He stayed around the bushy edges, laboriously pulling his craft westward. In his pocket was a map of the Land Between the Lakes ripped out of a tourist magazine in the prison library. It was the distant shore which now lay about four miles in front of him. That was his destination.

On land, the hunting party was still in pursuit. But by this time, it had lost both its intensity and momentum. Most prison officials were of the opinion that he had been picked up by an accomplice in a car, and was now out of the area. So Tate, perspiring in his labor, slowly made his way through the spring night unmolested.

By the early morning hours the dark mass which had been fixed on the horizon for most of the night began to come upon him. Only a tow boat, pushing two acres of barges, had crossed his path. Across the large span of open lake and the buoyed channel of the

Cumberland River, Tate at last reached his destination.

The Land Between the Lakes (LBL) is a wild and uninhabited wilderness. It is a national recreation and environmental education area managed by the Tennessee Valley Authority. The wooded peninsula is formed by Kentucky Lake on the west and Lake Barkley to the east. A canal runs through the northern neck connecting the two bodies of water.

This vast woodland is forty miles long, taking in parts of both Kentucky and Tennessee, and varies from six to eight miles in width. It covers 170,000 acres and has 300 miles of shoreline.

Over ninety percent of the area is forested, primarily with large, towering hardwoods. Prior to the impoundment of Lake Barkley the LBL was inhabited by about 2,500 people. This "Between the Rivers" section of far western Kentucky, although isolated by the adjoining streams, had always been blessed with good, stout-hearted people and various schools and churches.

But when Don Tate arrived just before dawn on May 4, 1978, all the residents had been relocated for some fifteen years. There were over 300 miles of roads, 200 miles of trails, and numerous facilities managed and maintained by TVA within the the government enclave. It was still—especially in early May—a land of entangling vegetation and woods, giving home to all kinds of wildlife including deer, bobcats, skunks, raccoons, opossums, beaver, rabbit, squirrel, river otters, coyotes, foxes, wild turkey, and over 250 species of birds. All of this is not to mention snakes of all kinds and the teeming insect population, which includes the dreaded deer tick.

It is not the land of Dairy Queen.

Into this world came Don Tate, as he dragged the boat up onto the gravel shoreline.

To conceal the vessel, he turned it over under some underbrush and carefully covered it with limbs and driftwood. Saying a sad farewell to the liquor, he loaded up as much food as he could carry and scurried up the bank into the woods. Satisfied that he was sufficiently hidden, he laid down on the ground and went to sleep.

Sometime in the afternoon, Tate awoke to the sounds of boaters on the lake. It was crappie season and he knew he would have to be careful. The full foliage of the deep and dense woods provided him ample protection. Pulling out his map, he assessed his current situation.

Running directly through the middle of the LBL, north to south, is the main artery called the Trace. It was Tate's goal to hike to the roadway and then follow it south into Tennessee. He would have to travel only at night to avoid being seen by motorists.

For the next two days the escaped convict trudged through the wild, searching for the Trace. The spring weather was miserable for one loose in the jungle without adequate provisions or gear. Evenings were cold and the days were hot. Occasional thunder showers would drench him and his wet clothing made for bone chilling and sleepless nights. One evening he spent on the floor of an old abandoned stone church. The remains stood hauntingly, defying the onslaught of nature's garden.

He kept running across gravel roads and narrow paved lanes, but they were not the main thoroughfare he was seeking. With the dense forest and towering trees, it was hard to determine directions. Finally he arrived at what he thought was the Trace and followed it. It seemed to meander and after a while he became disoriented and confused.

After two days and nights of traveling and with his food supply running perilously low, he became totally exhausted and demoralized. Even the thought of prison didn't seem so bad.

Then he arrived at a crest of a hill where the road bent down toward the lake. From there he was able to see a wide and open span of water. As he peered out upon the scene before him, a shocking and devastating sight filled his weary and tortured eyes. There, directly across the lake in front of him, was the Kentucky State Penitentiary.

For days he had been walking in circles. Dazed, he walked off into the woods and sat down near the water's edge to collect his awful thoughts. His dark and dismal mood contrasted with the beautiful sunlit May afternoon, and the sounds of nature all around him.

After a while he noticed something in the water, not far from the bank. It was a fisherman, floating along in an attractive fishing boat with a motor. The elderly gentleman was not far away, but Tate no longer feared detection. He was at the end of his rope and desperate.

As the fisherman and his craft drifted closer to the bank, an idea struck the dogged convict. If he moved down the hill just a bit, he might be able to jump on the unsuspecting fisherman and take his boat. By the time the old man walked out of the LBL to report the incident, Tate could be in Tennessee.

Creeping down the bank like a cat, he poised for the leap. The old man turned and their eyes met. It had to be a horrible sight for the startled angler. Here, in the middle of nowhere, lurking just above him was this crazed animal which looked a lot like a human being.

As Tate sprung from the ledge into the water, the old man dropped his fishing rod and abandoned ship. He was escaping from the escapee.

It was probably a surprise to both men to discover the water was only about waist deep. Tate waded hurriedly toward the empty boat, while its owner stumbled frantically toward the bank. They reached their destinations about the same time.

In an instant, the fleeing felon climbed aboard, cranked the motor and twisted the throttle. He sped away, leaving a churning wake behind.

The old man stood there, astonished and bewildered. He watched the vanishing vessel become smaller and smaller. Don Tate had found himself a ride to Tennessee.

❄ ❄ ❄

A mass break out is every warden's nightmare.

For over a hundred years the gallant guards and wardens at the stone castle have, for the most part, stemmed the tide of escaping prisoners to one or two at a time. But not always.

At about 9:30 on Thursday night of April 16, 1953, six inmates sawed their way out of five cellhouse. Using smuggled hacksaw blades over a period of several days, they cut out holes in their cells barely large enough through which to squeeze. Each night, when guards were feeding prisoners on other floors, they would come out on the walk and work on the door at the end of the walk. It opened to a stairway which in turn led up to the roof. Returning to their cells, the prisoners would then stick the severed bar back so that it was not noticed during the day.

On the night of the break, they crawled out of their cells, went through the back door, and up to the roof. They then proceeded to the exact location from which Don Tate would descend years later. Using ropes plaited from strips of their mattress covers and sheets, all six went down the face of the prison, one by one, in plain view of the passing traffic on the main street of Eddyville. No one noticed and they all landed safely and made their getaway.

Although the escapes were not discovered until the next morning, the sextet did not even get out of the area. An intensive and energetic manhunt had all of them back behind bars within forty-eight hours of their leaving.

The most significant mass break out in the history of the Kentucky State Penitentiary occurred in the early morning hours of June 16, 1988.

Three cellhouse lodges the segregation unit of Kentucky's maximum security prison. This is the end of the road for all felons. It is where the most incorrigible of criminals spend their entire days locked up, with only short respites for showers and exercise.

Shortly after midnight, twelve inmates in three cellhouse broke out of their cells. They had cut the bottom track on the cell doors, enabling them to push it out far enough at the bottom to squeeze through.

Once on the walk, they removed a steel mesh screen covering the window. They then proceeded to cut through a set of bars, broke a window and cut yet another set of bars. Eight of the convicts then lowered themselves to the ground by the use of an extension cord. Once outside the institution they broke away from its walls in a frantic run.

Three of the hopefuls were caught on the walk before they could effect their escape. Another one, discovered hanging from the window, was apprehended. Eight of the most dangerous criminals in the Commonwealth were loose upon the land.

At around 4:20 a.m. a pickup truck was reported stolen from the driveway of a house near the penitentiary. A major manhunt ensued, combining the forces of the prison, local law enforcement and the state police. Road blocks were established, helicopters circled just above the tree lines, and men combed the area on foot for days. Within forty-eight hours, three of the fugitives were found in the surrounding countryside and taken into custody.

Almost a week later, two more were arrested in Taylor County, Kentucky, after a brief exchange of gunfire. One week from the break out, almost to the minute, they were returned to three cell house at 2:30 in the morning.

That left three of them still at large. They had been the ones who had made their way out of the area in the stolen pickup truck. The trio motored along Barkley Lake over the narrow back roads to Dover, Tennessee. Near there, in a secluded subdivision, they broke into the home of an elderly couple and brutally murdered them. They then headed for Mexico.

Several months later, through outstanding police work and international co-operation, the Mexican authorities apprehended them and brought the three to the U.S. border where they were taken into custody by the FBI. After a lengthy extradition battle which was ultimately decided by the U. S. Supreme Court, Derrick Quintero, James Blanton and Billy Hall were returned to Lyon County and tried for the escape.

More importantly, they were tried and convicted in Tennessee for the murder of the Dover couple. They received the death sentence and are now imprisoned in Tennessee awaiting execution.

There was a tremendous outcry of public concern after the mass escape, and the news media spotlighted the need for additional security at the prison. Extensive investigations were conducted by both the Department of Corrections and the Lyon County Grand Jury.

As a result of all the attention and political pressure, the legislature appropriated additional money for the hiring of 47 more officers, and authorized six new maintenance slots. In addition, the state allotted two million dollars for capital improvement to enhance security at Eddyville, to include new perimeter lights and the renovation of three cellhouse. Also, at long last, hazardous duty retirement pay was finally approved for correctional officers.

Unfortunately, as attention was turned away from Eddyville and the state's budgetary crunch hit, many of the additional personnel slots and expenditures were slashed. As usual in the world of prisons, when the crisis cools, so do good intentions. Or, as one-time Eddyville warden Donald Bordenkircher liked to say, "Today's headlines become tomorrow's toilet paper."

Limestone being quarried for the building of the Branch Penitentiary; the land was owned by General Hylan B. Lyon and formerly belonged to his father, Matthew Lyon, Jr. The narrow gauge railway was built in order to transport the rock to the building site, approximately 3 miles away. (Photograph courtesy of Mr. and Mrs. Julian Beatty.)

Rock being unloaded from barges at the river front by inmates during the construction of the Kentucky State Penitentiary. (Photograph courtesy of Bob Bennett.)

This is a view of the front of the Castle on the Cumberland, made shortly after construction, and before the additions of four and five cellhouses. Notice the low water level of the Cumberland River, which existed prior to the construction of the lock and dam. (Photograph courtesy of Matthew W. McGovern and the Western Kentucky University Special Collections Library.)

A view of the back of the penitentiary taken from Pea Ridge shortly after the original construction. (Photograph courtesy of Matthew W. McGovern and the Western Kentucky University Special Collections Library.)

A baptism being conducted at the old water reservoir, around 1905. Originally a cooling pool for the old boiler room, it was later converted to a prison swimming pool. Finally, it was bulldozed under in 1990. Stripes disappeared from the yard in 1909 except for disciplinary cases.

The whipping stone, located in the old dungeon, across which inmates were held while lashes were being applied. Whippings were abolished in 1913.
(Photography courtesy of Barry Bannister and the Kentucky State Penitentiary Archives.)

"White line" lining up for chow.

The "colored line" coming out of three cellhouse on the way to the dining hall sometime around 1910.

"Castle on the Cumberland" as it appeared in 1911.

Inside of the old dining room, with porters ready to serve. Notice the striped curtains on the windows as well as the prison overseer seated on a platform to the upper right. Picture was taken around 1905. (Photograph courtesy of Matthew W. McGovern and the Western Kentucky University Special Collections Library.)

Warden John Chilton's wife, Lula (right) with daughter Sara (left) in front of the prison during the same time period as the Tex Walters siege. The warden's little nephew, Henry Payne Ashley, stands between them.
(Photograph courtesy of Bob Bennett)

Henry T. Haggerman, Warden of the Kentucky State Penitentiary, 1901 to 1912.

Inmataes loitering on the yard, sometime around 1905. Note several still dressed in stripes. (Photograph courtesy of the Kentucky State Penitentiary Archives.)

Inmate band performs on the prison yard around 1910, near the administration building. One cellhouse is in the background. (Photograph courtesy of Kentucky State Penitentiary Archives.)

A shot of three cellhouse as it appeared on Hodge Cunningham's last shift, October 3, 1923. It was converted into a segregation unit in the 1950's.

Old number one cellblock with lattice-covered doors operated by the "slam." This cellhouse has been renovated and converted into offices, inmate canteen, recreation hall, and chapel. It was in this general area that Hodge Cunningham confronted the Walters gang and was shot by Lawrence Griffith on the morning of October 3, 1923.

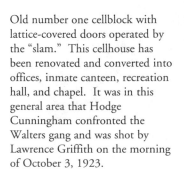

The prison library around the turn of the century, located inside the chapel. It was here that Daddy Warner worked for Chaplain Adolphus Hanberry.

The old dining hall at the Kentucky State Penitentiary around 1910. The wall clock which survived the Tex Walters siege is hanging on the wall between the windows. (Photograph courtesy of Bob Bennett.)

Prisoners at work in the garment factory, sometime in the 1950s. It was within this building that Tex Walters and Lawrence Griffith worked and launched their rebellion. (Photograph courtesy of Kentucky State Penitentiary Archives.)

The recreational shop for blacks. Photograph taken sometime in the 1940s.

79

Inmates drilling on the recreation field sometime in the late 1930s.

Warden John L. Chilton, who served the longest continuous term at the Kentucky State Penitentiary, from 1912 to 1929. (Photograph courtesy of George G. Harralson, III)

The electric chair at the Kentucky State Penitentiary, where 162 men have been electrocuted. It was constructed by P. W. "Pete" Depp, who was chief electrician at the prison at the time it was installed. He built the solid wooden seat in the back room of his home in Summer Shade, Kentucky. Depp also served as the first executioner. (Photograph courtesy of Kentucky State Penitentiary Archives.)

Chapter 6

◼◼◼

Hodge Cunningham was born October 3, 1880, and raised on a farm near Little River in rural Trigg County, Kentucky. He was the youngest of four and the only son of Perry and Sarah "Kitty" Cunningham. His mother and father were first cousins—not an unusual nuptial arrangement in those days in the vicinity of Goose Hollow. The "woods were full of 'em," you know.

Farming was a tough life, full of back-breaking work. Hodge grew up poor, as did most others in that community. There were few diversions from the bleak existence. Whiskey and making music were two of them. Both of these passions ran through the Cunningham clan. His uncle, Robert Cunningham, was called "Bob Tank" because of all the liquor he could hold.

Hodge fell right in step with family tradition on both counts, possessing a liking for good whiskey as well as a talent for music. By the time he was grown he had mastered three musical instruments: banjo, guitar, and fiddle.

His youth was filled with hard labor during the week, strong drink and making music for dances on Saturday nights. His weakness was that he could not do one without the other. So he gave up both on March 17, 1905, when he married Mary Emma Mitchell.

Their early years together were marred by heartache as they lost their first two children—Lucille at age three, and Loyd just after his first birthday. Death of the young was not that uncommon in that time and place. Two healthy boys were then born to the union—Perry, in 1909, and Mitch, in 1913.

Hodge's legs began to bother him from the hard, manual labor and he longed for something better than the dim prospects of the farm. When his sons were still small, the foursome moved to the county seat of Cadiz where Hodge obtained employment as the caretaker of the city cemetery. Next he became a city policeman.

He was a congenial and friendly sort, with a lively sense of humor. The tall and lean young man made friends easily. In 1920, through the political help of his friend, state legislator Adolphus Hanberry, he landed a job as guard at the Kentucky State Penitentiary. It was a coveted position at that time and the slots were allocated to the counties and controlled to great extent by the local political bosses.

His family moved into a comfortable wooden frame house just outside the wall of the prison. They all made friends quickly in the colorful little town of Eddyville. Hodge enjoyed his work at first. When he was struck by lightning his attitude changed. He began to feel the mounting pressure which comes with keeping hardened criminals on a daily basis. Hodge began to think of doing something else for a living.

Then the wife of inmate Sam Galloway died. As a relative and friend of the family, Hodge was allowed to escort Sam to Mayfield for the funeral. While he was there Galloway introduced him to a prominent businessman of the town. They talked about employment possibilities. Hodge made a good impression and Sam's friend assured him that he would be able to find him a job.

So on the night of October 2, 1923, as Hodge Cunningham walked through the prison to his assignment as officer of three cellhouse, he was both worried and hopeful. He was uneasy about the developments concerning Tex Walters, and hopeful that he himself would escape the castle before something dreadful happened.

In this segregated prison in 1923, three cellhouse was the housing unit for blacks. Not until thirty years later, when it would be completely renovated and converted into disciplinary housing, would the "colored" prisoners be moved to two cellhouse. There they would continue to be housed separately until 1968.

The penitentiary reflected the social mores of the outside world. Blacks and whites not only celled separately, but ate separately, and even had separate recreational facilities, called "shops". At chow time the "white line" was run first and the "colored line" last.

The convicted felons of different hues even worshiped in the chapel at different times and their educational classes, normally held at night, were separate and apart. The only time they mingled was in the work place, toiling away at the shirt factory, or making horse collars and brooms.

On this October night, as Hodge made his way to his duty station, keys rattled and metal doors clanged, echoing through the cavernous cellhouses. Under his left arm he carried his loaded .38 pistol in a shoulder holster.

The cell blocks, rising in the middle of the spacious rooms, were five tiers high, counting the basement. Cells were locked with individual padlocks. Running down beside the latticed door of each cell was a metal flange which was attached to a common axle. These latches could all be shifted simultaneously to secure each door on that row of cells by a giant lever, or "slam," at the end of the walk. Each cell was also secured by a padlock.

The walks—most of which were reached by a narrow staircase and rose to dizzying heights—were of wooden planking, five feet wide. Only a tenuous pipe railing separated prisoners from the abyss. It was not a place to meet your enemies.

Narrow doorways between the adjoining cellhouses were normally left open. This provided better circulation of air, especially on stifling summer nights.

Hodge arrived at three cellhouse and was greeted warmly by the officer of the second shift. He was playing checkers with a cellhouse trusty or "key boy" assigned to assist the guard. They exchanged pleasantries, bits of information and gossip—but not for long. Soon the outgoing officer checked out. Hodge then proceeded to his duties as cellhouse officer.

He first checked the transfer sheet to see what inmate moves had been made that day. This list would inform him of those convicts transferred to the hospital, discharged, sent out to court, or for some other reason were no longer under his watch. Inmate Andrew Hawkins' name jumped off the page, "Discharged by escape."

The dutiful guard then checked the board for the "okays." These were the names of the convicts authorized to be out of their cells on work detail. At this time of night there were usually very few—boiler room attendants, houseboys at the warden's quarters working a late party, and sometimes a shift staying overtime at one of the prison factories.

After checking the inventories, Hodge began to make his count. Slowly and methodically, with flashlight in hand, he moved from cell to cell making sure that the prisoners assigned to his keeping were where they were supposed to be. If he could see no flesh, but only bulging and knotted bed clothing, he would rap the door until there was movement.

During his rounds, the ray of his light swept across the gray hair and sleeping form of "Daddy" Warner. The old leather-faced convict serving a 10-year sentence was assigned to the prison library, located in the chapel. Even in his deep and peaceful slumber, he could not have dreamed of the extraordinary events about to unfold within the next 24 hours. They would totally transform his life.

The count took a while. Once finished, and all heads accounted for, Hodge sent the count to the shift lieutenant in the administration building by his "key boy" runner. Count was made every hour, but unless there was a problem, he was only required to report the first two.

He was so busy during the first hour of his shift that midnight came and went without notice. At that bewitching hour he became another year older. After the second count he locked up his sleepy "key boy." In between rounds, he sipped coffee, peeked at a day old newspaper, and listened for sounds.

Within the bowels of the Kentucky State Penitentiary, surrounded by a cathedral of stone, the sounds heard by a cellhouse officer in the dead of night are magnified. Even the beating of his heart may seem thunderous. A convict calling out in his sleep, a distant door clanging shut, the coffee pot purring, the piercing squeak of his chair—all intrusions into a world of silence within a dimly lit cavern.

Sharing these lonely hours with Hodge, in this castle of woe, were four men under sentences of death. They slept fitfully on their narrow berths of steel in the death house which adjoined three cellhouse. No one knows what unwelcomed dreams entered their tormented heads, as their victims lay cold and buried on some distant and lonely hill. Of these four condemned, Frank Thomas, age 70, was destined to become the oldest man ever to be executed at the Kentucky State Penitentiary.

In between counts, when the heavy summons of sleep begins to fall upon him, the cellhouse officer walks. Movement helps him survive until the morning. Fatigue and sleep become enemies number one. To sleep was to be fired.

At 4 a.m. Hodge began to let out his kitchen help—bakers first and then the set up men. By 6 a.m., the gray dawn began to seep in through the long, barred windows on the outside wall of the cellhouse. As prisoners began to stir, lights were flipped on.

The "white line" from the other cellhouses formed first, and then around 6:30 a.m., Cunningham began to "let out" the wards of his care. The "colored line" moved out the door of two cellhouse, up the walkway to the roadway which led past the great yard bell and into the huge dining hall.

A little before 7 a.m. the day shift officer arrived in three cell-house. By this time the early rays of sun covered the prison yard, and the whole place was alive with the sounds of morning. The smell of food drifted from the kitchen, mixed with the rattling of pots and shuffling inmates. The only voices were the commands of the keepers as the convicts moved and ate in silence. Moving along in the "white line" were Tex Walters, William Griffith, and Harry Ferland.

Just minutes before, in his cell, Tex had penned out a thoughtful and loving letter to his young wife, Lillian. He placed it—along with a map of Kentucky and a railroad passenger time table—into his coat pocket. Into his pants, he slipped a homemade dirk.

The threesome moved up the wide, wooden steps which led to the main entrance. Once inside the dining hall the "line" was halted. It waited until space opened up at the long, wooden tables arranged end to end. Then the guard would nod for a certain number to be seated.

This large room located on the second floor of the two-story, brick building would feed about 300 prisoners at one time. Food was brought up from the kitchen, found on the bottom floor, by a dumb waiter located in the middle of the hall. The black convict orderlies, dressed in crisp whites, ladled the grub from large buckets into sizable tin plates. The dining room officer, Lewis Hill, watched from his seat on the elevated, wooden platform in front of a window to the right of the main entrance.

At about 6:30 a.m. Harry Ferland left the dining hall and went to the first floor to the laundry where he worked. He was there early and he recovered the pistol and ammunition from their hiding place.

Tex and Griffith finished breakfast at roughly the same time. They headed in the direction of the shirt factory where they were to report to their work station at 7 a.m. On the way they stopped at the prison barber shop, where a number of convicts were gathered. Close to 7 o'clock they were joined by Ferland, with the pistol and ammo in his coat pocket.

The prison yard in 1923 was virtually a small village. There were buildings of all shapes and sizes, connected by sidewalks and encircled by the main road. Large shade trees and tall shrubs—still in their full summer dress—camouflaged troop movements on the hill. There were even telephone poles crisscrossing the terrain. It was a security nightmare, within which prisoners could literally disappear.

The only surveillance was from the officers walking the hill. Guards in the towers could do little else but keep prisoners from climbing over the walls. So no one noticed that Harry Ferland was away from his work place as he and his two confederates headed for the shirt factory.

The substantial four-story brick building was located behind the death house, next to the boiler room and toward the rear of the prison. Immediately behind it, next to the wall, was the harness shop—an adjacent structure of two floors. The buildings were joined by an enclosed walkway.

Their immediate target on this morning was 55-year-old guard, T. R. "Daddy" Scoles. He worked as the guard in charge of supplies and materials in the basement of the shirt factory. It was a secluded area where inmates came to check out needed wares for their work. Tex went there often and had became friends with the old man.

On this morning "Daddy" Scoles was returning to his duty station from getting a haircut. Tex and his two sidekicks intended to take him in the isolation of the factory basement. Instead, they jumped him on the yard. Griffith stuck the contraband pistol in his ribs and they ushered him to the supply room. There the crusty old critter put up a good fight. Had it not been for Tex's intervention, Lawrence Griffith would have killed him. Instead, Scoles was subdued, bound, gagged, and tied to a post. Ferland lifted his .38 caliber pistol and stuck it in his pocket. Armed with two pistols now and a dirk, the three convicts bounded up the steps from the basement. On the main cutting floor, guard William Gilbert was sitting on the platform overlooking the room of working convicts. He saw the armed threesome emerging from the downstairs and pulled his weapon. Before he could fire a shot, Griffith and Ferland riddled him with bullets. They then made their rapid exit from the shirt factory and raced across the prison yard toward one cellhouse.

Hodge wearily made his way back through the long spacious cellhouses toward the front. He felt relieved, as usual, and was looking forward to a birthday breakfast with Emma. The boys would be getting off to school. As he was let in the administration building from one cellhouse, he decided to celebrate the occasion with a shave and haircut in the officers' barber shop. It was located immediately to the left, coming into the administration building.

The main floor was alive with the sounds of activity. Some of the administrative offices were being opened as chattering clerks and secretaries arrived. Correctional officers were coming and going. The noisy concourse was a stark contrast to the lonely, midnight shift.

In the barber shop, there were a few bleary-eyed guards, hyped up with countless cups of coffee. Their shift over, they had hung up their weapons and were relaxing. Hodge moved into the room and began to joke and visit with his fellow guards, waiting for his turn in the chair.

Suddenly there was an unusual noise of yelling. It was coming from one cellhouse, the entrance to which was just a few feet away from where Hodge was standing. Still armed, and being the guard closest to the cellhouse door, Cunningham volunteered to check out the disturbance. He went to the key box in the hallway and took a large pass for the inside gate to one cellhouse.

The gatekeeper in the administration building, Roscoe Gumm, opened the rod gate leading to number one cellhouse. Just inside that portal was a small space just big enough for a couple of people to stand, enclosed by the rod gate and the solid door leading into the cellhouse. In accordance to security rules, Gumm closed the inside gate before Hodge slipped in his key to open the cellhouse door. The two were never to be opened at the same time.

Upon entering the cellhouse, Hodge immediately closed and locked the door behind him. There was definitely something going on, as he heard a commotion at the opposite end of the cellblock. He passed by the large stand-up desk and looked for cellhouse officer Ollie Catlett. He wasn't there.

He then heard someone yelling loudly, "Catlett! Catlett where are you?"

It was believed by many convicts that the number one cellhouse officer possessed the keys for passage into the administration building and out the front door of the institution.

Hodge turned the southeast corner of the cellblock and headed down the inside walk on the main floor. It was then he saw a group of prisoners coming toward him. Leading the way was Lawrence Griffith. The husky convict was coming on, almost at a trot. Behind him were Tex Walters and Harry Ferland.

"Where's Catlett?" Griffith demanded.

"What do you want him for?" Hodge inquired.

Then, when the charging inmates were still a good fifty feet away, the solitary guard saw Griffith raise a pistol and level the barrel down upon him. The make of the pistol was a brand new 32-20 Colt police special.

In that horrifying moment, Hodge Cunningham realized that he had made a terrible mistake. His pistol had not been drawn when he entered the cellhouse. It was still in his shoulder holster. He was a sitting duck.

One, two, three, four blasts of the pistol reverberated through the stone edifice like the echoing of dynamite. All four shots of the expert marksman caught Hodge Cunningham in the chest area. Mortally wounded, he staggered back from the blows, but miraculously stayed on his feet. Almost instinctively, he headed toward the front gate.

Another blast from the weapon, and the bullet tore through his thigh, causing his legs to buckle. Still he managed to stay on his feet.

The next ten seconds were some of the most pivotal moments in the history of the Kentucky State Penitentiary.

Inexplicably, instead of rushing the mangled officer and overtaking him and his keys, the mutineers laid back for just a short time.

Perhaps, because Cunningham remained on his feet, he had misled the mutineers into believing he had not been hit. They no doubt lost sight of him as he retraced his steps around the corner of the cell block, past the desk and toward the gate. Knowing that he was armed, they may have been just a bit wary. For whatever reason, they hesitated.

At last they gave chase. But the short space of time had given Cunningham just the lead he needed. Even in his terminal condition he managed to shortcut his route to the gate by jumping over a low railing that protected a stair casing to the basement. Frantically, he found the key hole, swung open the gate and, just as the desperados arrived on the scene, slammed the door behind him.

Thwarted, the rampaging prisoners turned and ran back through the cellblock and through the back door leading out onto the prison yard. Hodge Cunningham fell against the door.

"Let me out!" he yelled. "I'm shot all to pieces!"

Roscoe Gumm immediately opened the inner gate. Hodge fell onto the administration building floor, blood pouring from his wounds. Guards rushed in around him. His head came to rest on the marble flagging, his eyes fixed in a vacant stare at the ceiling.

The alarm was sounded, and guards swarmed onto the yard. One of them was V. B. Mattingly. He encountered the armed prisoners heading toward the dining hall. They exchanged fire. Mattingly soon expended his ammunition and retreated quickly to the administration building and reloaded.

They were ready for him when he returned to the hill. Ferland, armed with the pistol taken from Scoles, and Griffith with the 32-20 revolver, cut down the outmanned officer. Mattingly, seriously wounded, fell on a slight embankment outside the dining hall. The firefight spread through the entire yard.

Running back toward the shirt factory, the inmates were confronted by officer William Gillihan. Gunfire was exchanged. Walters and Ferland were slightly wounded. Gillihan was shot in the hip near the stand pipe at the top of the hill. He managed to crawl around behind the brick foundation before further damage could be inflicted upon him.

The murderous convicts were now like trapped animals desperately looking for a hole in which to crawl. Finally Walters, Griffith, and Ferland headed toward the dining room. They bounded up the wide flight of steps and burst through the doorway into the large hall. Some inmates were still cleaning up. They immediately scattered and headed out the main exit.

Officer Hill leaped from the platform and dashed through the door and into a small coal shed attached to the building.

In less than a minute, Tex and company had the the entire floor to themselves. Immediately they moved to the large windows and began to lay down a field of fire upon the prison yard and pursuing guards. Inmates and guards in the open scampered for cover.

V. B. Mattingly lay moaning and bleeding within easy shooting distance of the upstairs windows.

Lawrence Griffith, relishing the violent havoc they were inflicting, taunted the guards from his lofty and invincible perch.

"Come and get us, you hundred dollar men!" he yelled, and proceeded to laugh and yelp with each blast of his pistol.

On the second floor of the brick building, in command of the prison environs below, Tex Walters, Lawrence Griffith, and Harry Ferland had taken the higher ground. They possessed weapons and an ample supply of ammunition. The siege was on.

Chapter 7

When Hodge Cunningham was killed on October 3, 1923, he became the first employee of the Kentucky State Penitentiary to die in the line of duty. V. B. Mattingly and William Gilbert were soon to follow. The third and fourth fatal victims of inmate violence were not strangers to the first.

Prison guard William Lewis Moneymaker and Hodge Cunningham were good friends. In fact, the fun loving Cunningham kept Moneymaker in stitches a great deal of the time with his pranks and jokes. Moneymaker had an unusually loud and infectious laugh. It was reported that on a still day, the sound of his laughter at one of Hodge's jokes would carry all the way from the prison yard to the school, which sat upon a hill, half a mile away.

At age 57, Moneymaker was working the evening shift April 21, 1931. While on routine patrol of the yard around five o'clock, an enraged convict named Sam Long slipped up behind him with a hatchet he had stolen from the broom factory. Long buried the hatchet into the unsuspecting guard's skull behind the right ear. Moneymaker fell at the convict's feet. Immediately, Long grabbed his victim's gun and shot himself in the head, dying instantly. The mortally wounded officer was rushed to the prison hospital, where he died two and one half hours later.

The reason for the killing has remained a mystery.

Moneymaker, who had worked at the prison for twenty years, was well liked by prisoners and fellow workers.

First reports stated that Long had been involved in a skirmish and was chasing some other inmates out of the broom factory, picked up a hatchet, and clubbed the unsuspecting guard by mistake. Discovering his terrible error, he became crazed by fear and remorse, and used the guard's gun to commit suicide. Officials at the penitentiary later denied this version of the tragedy.

By any account, on the surface at least, it was a totally senseless and unexplainable slaying.

⁂

The acting warden at the time of Moneymaker's murder was Roscoe Gumm. Less than eight years before, he had caught the dying Hodge Cunningham when he fell through the door of one cellhouse.

The soft-spoken and mild-mannered native of Summersville, Kentucky, put in an illustrious career at the prison, spanning over 30 years, beginning around 1915. They were not continuous years, for prison jobs have always been, if to a much lessor degree today, political positions. Employment would come and go for many with the political power in Frankfort. Unless you were tight with the patronage man at the time, your chances of getting a coveted job with the state were zero. This was especially true with wardens, who would not know civil service protection until recent times.

In 1929, Warden John Chilton—who had weathered several different regimes in Frankfort—died in office. But no replacement was named.

A word about prison and politics.

Most all governors view penitentiaries—especially big bad maximum security types—as monsters which need to be kept locked in the closet. They wish to simply tiptoe past the door throughout their term, and hope the confined beast will not come tearing out into the room. Occasionally they will crack the door, and heave in some slices of legislative largess to keep the animal alive and satisfied. Prisons are never a political plus. But they are time bombs, ready to explode at anytime into riots, violence, corruption, or some other unpopular happening.

Most state executives—Blackburn a rare exception—simply want to nurse the correctional system through their term without any major damage being done on their watch. Consequently, while governors liked to reward their friends with jobs, including warden, they wanted to make sure that whoever was appointed to that terribly important position knew what they were doing and were capable of keeping the lid on.

After much soul-searching, one governor had finally been convinced by his aides that he had to fire a controversial and possibly corrupt warden. "Okay, okay," he gave in, "but which one of you bastards are going to go down and run that place until I get a replacement?"

The "Attica complex" was alive and well, long before that New York prison exploded in the early 1970s.

Back to Gumm, and a little political speculation.

When Republican Governor Flem Sampson started looking around in mid-term in 1929 for a replacement for Chilton, the pickings were slim. First of all, far western Kentucky, at that time, was a strong Gibraltar for the Democratic Party. Republicans in these parts were as scarce as the offspring of a monk. Therefore, it was difficult to find a warden from that area with both the right political party and the ability to run a prison. Insomuch that Sampson was already half-way through his tenure, no one from another part of the state was interested in pulling up stakes and moving out west to Eddyville for what could be just a two-year stay. Besides, the job was easily the most intimidating one in state government.

So the fully capable deputy W. R. "Roscoe" Gumm was appointed "acting" warden. He served in that capacity for three years until 1932, when western Kentuckian Ruby Lafoon was elected governor and returned the Democrats to power. Lafoon appointed his Madisonville friend Tom Logan as warden, and Gumm gracefully went back to serving as deputy warden. He was a good soldier—the kind of man every prison jailer would like to have.

He was serving in that capacity under Warden Guy Tuggle in December, 1945. It was the holiday season, and one anticipated by the American people with special excitement and joy since all the boys— those who had survived—were home from the war. The world was at peace, and America's power was at its zenith.

On the weekend of December 17, Warden Tuggle was out of town visiting his home in London, Kentucky. Deputy Gumm was in charge.

At about 1:30 in the morning he was asleep at his home on Franklin Street in Eddyville, across from the Methodist Church. The telephone rang and he was awakened from his slumber.

"There's trouble at the prison," he reported to his wife, hanging up the phone. "A gun got in."

He dressed quickly and left.

The night was cold and the little town was deadly still. Colorful Christmas lights strung along Main Street were aglow, contrasting sharply with the grim task before him. He passed up Penitentiary Hill between the darkened court house and the Kentucky Theater.

Showbills on the front of the theater proclaimed upcoming features including "For Whom The Bell Tolls," with Ingrid Bergman and Cary Grant.

Upon arrival at his office, Gumm immediately met with his shift captain and a handful of guards. Over steaming cups of black coffee, they began the grueling and stressful investigation. With bits of information, interrogation of informants, and an abundance of prison intuition, they slowly drew in their nets over a period of the next few hours.

The pistol had been smuggled in by mail, along with six cartridges, in a cigar box. It had been inside for over three weeks. By 5 a.m. they had their man.

The pistol was in the cell of Earl L. Tunget, a 23-year-old convicted murderer out of Jefferson County.

Gumm told reliable and tough Dallas Gray to pick a man and go and shake down Tunget's cell. Gray picked another ace, Tom Underwood, and they headed for one cellhouse. Toad Manley, captain of the guards, and Jim Bales, the cellhouse officer joined them.

The four guards, armed only with clubs, approached Tunget's cell and opened the door. As soon as they did, the convict pulled the loaded pistol on them, took their keys and locked all four of them in his tiny cell. He then proceeded down the walk toward the main cellhouse door which led into the administration building.

Gumm, growing restless with anticipation, left his office and headed for two cellhouse. For some unexplainable reason, he forgot to take the little .32 snubbed-nose pistol which he normally carried with him, but left it instead in his top desk drawer. He went through the two doors into one cellhouse, turned right and passed under the dog trot outside the cellhouse office. He then started down the walk toward Tunget's cell. There on the walk the two men met. Tunget pointed the gun at the veteran prison man and chased him back toward the entrance to the cellhouse.

The deputy warden did have his walking cane. It was an attractive cedar stick, nicely varnished and tapered from a two-inch handle down to a pointed end covered with a rubber tip—prison made. He held it out toward Tunget, protecting his space, as the convict backed him into the tailor shop which was located in the open space of the main floor of the cellhouse. Gumm instructed Tunget to put down the gun.

Two guards, Walter Stephens and Josh Lewis, armed only with

clubs themselves, looked on with terrible apprehension at the deadly standoff.

As Gumm moved behind a cutting table, the desperate convict shot him point blank. The 61-year-old prison veteran fell dead just a few feet from the door leading into the administration building.

Stephens and Lewis immediately went after the armed convict. He fired again, wounding Lewis slightly. After a short struggle, he was disarmed and cuffed.

Deputy Warden Roscoe Gumm lay dead, defending the same door which the mortally wounded Hodge Cunningham had closed upon his murderers over 22 years before, thwarting their attempt to escape. The anxious turnkey on the other side of the portal on that fateful day had been Roscoe Gumm.

On April 11, 1947, 23-year-old Earl L. Tunget was electrocuted at the Kentucky State Penitentiary for the murder of Gumm.

There was a dark irony in the execution of Tunget.

While acting as warden, Gumm had been in charge of over half a dozen executions. He had been in attendance at numerous others. But he was opposed to capital punishment. Many times he voiced his opinion that a true life sentence—no parole, no time off—would do more to deter crime. At each execution he attended, he always turned his head when the condemned was electrocuted.

The only death he ever saw inflicted was his own.

It is universally a great mystery, to those not familiar with corrections, as to how weapons and other forms of contraband find their irrepressible way into prisons.

The most valuable thing in the world, and that which none of us can replenish, is time. And convicts do it for a living. While most people go about their daily struggle to make a living and survive, the convict has the luxury of countless hours of time to think and to scheme.

Until recently, much of the contraband would come in through the mail. Not in letters, but in packages. All incoming mail at Eddyville was censored. It can still be examined without a court order. All packages were opened and inspected. But a shortage of personnel, slipshod work by the mail officer, and ingenious tricks utilized by the sender caused a lot of bad stuff to get in behind prison walls.

Take the Tunget gun, for instance. It came in concealed at the bottom of a cigar box. Mail officer Dallas Gray, a man with a reputation for doing the job right, was off the day it arrived. Someone standing in for him was asleep at the switch.

A small bit of a hacksaw blade in the heel of a shoe, illicit dope hidden in a neatly cut out hole in the middle of a thick book, or a weapon in the pocket of a coat were all common and sometimes successful means. With sophisticated x-ray scanners, these methods have diminished. In modern times, most contraband—weapons and drugs—is brought in by people.

Prison guards make poverty-level salaries. Shrewd convicts learn of financial problems or other weaknesses of a particular guard. He pays him to bring in contraband. It's happened since the first stone was laid. Dirty guards, while few in number, help supply the yard with trouble.

Visitors are primary merchants of prison contraband. Mothers, wives, girl friends, and even children are used as mules to get things in. Once again the methods are often extreme, including the use of body cavities.

The most disruptive effect of drugs upon the yard is not the mood-altering potential of the contraband—although that certainly causes a peck of trouble. But the illicit drug business on the yard causes loan sharking, which leads to violence. The cost of illegal drugs inside the prison is inflated tremendously from the price on the outside. It's the law of supply and demand. A prisoner borrows money—or some other prison medium of exchange—to purchase reefers. He builds up a tab he cannot pay back. If a convict cannot collect his debts, he's considered weak by the inmate community and loses face. He collects it or else. Usually violence ensues.

Green money is prohibited on the prison yard. Prisoners must use vouchers drawn on their accounts to purchase items at the inmate canteen. Some other medium of exchange has to be substituted for currency in the convict business of purchasing items from each other, compensating legal aides for services, and paying off debts. Traditionally the accepted legal tender has been cigarettes. Where there are criminals, and where there is commerce, there will be counterfeit money—or cigarettes. At one time, saw dust was rolled and packaged into fake cigarettes. The wary businessman on the yard knew how to test the coin of the realm. Packages of real cigarettes were lighter and would bounce when dropped on the ground. The saw dust counterfeit would not.

Drugs and hacksaw blades must come in from the outside. Weapons are most times manufactured from within.

Before the yard was cleared of most all extraneous fixtures and vegetation, it was easy for prisoners to find ample material for the making of deadly instruments. Sharpened and carefully fashioned pieces of bed springs, chair legs, and other objects made for lethal hardware. When the factories were operating, it was almost impossible to control all of the available resources for weaponry. With the later day construction of the vocational schools out back came a steady flow of raw material through the back gate.

The old, cast-iron padlocks used to lock the ancient cells were often times removed from the latch, placed in the toe of a sock and wielded about as a mace. Until recently removed from the yard, the bars and heavy disks of the free weights, clustered for body building at the "iron pile," have been used as fatal assault weapons. Guns—both real and decoys—have been made by convict hands and used to wreak havoc.

The standard "zip" gun is a homemade firearm. Ingenious methods are used to manufacture cumbersome, and in most instances, ineffective weapons. They are usually put together with some kind of pipe for a barrel, attached to a handle by tape or soldering. A fuse is inserted through a small hole at the base of the chamber to set off a round of gunpowder, either produced by inmate chemistry, or smuggled onto the yard. This unwieldy piece of hardware is constructed to fire ball bearings or nails. Recently, an unusually sophisticated gun was found, capable of firing a .22 bullet.

The purpose for the manufacture of a zip gun is not quite clear. Usually they are one-shot tools which would probably be ineffective in perfecting an escape. Most likely they are for self-protection—or assassination.

Less dangerous, but much more practical, is the fake gun, carved from soap or wood and painted black with shoe polish. Looking down the wrong end of one, it can look as menacing as the blue steel of a Smith & Wesson. They have often been used in kidnapping and escape attempts. At Eddyville, they have never been used successfully in gaining freedom for the perpetrators. But they almost always create fear and chaos. One such occasion was just after midnight on October 3, 1982.

William Woolum was one of the most dangerous people at Eddyville at that time. In addition to all kinds of trouble with prison guards and staff, a year before he had killed another inmate by stabbing him 56 times.

At about 1:30 in the morning, he freed himself from his prison cell by cutting the cell bars. He then proceeded to take a correctional officer hostage by using what appeared to be a .45 caliber revolver. He held the officer for seven and one-half hours on the walk of the segregation unit, making demands upon the prison administration and placing the captured guard in grave danger.

Through the cool and persistent negotiations conducted by future warden, Phil Parker, Woolum finally gave up. The only concession given by the administration was the radio broadcasting of his list of grievances. The hostage was released unhurt.

As it turned out, the "weapon" was only the carving of a pistol, fashioned from two bars of soap, blackened by shoe polish. In the dimly lit cellhouse in the middle of the night, it looked like a real pistol—and as big as a cannon.

There are also the legitimate tools which find their way onto the prison yard in the day-to-day operation of the penitentiary. Maintenance employees, most times utilizing inmate laborers, use an elaborate inventory system to account for each tool when their work is finished. Like in everything else, human errors are made.

It was a seemingly innocuous putty knife which inmate Virgil Moore, age 22, sharpened into a devastating murder weapon on a hot summer day in 1956.

At about 2 p.m. on the blistery July afternoon, Lieutenant Owen Davenport, a 13-year veteran was sitting at an open guard station on the prison yard watching an inmate baseball game. Moore slipped up behind Davenport and without warning jumped on his back, stabbed him and cut his throat with the homemade knife.

A tower guard saw the attack and gave the alarm. But he hesitated to fire his weapon at the assailant because he couldn't get a clear shot at Moore. He didn't know until it was too late that the inmate had a knife.

Guards rushed onto the yard and captured Moore without resistance. The bleeding guard was lying on the ground semi-conscious. He died before guards could get him to the prison hospital.

The diminutive Moore, who weighed only 97 pounds, was a pawn of other strong-arm inmates led by Dago Reese.

Davenport, who was well liked by inmates and staff, was heading up an investigation which threatened to dry up illicit drug flow coming into the prison. The young inmate was doped up the night before and given twenty dollars, a Cuban penny, and a bottle of cough medicine laced with codeine to kill Davenport. Moore related that he drew straws with Reese and another convict and was told that there was "a job to be done" and that he had to do it. He was then given his mission.

The lightweight Moore was able to overpower the 240-pound guard, in part, because he was hyped up on some kind of drugs, probably amphetamines. Moore received a death sentence from a Lyon County jury, but it was subsequently reversed by the appellate court. On retrial he was given life.

⌘⌘⌘

Assaults upon correctional officers and staff by inmates at Eddyville occur almost on a daily basis. A shove, a push, the slinging of an arm, an elbow to the nose—it happens constantly. This is especially true when dealing with the prisoners in the disciplinary unit of the penitentiary.

Perhaps the most galling type of assault to the prison guard working within the bowels of the beast is the throwing of human urine and feces upon the unsuspecting officer. It happens often, and these centurions within the walls, making so little pay that some qualify for food stamps, must maintain the cool of a saint and not retaliate with excessive force. It's all part of the course.

It is a maximum security prison, and many of the residents are staring at so much time that they have little to lose by attacking anyone, including prison guards. The dastardly methods utilized by inmates to inflict harm upon their keepers know no bounds.

Carl Reidling was a 27-year-old World War II veteran working one of the back wall stands on the morning of July 26, 1950. Four prisoners, attempting to escape, slipped up to within thirty-five feet of Reidling's stand. Hidden behind a small building, one of the prisoners hefted a Molotov cocktail—a blazing bottle stuffed with gasoline soaked in cotton—into the guard station.

The bottle hit the mark. It burst into flames which engulfed the cribbed watchman. Each of the other three convicts hurled additional bottles into the tower. His clothing in flames, Reidling managed to get off a shot from his rifle and the assailants fled in all directions. Miraculously, the beleaguered guard survived the attack, although he suffered searing burns about the face, head, arms and hands.

⌘⌘⌘

The pillbox guard stands atop the stone walls compose the last line of defense between the inmate population and the outside world. Perhaps no job in the penitentiary is more critical. Certainly none is more tedious. An eight-hour shift can seem like an eternity.

The mission is to do nothing but watch. No reading material, no radio, no television. Watch the yard, watch the wall, watch the cellhouse, watch the outside perimeter for unauthorized personnel. . . . watch, watch, watch.

One must climb to the perch on an enclosed ladder that leads up from outside the wall. If anything is sent up, or sent down, it is done with a bucket on a rope.

The square chamber is sparsely furnished. A weapon—usually a 30-30 rifle and maybe a shotgun—telephone, hand held radio, and sometimes binoculars. Anything else left there will be torn up out of sheer boredom.

One must constantly be working at staying alert, and attentive. More than one guard has been caught napping, day dreaming, or watching a baseball game on the yard while a convict scampers over the wall. That means instant death to the job.

Through all seasons and around the clock, the benumbing job makes many a guard anxious for yard duty. The night shift almost welcomes the check in call to the front which they are required to make every fifteen minutes.

But on this sea of endless monotony a ship may come calling. And when it does, it can bring high drama.

Sam Hooks—a distant relative of Hodge Cunningham—was a wall stand specialist. For twenty years he worked number six wall stand, which is located to the rear of five cellhouse and the dining hall. It is a critical vantage point, covering the entire south side of the penitentiary on both sides of the wall. In addition, it controlls electronically the sally port gate just below it and through which most all of the prison trucking traffic passes.

Hooks was a hunter and an outstanding shot with a rifle. He always qualified near the top at the prison range. On his stand he was armed with a shotgun, .38 caliber pistol, and a Model 94 Winchester 30-30 rifle—lever action and open sight.

When the 53-year-old Hooks climbed the wooden ladder to his familiar duty station on the morning of June 21, 1970, he had no reason to anticipate that day being any different than any other.

It was a Sunday—Father's Day. The general population would spend most of the day on the yard.

The weather was hot and sunny. Before the day was over, American forces would encounter some of their hardest fighting in Vietnam in more than two months, as U. S. troops began their major withdrawal from Cambodia.

Attorney General John N. Mitchell announced a major crackdown on organized drug trafficking involving Cuban refugees—Operation Eagle.

In the afternoon, Hammerin' Hank Aaron smashed two homeruns to lead the Atlanta Braves past the Houston Astros as the future hall-of-famer passed Lou Gehrig in the all-time extra base hit parade.

People lined up at the Arcade Theater in nearby Paducah for the afternoon matinee to see "Goodbye, Mr. Chips" starring Peter

O'Toole and Petula Clark.

But on the prison yard at Eddyville, convicted felons loitered around in the sun, lifted weights, played basketball, swam in the old reservoir, or gathered in small groups to kill the time. The prison population had ballooned to about 1200 and the yard was teeming with convicts. Beautiful Barkley Lake, which had created a peninsula out of Penitentiary Hill, was bouncing to a slight breeze. A few fishermen shared the broad span of water with skiers.

Sundays provided the wall guards with more activity to watch. Even slow moving vehicles on the street outside and just a few yards from Sam's stand had to be given some heed. Weekend visitors, most of them down from Louisville or Lexington, would sometimes attempt to drop contraband on the grounds.

On that morning inmate Billy Houchin, one of the prison's "tushhogs"—a term applied to a small number of prisoners who attempt to run the yard by force and brutality—got high on some homemade brew. He pulled a knife on a guard, momentarily holding him hostage. After a few tense moments, Houchin surrendered and was locked in segregation.

Carl "Rainbow" Beamer was a friend and running buddy of Houchin. The two had been terrorizing the yard for some time. In February of 1969, the pair had been involved in a television and window smashing spree in two of the shops, causing about $1200 worth of damage. They were finally subdued after guards arrived on the scene with weapons, but not until Beamer had threatened one guard with a shovel and was backed down by a pistol in his face.

The previous August, the two had stabbed inmate Alonzo Brister to death with a homemade knife. Suffice it to say, they were bad actors.

After Houchin was locked up on that Sunday morning, Beamer apparently got into the same batch of spirits which had sent his friend Houchin on a tear.

About three o'clock, Beamer showed up on the yard drunk from the home brew. He was also wielding a homemade knife made from a toggle bolt approximately thirteen inches long, including a built-up handle. It had a nine-inch blade, made by grinding off the bolt threads on two sides, down to a sharp and deadly point. It was strikingly similar to the weapon he and Houchin had used to kill inmate Brister.

Beamer first approached guard C. L. Pritchard. Pointing the knife at his chest, he demanded the release of Houchin from segregation. At this time, officer Henry Phelps came upon the scene. The inebriated convict then put the knife on both of them. At least five of

Beamer's buddies had now encircled the group, some of them most likely armed with knives. There was very little the unarmed and out-manned guards could do.

Beamer finally decided he would take the two guards with him to the prison canteen, ostensibly to get a cup of coffee. His real intention was to show off his captives to the yard full of inmates.

Beamer was thoroughly enjoying himself, jousting and terror-izing the guards. He took Pritchard's cap and placed it on his own head, to the laughter and enjoyment of the growing number of convicts now congregating around the entourage.

A third guard, George Claypool—who was from the same hometown as Beamer—came upon the gathering, and seeing trouble brewing, started to go for help.

"Come back here 'hometown boy' or I'll kill these guys!" Beamer yelled after him. Claypool returned.

The prisoner canteen was located on the back part of the loop which encircled the prison yard. It was in clear view of number six stand where Sam Hooks was now watching the dangerous development through binoculars, about one hundred yards away.

When the group reached the canteen, they found it closed and Beamer ordered Pritchard to call the warden to open it. He called from the nearby laundry phone but was unable to reach him.

By now around three hundred inmates had gathered. Beamer was ranting and raving, brandishing the knife, and building up his courage. The situation had clearly escalated to the critical point.

There is a certain sickening and paralyzing sense of terror which falls across combat zones and prison yards just before something really terrible is about to happen. The sensation is almost tangible, like a flash of static in the air. This crisis had reached that point.

Sam Hooks had put away the binoculars. He was now on the front narrow platform of the guard stand with the 30-30 shouldered and sighted.

Claypool tried to leave the group. Beamer lunged at him and nicked the retreating guard on the forearm. The prisoner turned back to Phelps, whom he now had by the collar of his shirt. He raised the dagger above his head and was poised to plunge it into the chest of his captive.

A lone rifle shot echoed throughout the stone canyon. The bullet went crashing through the head of Carl Beamer. Guard Henry Phelps felt the wind of the bullet as it passed him.

The courageous and deadly marksmanship of Sam Hooks saved the life of at least one prison guard, and probably more.

He was not the kind of man to savor his heroic act. He regretted deeply the taking of a human life, and felt genuine anguish for the inmate's family. He agonized over his decision to shoot, in spite of continual reassurances from his fellow officers that he had done the right thing. Long before his death on June 18, 1994, this good and humble man had become a legend.

Reluctant hero that he was, at the Kentucky State Penitentiary, Sam Hooks is the patron saint of wall guards.

※ ※ ※

By 1984, new faces were put upon the work force at the prison. Women were being hired to work behind the walls. They had been employed for years in clerical and administrative positions, as well as nurses at the prison hospital. Now they were being employed as correctional officers and other positions which placed them with inmates on a routine basis.

On March 1, 1984, Patricia Ross was a 37-year-old divorcee, with one young son, working as a vocational teacher in the prison dining room. Her duties were to teach a cooking class for the inmates. The class and the operation of the dining room were so functionally intertwined that both she and her students were considered a part of the food preparation crew.

Fred Grooms was a 28-year-old inmate from Tompkinsville, Kentucky, who was a vocational student in the dining hall. He had been convicted of several sex offenses. Grooms, who had suffered from polio as a child and walked with a limp, had become infatuated with the attractive Ross. He was scheduled to be moved in a couple of days.

A little after three o'clock in the afternoon Ross went into the large storage room of the kitchen area to pick up some silverware. The storage room had no windows and the solid door was normally kept shut and locked.

Fred Grooms followed Ross into the secluded area, and tried to have sex with her. When she refused, he picked up a large commercial can opener, which is equivalent in size and weight to a sledge hammer, and proceeded to strike her repeatedly about the head. She died almost immediately from the massive head trauma and excessive skull fractures.

While the murder was taking place, inmate Larry Lehner walked into the pantry. Grooms then bludgeoned him with the can opener.

Lehner survived, but Patricia Ross became the seventh prison employee in the history of the Kentucky State Penitentiary to lose their life in the line of duty.

103

Grooms was tried and received the death penalty. On appeal, however, his conviction was reversed. After a long and complicated delay, Grooms finally pled guilty and received a sentence of life in the penitentiary without eligibility for parole for 25 years.

Chapter 8

W arden John Chilton's dining room windows looked out over the prison yard. The entire second floor of the administration building provided the livng quarters for wardens and their families, until 1955 when a separate residence was constructed two doors down from the prison. On many summer Sunday afternoons, just below these windows, the prison band would serenade the superintendent, his family and friends.

Directly out from the well-furnished dining room, across less than two hundred feet of prison yard, stood the inmate dining hall. The kitchen and laundry were on the bottom floor, with the main eating room upstairs.

The tall, full windows, behind which convicted felons ate their daily meals in silence, were directly across the great abyss from the steel-grated windows of the Warden's dining room. Only two hundred feet, but a world away.

When Warden Chilton was called from his comfortable residence early on the morning of October 3, 1923, to the chaotic cauldron of violence below, he had little notion of what lay ahead. He went, however, with the confidence and self-assurance of a man who had eleven years of experience at the helm of the state's only maximum security prison under his belt.

Fifty-two-year-old John B. Chilton was born January 19,

1871, on the family farm ten miles out of Hopkinsville, Kentucky. As the third of six children, he learned the value of hard work and good morals. On reaching his twenty-first birthday his father awarded him a gold watch for not drinking alcohol.

His wanderlust was satisfied after spending over three years on a ranch in North Dakota. Back to the family farm he came and at age thirty, married Lula Irvin in Adams, Tennessee.

For five years he was Superintendent of Western State Asylum in Hopkinsville—a stint which no doubt provided him valuable experience for his future job as warden of a maximum security prison.

By the time of his marriage, Chilton had developed a love for politics, and he became active on the local level in various state-wide campaigns. In 1909, as Chairman of the County Democratic Executive Committee, he masterfully led a sweep of the county offices for his party. Both affable and smart, he gained the attention and respect of the political kingmakers in Frankfort.

On September 1, 1912, Democratic Governor James McCreary appointed Chilton as the fifth warden at the Kentucky State Penitentiary at Eddyville. He and his wife, Lula and their five-year-old daughter, Sara Elizabeth proudly moved into their second floor residence at the castle on the Cumberland.

The job paid 300 dollars a month with many fringe benefits. The living quarters were not only spacious, but plush for that time. A front porch, hung over the entrance and provided the prison's first family with a breathtaking vista of the Cumberland River valley. Prison trusties—dressed out in crisply starched whites—scurried around waiting on them hand and foot as houseboys, cooks, babysitters, and valets. As the slaves in a bygone era, these inmates became like family.

Ample food for family and entertainment was provided.

And entertain he did! Standing less than six feet tall, the stocky boss man with the reddish hair and kind face looked more like a school teacher than a warden. The convivial politician and his wife loved to entertain frequently, and family and friends were readily welcomed to their second floor suite. Parties and balls were a regular part of their social agenda. They especially courted the political bakers and shakers, always cognizant of where his bread was buttered.

Just that past weekend, he and his wife had played host to General Percy Haly of Frankfort, one of the best known politicians of the day. The warden's political astuteness and popularity paid dividends. Chilton survived two Republican administrations in Frankfort and would serve a total of 17 straight years until he died in office on July 11, 1929. No other superintendent would ever equal his length of service.

It was an active and historic tenure. Stripped uniforms for convicts had just departed from the prison scene. The electric chair had been in use for just a little over a year when he arrived. During his watch, he would direct and supervise fifty-four executions, including the historic seven of Friday the 13th, 1928.

In 1913, he abolished the use of the whipping stone for prison punishment. In that same year, Chilton's prison population was hit with an outbreak of typhoid fever, requiring all cooking and drinking water to be boiled.

He would live to see the first professional commissioner of corrections when Joseph P. Byers, General Secretary of the American Prison Association was appointed as head of Public Institutions in 1920. Byers attempted to remove politics from corrections' hiring practices. He failed, and five years later the "carpetbagger" resigned after a long, public battle.

But on this October morn in 1923, with Tex Walters, William Griffith, and Harry Ferland firing hot lead out of the top floor windows of the dining hall, he faced the biggest challenge of his career. His mettle was about to be sorely tested.

The crisis confronting Chilton when he descended from his quarters to the main floor was staggering. There, in the frenzied din of pandemonium, Warden Chilton received information of the deadly uprising. The revelations were terrifying.

One guard was dead, his blood still pooled upon the marble flagging. Two others were mortally wounded—one removed to the hospital, the other lay on the yard, trapped in the line of fire of the armed convicts. A third, also wounded and his condition unknown, had taken cover behind the base of the stand pipe.

The three killers, who were armed with at least two weapons and an abundant supply of ammunition, were aloft in the dining hall and holding the prison yard at bay. Initial reports indicated that they were holding dining room officer Lewis Hill as hostage.

Compounding these grim prospects was the unsettling realization that the entire prison population was still out of their cells—roughly six hundred men scattered over the grounds. Most of them were at work in the three factories which were located to the rear of the walled in yard. Unquestionably, they now knew about the uprising taking place at the front part of the prison.

As Warden Chilton sized up the harrowing conditions, he was no doubt shaken by the deadly violence. The first employee killed in the history of the institution lay on a stretcher, covered by a sheet in the room just across the hall. Other guards were down and dying.

Subconsciously, Chilton's future acts would be guided by this stunning avalanche of bloodshed and killings. All efforts to bring the prison under control would be carried out with the least amount of risk to the loss of additional lives.

As any warden in battle would recognize, the first priority was to get the prison locked down—to get the mass of criminals still at large upon the hill, safely put away in their cells. Unless this was done, and done quickly, Warden John Chilton might just lose his penitentiary. But this task would not be easy. For the prison warden and his hastily-assembled battle crew faced a most hazardous predicament, uniquely made by the three gunmen in the dining hall.

Strung along the inside of the back wall was the prison industrial complex. Three major contracts were in effect at the Eddyville prison. These called for the manufacture of shirts, horse collars, saddles, whips, mops and brooms. Over four hundred inmates were at work in four separate buildings. Scores of laboring convicts with tools in their hands which, upon a thought, could be converted to lethal weapons of revolt.

Over one hundred fifty more were dispersed over the prison yard and cellhouses assigned to various jobs. Of the entire population, only about 20 were confined to either the hospital, solitary confinement, or to death row.

Between the factories—where the bulk of the prisoners were located—and the cellhouses, stood the hulking presence of the dining hall. From the large upstairs windows, Walters and company had a clear view to the entrances of these buildings. In short, to complete the lock down, hordes of prisoners would have to be herded across this free-fire zone to their cells.

It was unlikely that the cornered desperados would fire upon their fellow prisoners. But one never knew. They might at least shoot toward them in an attempt to incite panic, and a stampeding riot. And the guards required to patrol the move would be at grave risk. Besides, it was an explosive tinder box. Moving the inmates across such perilous grounds would be like transporting five hundred human-sized packages of nitroglycerin from the back of the walled quadrangle into the cellhouses.

Meanwhile, Chilton and associates were trying desperately to patch together some manpower. It was a thin gruel. The total guard force at the penitentiary at that time was less than fifty. Walters, Griffith, and Ferland had already knocked four out of commission. Some were out in the hills and hollows trying to track down escapee Jim Hawkins. It would take some time to get them back. The night shift was held over, and calls went out to those at home. The clerks and secretaries from the administrative offices were sent home and to scour the town for off-duty officers. Fortunately, a few were still around as the third floor of the administration provided quarters for some of the correctional officers.

Most of the guards on the scene surrounded the dining hall at a safe distance. Lying prone on the ground and protected by the sloping grade, they exchanged gunfire with the three gunmen on the second floor.

With the situation critical and the prison population still on the hill, Warden Chilton placed a telephone call to the governor.

Governor Edwin Morrow was not in Frankfort. With the general election only a month away, he was on a speaking swing through far western Kentucky. He was finally located at LaCenter, in Ballard County.

After briefing the chief executive on the crisis, the distraught warden requested the activation of the National Guard. He urged that troops be sent at once to reinforce his meager line of correctional officers.

Governor Morrow readily agreed. Company B, Fifty-fourth Machine Gun Squadron of Hopkinsville was immediately mobilized.

About this time little Mitch Cunningham came running up the utility road which ran between his house and the prison wall. He was answering the dreadful summons received just moments before at his home. As he approached the substantial front steps, he met a prison employee who sprinted past him on the way to a wall stand. The young lad's heart sunk to his heels. He spotted, in the man's right hand, a familiar object. It was his father's pistol.

The firing continued on the prison yard. Everybody within range of the dining hall was subject to the barrage. Even those who thought themselves secure within the administration building were in danger. One of the bullets crashed through a window and entered the lower hallway of the main building.

But a solution was fortunately discovered for the lockdown problem.

The death house, or "annex" as it was called, clung to the end of three cellhouse. Only one corner of the roof was visible from the dining room. The rest of the building, including its back entrance, was obscured by both the prison chapel and the slope of the hill. Ironically, the death house would provide a life line to the rest of the prison.

The back doors were swung open and hundreds of convicts began to file through. They passed the electric chair, by the condemned residents who stood at their cells and gawked in amazement. Into three cellhouse they went, into two, and one. Quietly and in perfect order they climbed to the upper walks, waited for the slams, stepped in and were locked down.

Finally, the last contingency of prisoners marched through the administration building and into four cellhouse. They shuffled through the corridor, most of them unmindful of the blood smears upon the marble floor.

By 9 a.m. there was a collective sigh of relief. The inmate population was locked down. For once the antiquated classification system had actually helped. For among this mass of hardened criminals was an ample smattering of chicken thieves, horse stealers, and cold checkers. They had very little time hanging over their heads, and wanted nothing to do with the trouble spewing out on the yard.

The next order of business was cleaning up the carnage. Hodge Cunningham's corpse still lay under a sheet in a room off the main corridor. There had not been any men available to bear his body home to his grieving wife and sons.

At about the same time the door was slammed shut on the last inmate locked down, guard William Gillihan was rolling away from the brick foundation of the stand pipe at the center of the prison yard. He had gained protection there from the constant volley after he was shot in the hip. It was a painful wound, but not life threatening. Finally, after almost two hours of exchanging fire with the barricaded men and being in great pain, he decided to try to make a go for the back of the hospital.

The prison infirmary—the elegant two-story Cobb house which had been standing before the prison was built—stood less than a hundred feet directly behind the mess hall. Its front was easily and dangerously exposed to the deadly intentions of the Walters gang. In fact, Deputy Warden E. B. Miller had narrowly escaped being killed when he dodged the whizzing bullets from Lawrence Griffith's pistol and barely made it through the front door to safety.

Behind the hospital, the prison yard sloped to the roadway which circumvented the hill. The declining terrain provided protection to the back of the prison quad. One could move with safety in and out of the back of the hospital, along the road to the death house, and through the cellhouses to the front. It proved to be a valuable passageway.

Gillihan rolled down the embankment to the hospital, where he received medical attention.

But where was dining room officer Lewis Hill? It was first thought that he had been taken hostage by the three convicts now holding the yard captive. But as time passed, they began to fear that he had been killed inside the dining room. Their growing anxiety was joyfully relieved when guards inside the chapel spotted Hill peeking out of the small, brick, coal shed within a few feet of the dining room. Throughout the rest of the day he would proceed to take occasional shots at the upper floor windows. Finally, at dusk he made a successful dash to the chapel and safety.

The plight of guards William Gilbert and V. B. Mattingly would be quite different.

Gilbert had been shot in the abdomen with the bullet piercing his colon. With the assistance of other guards, he managed to make it to the prison hospital. There the penitentiary physician, Dr. D. J. Travis, and nurses—including some inmates—did the best they could. But it was a serious wound, and they were limited mostly to desperate attempts to alleviate his pain.

Chilton put in a call to Paducah, asking for surgeons. He was not only concerned for the wounded now on his hands, but he also anticipated that the casualty list might grow—and grow in a hurry. Several doctors and nurses left Paducah at once by train for Eddyville. Others from nearby Princeton also arrived.

Meanwhile, the source of all the bloodletting had been successfully contained. While the three rebels continued throughout the day to fire from their barricade, a sufficient armed line of defense was positioned around the dining hall from various buildings and points of cover. The front gate of the prison had been besieged by citizens of the town and local law enforcement offering their assistance. Some of the more responsible ones known to Warden Chilton were pressed into service in order to supplement the prison force until the National Guard arrived. A steady stream of lead was being poured into the dining hall from the chapel, hospital, cellhouses, and wall stands. As the day wore on, the most excruciating and painful development was the predicament of V. B. Mattingly.

The thirty-seven-year-old officer had been shot down by the rebels around eight in the morning. The bullet had pierced his liver, and he fell to the ground outside the laundry and just below the windows of the dining room. Bleeding profusely and withering in pain, the pathetic figure lay in the deadly fire zone for hours as his friends and fellow workers looked on helplessly.

No prison wall, nor convict garb, can suppress the sterling virtue of courage. Up to the line stepped an unexpected hero.

A. C. "Daddy" Warner of Paducah, Kentucky, was a 70-year-old, wrinkled black man, with a shock of white hair. He was sent to Eddyville in 1919 to serve a ten-year term for a statutory rape sex charge, alleged to have been committed ten years before he was tried. Some citizens of McCracken County had tried repeatedly to have him pardoned. Having served almost half of his sentence, he had, just days before, received word that there was no prospect of immediate action on application for a pardon. He dreaded the thought of another five years of incarceration—a stint he did not believe he could outlive. The likable old man had instructed his four children never to visit him at the prison. He was of the opinion that he had disgraced them and they must not regard him as their kin.

As assistant to the prison chaplain, Daddy was at work in the prison library in the chapel at the time of the outbreak. He and several other trusted convicts were allowed to remain outside their cells after the lockdown.

By mid-day, the autumn sun had warmed up the day considerably. Mattingly was suffering even more because of the terrible thirst which torments anyone who is bleeding freely.

Daddy Warner could not bear to watch his suffering. The guards found him inside the chapel door crying. He begged for permission to take water out to the wounded guard. Warden Chilton was summoned. After a great deal of discussion, permission was granted.

No one had risked their life to bring in the wounded guard. But this enfeebled, old convict, compelled by human compassion which transcends race, rank and fear, walked out onto the lonely battlefield with a bucket of water and dipper in his hands.

Mattingly's position was such that the besiegers could not protect Daddy with a blanket of fire upon the dining room. There was too great a danger that he would be struck by ricocheting bullets. So the guns were silenced and the aging Samaritan moved out toward Mattingly as eyes looked on from various protected nooks and crannies of the quadrangle.

As later noted by a news reporter:

> "As 'Daddy' knelt by Mattingly's side, raised his head and put the cooling cup to his lips, no one knew but what the next moment a shot from the mess hall would send him to Kingdom Come. . . ."

Whether Tex Walters, Lawrence Griffith, and Harry Ferland were similarly moved by compassion to spare Warner, or simply were not in a position to see what was going on, is not known. Most likely it was Tex Walters who protected the life of Daddy Warner that day. As opposite as they were, he and the old black man were friends. Tex was a frequent visitor to the prison library. There he treated Daddy with courtesy and respect. Warner, impressed with Walters' unsatiable love for books, took pride in scrounging together all the tomes he could gather for the convicted murderer. From time to time they even engaged in serious conversation on religion and psychology. Daddy had been converted by the prison chaplain and had enlisted in the Salvation Army. Tex was still searching for a spiritual center in his life, and Lillian's father was a captain in the Salvation Army. In short, these divergent personalities found common ground on which to become friends. And as one old convict who had served time with Tex later said of him, "he was mean as hell, but he took care of his friends."

In the midst of this murderous revolt, Tex apparently took care of Daddy. The guns above their heads in the dining room remained silent.

Once Warner got to Mattingly's side, and saw up close his terrible condition, he attempted to remove him and take him to the hospital. But he was too old and too weak to move the victim on his own. Mattingly—afraid for both Warner's safety and recognizing his frailty—waved him away.

Not to be thwarted, old Daddy retreated to the chapel, and returned with another black inmate, Homer Crutchfield, who was a powerful young man. Together they removed Mattingly from the yard and took him to the hospital.

With his prison population locked down, his dead officer finally removed, and the wounded receiving treatment, Warden Chilton now turned his full attention to long-range strategy in dealing with the nest of rebels in the heart of his penitentiary.

He was determined that there would be no more loss of innocent human lives. To this he vowed, and all his following acts would be guided by this controlling consideration.

For the first time in his career, John Chilton carried a pistol protruding from his hip pocket as he moved about the prison directing the work of attempting to dislodge the three convicts. The barricaded gangsters continued to fire freely at guards and the administration building. Apparently they were not worried about their supply of ammunition. Window panes on the third floor of the administration building—the guard dormitory—were shot out by the convicts.

The huge dining hall building was a formidable fortress. Hardly a structure in the institution could have provided a more secure and seemingly impregnable sanctuary.

It was a gigantic brick structure, with two spacious levels. The tall structure was covered with a massive hip roof, broken at the very top by a rectangular boxed cupola with windows which capped the building. Wide and elongated windows graced the second floor.

The bottom level consisted of the kitchen—which took up most of the north side—and the laundry next door. Entrances to both were from the side facing the administration building. The only entrance from the outside to the upper floor dining hall was a wide set of steps leading up to a double doorway. This access was located on the opposite side of the building and away from the front of the prison. Less than two hundred feet out from these steps, over sidewalks and the lawn, sat the hospital. It was up these steps the convict lines moved for meals. More recently, the three mutineers now held up inside had bounded up the stairway seeking refuge in the cavernous mess hall.

Inside the huge dining room, narrow wooden tables sat end to end. A "dumb waiter" or elevator punched a hole in the middle of the room. It was utilized to crank food up from the kitchen below. Usually it was manned by a large, muscular inmate. The high ceiling tumbled into the upper reaches of the clerestory skylight inside the cupola.

The *Paducah Sun Democrat*, in its coverage of the siege, cited the advantages of the stronghold:

> "The dining room on the second floor is filled with tables, which can be utilized as embattlements, while in the basement there is a large oven constructed of bricks and lined on the inner side with sheet metal, affording an ideal protection from the most powerful rifle. In addition, there are metal bread mixers in the kitchen, giving the mutineers another chance to protect themselves from attack. The dining room proper is about 80 feet square and the only connection between the ground and the second floor is an elevator."

The steady exchange of gunfire could be heard throughout the little town of Eddyville, where people were beginning to receive regular accounts of the developments.

In the early going, the three convicts—especially Griffith—taunted the guards, challenging them to charge the building. A steady stream of lead continued to come from the upstairs windows. At one time officer Hill—caught in the coal shed—could hear the trio singing and yelling.

By 3 o'clock in the afternoon, the occupants of the dining hall had grown quiet. Their besiegers, assuming that they were conserving their ammunition, continued to fire upon the building. It seemed to several of the guards that any firing from the building was now coming from one pistol.

In late afternoon, the Hopkinsville guardsmen arrived on the scene. When the four officers and twenty-one enlisted men smartly marched into the prison, in full combat uniform and loaded for bear, a sense of relief and confidence surged through the prison ranks. Several of the soldiers were veteran "Doughboys" of the Great War.

The troops of the machine gun squadron began moving throughout the penitentiary to various vantage points. Some of the guards were given much needed relief.

A strategy meeting was held between Warden Chilton and commanding officer Captain Allan Radford. Contractors working on the construction of the U. S. Corps of Engineers' lock and dam just below the prison on the Cumberland River were in attendance. They offered dynamite for the occasion. It sounded good to Radford. He had a mission to accomplish. But Chilton had a penitentiary to run. Winter was coming on and there was no alternative facility for the feeding of prisoners. The idea was put on the back burner.

A basic game plan was agreed upon.

Simply put, they intended to intensify and maintain a steady barrage of firepower upon the den of outlaws, until they had either killed them or caused them to surrender. Hours earlier in the day, Warden Chilton had placed a call to law enforcement agencies in the Louisville area requesting gas guns. Not long after the troops were in position, Detective Sargent Charles Scheffer of the Louisville Police Department arrived by train with the gas guns. Coincidentally, it had been Scheffer, along with another detective, who had arrested Walters for the murder charge for which he was now serving time. He knew the subject well. Sargent Scheffer had become fascinated with the almost mystical relationship between Tex and Lillian. He had been present many times at meetings between the couple at the Jefferson County Jail.

"I never heard him say as much as 'damn' in front of her," he told reporters at the prison.

The Louisville policeman had not brought with him the gas canisters. They were scheduled to arrive on the early morning train the following day. Hopefully, by that time the crisis would be over and the bombs no longer needed. It would prove to be wishful thinking.

Sharpshooters armed with high powered rifles, along with two machine gun crews, positioned themselves at strategic locations. One of the machine guns was set up in a window of the third floor of the administration building. It began pouring out a deadly stream of high caliber flak across the narrow strip of prison yard and into the brick fortress. The second machine gun did its work from the chapel. Other primary battle stations for surveillance and assault were the main floor of the hospital, and the wall stand located to the south of the administration building. These points encircled the embattled tower of resistance.

There was no avenue of escape. Except, perhaps, under the cloak of darkness. And it was to this very real and increasingly imminent eventuality that the warden gave attention, as the shadows began to grow long on this October afternoon.

The prison engineer and his crew gathered all available acetylene tanks and began to rig torches which would light up the face of the dining hall from all sides. They were careful to make sure the containers were protected from the gunfire of the besieged convicts.

A team of surgeons and nurses had arrived from Paducah around noon and were ushered through the protected passageway and through the back door of the hospital. Guards William Gillihan—whose wound in the hip was painful but not life threatening—and William Gilbert—who was not expected to live—were transported to the Riverside Hospital in Paducah in mid-afternoon. A part of the Paducah medical team began surgery on V. B. Mattingly.

Giant shadows from the towering cellhouses began to darken the prison yard. Finally dusk began to settle in on the deadly standoff. Officer Mattingly's wife arrived at the prison hospital from Breckinridge County at 5:40 p.m. and began her night-long vigil.

As supper time approached, Warden Chilton was confronted with another administrative hassle. The general population now locked in their cells had to be fed. But all the prison's foodstuff was in the kitchen of the dining hall.

Chilton sent prison employees out to raid the local businesses for all the baloney, cheese, bread and milk that they could buy. The little town of Eddyville searched every nook and cranny for available food. Through this joint effort, a sufficient number of sandwiches was put together to feed the prisoners their evening meal. But the warden wisely looked ahead. He placed an emergency order for various food staples to be delivered from Paducah, beginning that night by train.

He also assigned a team, consisting mostly of trusties, to handle the task of feeding and watering the locked up prisoners. Cold cuts and pork and beans might go for a while. But every good warden knows that the quickest way to a rumble is through the prisoners' stomachs. So plans were made to begin preparing hot meals, the next day, out of the hospital galley, and—even at some risk of straying bullets—the warden's kitchen on the second floor of the administration building.

Steps also had to be taken to make sure the cribbed convicts received sufficient watering, and that their respective latrine buckets were taken out as needed. Sewer gas had been known to kill in the castle.

People continued to show up at the front gate to offer their assistance. Individual citizens and law enforcement from the surrounding community gallantly volunteered to storm the barricade. Most were politely turned away, although some of the town's known sharp shooters were invited in.

And, of course, the newspaper reporters began to arrive in full force. They came from far and wide—both larger dailies from Louisville and Nashville, as well as the smaller weeklies. There were only two outside telephone lines into the penitentiary at that time, and they were constantly jingling with incoming calls inquiring about what was being called the "Battle of Eddyville." But Chilton, ever the consummate politician and diplomat, treated the media with gracious hospitality and respect, affording them a separate room with desks and typewriters from which to work. He allowed them unlimited access to observation points throughout the institution, including the dangerous positions of the chapel and hospital.

With the inmates fed, and machinery in motion for their continual care, the tired and bedraggled warden turned his attention back to the siege.

Darkness came and an eerie quiet fell upon the scene. The pale flickering glow from the acetylene torches cast a ghostly glare upon the buildings. Lights in the basement kitchen and laundry were glowing. But the windows on the second floor were narrow boxes of black.

Both sides settled in for the night. Periodically, the surrounding forces would open up with a burst of firepower. Once when this happened, steam began to pour out of the dining hall building in the area of the laundry. A steam pipe had been punctured by a rifle bullet. Once again, the penitentiary engineer Charlie Collier was called into service, turning off the lines leading into the dining hall.

Late into the night, a soldier on guard in the wall stand near four cellhouse saw some movement near the laundry. Thinking that it was one of the convicts attempting to sneak out of the building, he opened fire. A sharp yelping of a dog pierced the midnight air. The edgy marksman had shot and wounded a prison pet.

※ ※ ※

At 4:45 a.m. on Thursday, V. B. Mattingly died in the prison hospital. His body, shrouded in a white sheet and followed by his widow, was borne on a stretcher out the back door of the hospital. Quietly, the litter bearers carried the body around the protected roadway, through the cellhouses and administration building, down the long steps in front to the waiting hearse.

It was a somber procession, reminding the sleepy-eyed sentinels along the way of the grim harvest still being reaped by the dining room trio.

Shortly thereafter the gray dawn crept onto the hill, as a silent and dreary drizzle began to fall.

Soldiers and guards, alternating watches throughout the night, had caught fragments of sleep where they could—on tables, floors, and even the pews in the chapel. No one was sure how the boys in the dining hall had slept.

At 5:00 a.m. guards thought they heard a single report from the upstairs windows. It was answered by a barrage of lead from rifles and machine guns.

Day number two of the siege began. Chilton and his associates huddled in his office with Captain Radford over mugs of steaming coffee.

There was growing pressure to storm the building. They were growing impatient with the waiting game. It was suspected that at least one of the convicts was wounded, maybe dead. With only one weapon reportedly being fired, it was generally believed that they were precariously low on ammunition.

Chilton resisted. The sight of V. B. Mattingly's corpse passing his office and through the front gate was still fresh on his mind.

"Of course we could go and get them," he exhorted, "if we want to lose more men to get them."

But the tired warden was not only affected by the death and dying of his guards. He was also immensely intimidated by the looming brick fortress.

As he told the press, "The main difficulty encountered in dislodging the men are the effective places of hiding afforded them by the construction inside the building.

"There are four, heavy, ninety-gallon steam boilers on the first floor. These are thick and round and will deflect any bullet from high-powered rifles or machine guns. In one corner of the kitchen on the floor are two, steel-sheeted bread mixers in which two men could hide. These command the rear entrance—the boilers control the front entrance.

"It would be possible for one man at either of these points to stand off a regiment from either entrance."

The military men shared their doubts of Chilton's assessment with each other only. Some of the warriors were veterans of the deadly trenches of France. These boys in the mess hall were armed and dangerous. But they were not Alvin Yorks.

Life in the little town of Eddyville was turned upside down.

People poured in from all over to view firsthand the event which was catching national attention. Many gathered on Pea Ridge—the hills overlooking the town—and patiently looked down on the prison yard in hopes of seeing some action. One of these spectators was little Forrest Pogue, age eleven, who was brought over from the nearby hamlet of Francis, by his grandfather, to get a glance at the historic happening. Pogue would grow up to become a combat historian during World War II, recording interviews with men from Omaha Beach to Czechoslovakia, winning the Bronze Star and Croix de Guerre. Born in Eddyville, he became an internationally known biographer, writing the official history of General Dwight Eisenhower's command, and the exhaustive and definitive work on General George C. Marshall. On this autumn afternoon in 1923, the youngster was getting his first, small taste of combat.

Many continued to crowd the front gate, volunteering their services. But there was also apprehension shared by most of the local citizens as bullets from the battle on the hill would occasionally whiz overhead. School was closed. Hotels filled up with reporters and photographers. Even a food shortage developed.

About the distance of a long fly ball from where Lillian Walters and Jim Sparks hid the pistols under the bridge was the Eddyville depot. In fact, most locals referred to the narrow span as the "Depot Bridge." This train station was now a beehive of activity. Each locomotive which chugged and whistled its way up to the platform brought a wide assortment of travelers sharing a common destination—the castle on the Cumberland. Reporters, politicians, troops of soldiers, bureaucrats from Frankfort, representatives of various law enforcement agencies, and the simply curious, were disgorged from the cars.

Rickety and coughing automobiles did a land-office business shuttling people back and forth to the penitentiary a mile away. Some horse drawn carriages were even pressed into service.

Arriving on the early Thursday morning train was the riot squad from Louisville bringing with them the gas bombs left behind by Detective Scheffer the day before. Now armed with gas, Warden Chilton decided to go on the offensive—to some extent. Remembering the punctured steam pipes in the dining hall, Chilton directed that gas be mixed with cayenne pepper and forced through the lines into the building. This was attempted, but fizzled miserably.

Chilton then had to take time out to receive the Democratic candidate for governor, William Jason Fields, accompanied by First District Congressman Alben Barkley. Like all good politicians, they had the knack of showing up where news was being made. Actually, the two had reached Eddyville on Wednesday night from Cadiz, where they had spoken that afternoon. Because of the state of emergency existing in the Lyon County capitol, they wisely canceled their political rally slated for that evening. Chilton briefed them on the pending crisis. It was doubtful that much politics was discussed.

After the short visit, the pair departed by car for Marion, Kentucky, where they were billed to deliver speeches in the afternoon. It was Mr. Fields' first visit to Eddyville. And one that the future governor would never forget.

At 10:30 in the morning, a dark mood once again settled over the prison. Word was received that William Gilbert had died in Paducah.

By late morning, plans had been finalized to utilized the gas guns and bombs. Soldiers Joe Kelly and Gilbert McCollum were to make a run toward the laundry and fire gas canisters into the window. They would do so under cover of heavy fire from all corners of the prison yard.

Just a few minutes before noon, the order was given to commence firing. Machine guns anchored in the third floor window of the administration building and the chapel began cranking out a steady stream of fire upon the upper floor of the brick dining hall. Rifle fire erupted toward the same target from the hospital and a guard stand. The fusillade raining down upon the barricade was awesome.

Kelly and McCollum broke from the chapel, each carrying one of the gas guns brought from Louisville. Kelly also wore an armored vest. They charged toward the doorway of the lower floor kitchen, which faced directly into the administration building a scant hundred feet away.

They successfully set off the guns, leaving them in the mess hall kitchen. But as they began to make their retreat a strange thing happened. Fanned by the draft rushing through the open doorway and bullet-riddled windows of the kitchen, instead of permeating the building, the dense tear gas reversed its flow and began to chase the soldiers as they sprinted back toward the chapel. A wave of the tear gas enveloped Lieutenant Kelly causing him to stagger. His anxious comrades watching from the chapel thought he had been shot. He recovered, and managed to blindly wobble back up the hill and dove through the chapel window into the arms of Detective Scheffer. McCollum also managed to get back to cover safely.

The thunderous barrage lasted for twenty minutes. While there had been at least five hundred rounds of ammunition fired into the dining hall the day before, this onslaught of over a thousand bullets was devastating. Hardly a square foot of the old building was untouched. Flying glass, splinters, plaster and fragments of brick cascaded around the structure kicking up massive clouds of dust and debris. Even the trunk of a good-sized maple, between the hospital and the riddled dining hall, was shredded.

So exhaustive was the outpouring of firepower that Captain Radford immediately requested 25,000 additional rounds of ammunition be brought from Hopkinsville to replenish his munitions.

Unbelievably, it was reported by front-line troops that during the concentrated fire, the beleaguered prisoners managed to return twelve or more shots.

The firing ceased and a quiet stillness settled in with all ears still ringing. After all the fireworks and noise, the building was still free of gas and the rebels still entrenched.

It was decided to use a ruse. One of the National Guard officers went to an open window on the third floor of the administration building overlooking center stage. With the assistance of a megaphone, he called out to Tex Walters, Lawrence Griffith, and Harry Ferland. "Tex Walters, are you willing to surrender?" barked the husky lieutenant, "If you are willing to surrender we will cease firing. We will give you fifteen minutes to march out of the building or we will destroy the building with dynamite."

A few shots were fired from the guards and soldiers in the chapel who had not received instruction on the temporary truce. After they were silenced, the officer repeated the message.

The whole prison held its breath as the minutes ticked by. Only the wind, sweeping up the river valley and around the giant and lofty boulders of the castle's walls and cellhouses, could be heard.

Not a word came from the dining room. Finally, when the time had elapsed, the disappointed and fatigued guards and soldiers resumed firing upon the building. It continued throughout the day.

Five thousand rounds of ammunition would be heaved into the air by the besiegers that Thursday. It was a miracle that they did not accidentally shoot themselves. It was equally miraculous that innocent citizens of the town were not hit by errant and ricocheting bullets.

Men at work in front of the prison on the construction of the lock and dam could hear ballistics streaking overhead and landing in the water. At one point, the laborers threatened to quit if the hazard continued.

The whole area was becoming a combat zone.

Number five cellhouse had not been constructed in 1923. Only the prison wall in a low-lying area of the stockade extended from four cellhouse around most of the southern perimeter of the penitentiary grounds. All of the business and most of the residential area of Eddyville was exposed to the vicious gun battle taking place on the prison yard.

From their perch atop the dining hall, Tex Walters and friends could look right down the main street of Eddyville. The good people of this normally peaceful village were living a charmed life.

Inevitably, the continual avalanche of lead began to take its toll on the old brick structure. The high caliber bombardments from the machine guns were especially destructive. Concentrated drilling by these guns began to open up holes in the masonry. By far the larger cut was on the southwest corner of the dining hall, just to the right of the upper window. This growing wound was directly in line with, and a short distance from, the machine gun positioned in the third floor window of the administration building.

Ostensibly, the mission was to open up a gaping breach so that the gas grenades could be hurled directly into the midst of the top floor gunmen. This stated purpose, in retrospect, makes little sense. Numerous large windows on the upper floor provided ample and unobstructed openings into the large room.

Tedium no doubt played a role in the hole making. With time and ammunition on their hands, the frustrated gunners found themselves something to do—like children who start out baking cookies, and end up throwing dough.

A steady stream of fire continued upon the fortress for most of the day, interrupted only by occasional breaks for reloading and reassessment. Under the deadly deluge, no signs of resistance were noted. A narrow balcony hung onto one side of the upper floor. Steps, now long removed, once led down from the porch. Some guards noted in the afternoon that one of the open double doors which led to the landing had been shut by one of the inmates.

That was the only activity cited in the building after the late morning onslaught. And it was of questionable importance. Heavy fire throughout the siege had opened the door. The same could have closed it.

By three in the afternoon it was decided that another gas attack would be made upon the building. Grenade rifles would be used to propel the bombs into the various openings in the structure in an attempt to rid the interior of its vermin.

At 4:10 p.m. a new wave of heavy shellacking of the building began. Under the intense cover of fire, a few soldiers armed with gas dispensers moved in close enough to dislodge their loads. Gas grenades headed into various openings, to include the yawning punctures recently carved out by the machine gun fire. This done, the grenadiers quickly retreated.

A dud grenade landed on the ledge of the laundry room window, and burst into flames. The mess hall was on fire. An electric flash of panic ran through the assailing troops. Such a drastic development would no doubt take care of the immediate problem at hand. But orders had been sternly given that the building itself had to be salvaged—the dynamite idea had been solidly rejected by correctional authorities.

So the encircled soldiers and guards looked on with consternation. Prison guard Roscoe Gumm, in hopes of extinguishing the blaze, began to fire into the flames leaping from the window sill. Then a very peculiar thing happened. The fire began to subside, and vanish. Soon it was reduced to a few finger-sized tapers, and then wisps of smoke. Staring into the laundry, the onlookers could now see water trickling down and around the window encasement.

Apparently the corralled convicts had managed to douse the flames. When the realization of this startling occurrence hit home, the armed company of men immediately sprung into action and began pelleting the laundry area with bullets.

With the dust settling on the newest advance, it became obvious that it had been no more effective than the gas attack of that morning.

As dusk came on the second day of the siege, the thirty-nine guards, some twenty-five soldiers, along with several volunteer sharpshooters, began to settle in for another night of watching. Sleeping and eating in shifts, and alternating between moods of intense excitement and numbing boredom, they were growing increasingly weary and tired. Several guards had been on duty for almost forty-eight straight hours. They were physically and mentally depleted. Some were even beginning to doubt their own powers of perception.

The acetylene torches were once again adjusted and lit to cast a yellow glow upon the battle-marked dining hall now outlined in the gathering darkness.

Early in the evening, bleary-eyed watchmen in the hospital reported seeing one of the convicts appear at the dining room doorway. They opened fire and the form vanished. Later, close to midnight, guard Guthrie Ladd stepped from the chapel to replace one of the acetylene lamps. Three shots landed near him, and he quickly returned to cover.

The guards and soldiers knew that they must eventually win. But at what cost? Their enemies were ensconced within a seemingly impregnable fortress, with open firing lanes in all directions. They possessed an inexhaustible food and water supply and apparently plenty of ammunition.

The wearing and stressful situation was certainly not lost on the prison warden. He was constantly keeping in touch with the governor and Chairman E. S. Tachau of the State Board of Charities and Corrections.

On Thursday night, Governor Edwin Morrow ordered 30 members of Company L, 149th Infantry, of Mayfield, Kentucky to mobilize and entrain to the Kentucky State Penitentiary.

⁑ ⁑ ⁑

On that same Thursday afternoon while the rattle of musketry and heavy roar of machine guns engulfed the prison yard, Hodge Cunningham was laid to rest in Cadiz, Kentucky, some 25 miles away.

His body had been removed from the prison on Wednesday morning and taken to Glenn's Funeral Home in the neighboring burgh of Kuttawa. After preparation for burial, he was brought back late that afternoon to his home just outside the wall of the penitentiary.

By the time he was laid out for viewing there in the modest living room, hordes of friends and relatives had descended upon the humble home, giving loving and caring embraces to the bereaved widow and two small boys. Food of all kinds—offerings of love meant more for the soul than the body—arrived from caring neighbors and friends.

Men folk stood in the front yard under shade trees, smoking and talking in low voices. The women gathered inside, staying close to Emma, reaching out and touching, holding, and circling the wagons against the uninvited anguish now visiting this family.

Adding a dreadful backdrop to the fellowship of grief was the constant interruption of gunfire just behind the house and over the prison wall.

Children came, not really sure as what to make of it all. Little Mitch and Perry, trading hugs and tears with their relatives, seemed stunned by the enormity of death and its consequences.

Among those arriving to give solace and support for their stricken kin was Hodge's sister, Pocahontas, and her husband George Cunningham. Their 13-year-old daughter Mary Grace was also along. They spent the night and the young niece of the stricken guard was kept awake by the sounds of battle just a short distance away. It was a harrowing and haunting experience for the impressionable young girl. At that time, she would not have been particularly happy to know that she would return to Eddyville someday as the wife of Luther Thomas, the fifteenth warden of the Kentucky State Penitentiary.

Arrangements were made to transport the body to Cadiz for the funeral on Thursday afternoon. On Wednesday night, it was reported that backwater from the swollen Cumberland River covered a low-lying stretch of the Eddyville to Cadiz road. The body would have to return home by

124

train. By Thursday morning, however, the water had receded to the point that the remains of Hodge Cunningham were carried by hearse to the First Baptist Church of Cadiz for the funeral services.

Numerous people gave eulogies to a large gathering which packed the lovely brick chapel known for its graceful lines and stained glass windows. Among those speaking was the Chaplain of the penitentiary, Adolphus Hanberry, a long time friend of the deceased and the one responsible for landing Hodge the coveted state job.

The early morning rain clouds had departed and a brilliant blue sky looked down on the funeral procession as it moved to the East End Cemetery. There, beside a walnut sapling and a young evergreen, Hodge Cunningham was lowered into the ground, as his heartbroken widow and two small sons looked on. They stood in the same cemetery which their beloved departed had once maintained. Out of respect and appreciation, the City of Cadiz provided the burial plot without charge. Only a stone's throw away from his final resting place stood the small frame house in which he and his young family had once lived.

Graveside Masonic rites were conducted. A long line of somber-faced men gathered around the grave, each appareled with the traditional white apron. As the sun began to fall behind the trees, and shadows lengthened, there was just a touch of autumn coolness in the air. A hush fell over the gathering, as the ceremony was conducted.

"It is appointed for all men to die," so it went in part. "In the grave, all men are equal. Only the good deeds, lofty thoughts and heroic sacrifices remain to bear fruit in the lives of those who strive to emulate them."

The grave was covered, and the crowd quietly dispersed into the gathering dusk.

The shoes and hats of inmates Harry Ferland and Lawrence Griffith, discarded underneath the dining room supervisor's platform during the 1923 siege. (Photographs on this page courtesy of Kentucky State Penitentiary Archives.)

General view of the dining hall immediately after the siege. The wall clock, which survived the onslaught, can be seen between the two windows to the left of the guard platform. The dumb waiter leading to the kitchen below is in the left of the picture.

The dining hall taken during the 1923 siege looking from a window in the administration building. Doors leading to the inmate kitchen (left) and laundry (right) are at the bottom of the picture.

A view of the gaping hole chiseled out of the dining hall wall from the constant machine gun fire by the National Guard during the "Battle of Eddyville." (Photograph courtesy of the Louisville *Courier Journal*.)

Citizens of the area on tour of the devastated dining hall after the Tex Walters siege. (Photograph courtesy of Kentucky State Penitentiary Archives.)

Lester Hotel in Eddyville, about the same time when Lillian Walters stayed there during her trials. (Photograph courtesy of Bob Bennett.)

A view from the roof of three cellhouse in the late 1930s. It depicts the old dining hall and the ongoing construction of five cellhouse. Note the steps to the dining hall up which the National Guard charged. To the right of the steps is the coal shed, in which guard Lewis Hill hid. The winding Cumberland River and the old town of Eddyville are located toward the top of the picture. (Photograph courtesy of Kentucky State Penitentiary Archives.)

The prison hospital which had formerly been the home of R. L. Cobb (White Hall) before the penitentiary was constructed. The old dining hall was located in the foreground in the approximate location of the "KSP" flower beds. (Photograph courtesy of Bob Bennett.)

An aerial view of the prison and old Eddyville, taken in the early 1950s.

Football being played on the recreational field during the 1930s. The garment factory, also known as the shirt factory, is to the left in the background. This is the building the inmates seized and where they held Fred McChesney hostage during the 1952 riot. (Photograph courtesy of the *Courier Journal.*)

Inmates lounging on cots in the overcrowded four cellhouse during the 1930s. (Photograph courtesy of Kentucky State Penitentiary Archives.)

The prison band poses on the prison yard with Warden Luther Thomas sometime between 1961 and 1965. Note historical old chapel in background.

Three towering prison wardens of the past. From left to right: Jess Buchanan, Bill Jones, Chuck Thomas.

Warden John Chilton (center), flanked by Jim Noble Smith (left) and John B. Beatty (right), who operated the Reliance Manufacturing Company, which made shirts inside the prison with inmate labor. This photograph was taken in 1915. (Photograph courtesy of Mr. and Mrs. Julian Beatty.)

Inside the current dining room on the bottom floor of five cellhouse, before recent renovation. The gun alley runs above the doorway.

Guard Fred McChesney (on the right) and an unidentified inmate prepare to exercise the bloodhounds, around 1960, outside the walls of the prison. Behind them, and in the edge of the woods, was Vinegar Hill, the old inmate burial ground.

The Castle as it appears today, from the waters of Lake Barkley. The picture is taken near the old lock and dam, now covered by the lake.

Lloyd Armstrong, highly respected and long-time prison official at the Kentucky State Penitentiary.

Warden Luther Thomas is flanked by two inmates in the officers'barber shop. Thomas was warden at the penitentiary between 1961-65. He was responsible for the construction of the prison school building and supervised the last electrocution in 1962.

Charles C. Grassham, outstanding trial lawyer who defended Lillian Walters. (Photograph courtesy of Tom Grassham.)

Judge Charles H. Bush, who presided at the trials of Lillian Walters. (Photograph courtesy of William Turner.)

The face of Tex Walters (top), peers out through the headlines of the siege. Also pictured are Lawrence Griffith (left) and Harry Ferland (right).

Chapter 9

The death house was a block-shaped, one-level building tacked on to the end of three cellhouse. Constructed in 1910 for the grim purpose of executions, it was referred to simply as the "annex" for many years.

For some time, no additional space was needed to house those hapless men who were under sentence of death. Justice was more swift in the early days of the chair, and there was a rapid turnover of tenants. Silas Williams, a black man convicted of murder in Woodford County, arrived at the penitentiary on March 21, 1913. He was executed on the same day.

As the electric chair became more popular with juries and judges, and as the appellate process lengthened, the number of prisoners awaiting electrocution increased. Finally, the death row inmates overflowed the death house and had to be housed in other areas of the prison. For a long time, cellhouse one was used as the death row extension. Finally, with the renovation of three cellhouse, cells were extended down the walk in the basement of that building to provide eleven additional cells for death row.

Today, with men remaining for years on death row until their appeals are exhausted, the population of the condemned has grown even more. The influx has caused the condemned to be moved to the newly constructed six cellhouse. The old death row cells are left empty, used for temporary isolation of unruly inmates. They will be used again for future executions—if and when they occur. Because of this potential, the basement of three cellhouse is still the "death house."

In the center of one of the windowless rooms is the ominous and substantial oaken chair. P. W. "Pete" Depp of Metcalfe County, who served as the chief electrician at the prison at the time, built the solid wooden seat in the back room of his home in Summer Shade, Kentucky. He also served as the first executioner. The chair sits on a slightly elevated wooden platform. A large window separates the electric chair from the witness room, which is large enough to accommodate two dozen people.

Adjoining the death chamber on the other side is the small control room where two, large, gray levers engage the awful workings of the powerful transformer. The old dynamo, which whined and groaned to build up sufficient voltage before each execution, has been replaced by modern electrical equipment. It's hooked to an independent source of power.

There have been 162 men executed at the Kentucky State Penitentiary. They have ranged in age from a mere 16 to the gray-bearded Frank Thomas, who died at 71.

The death march, beginning with James Buckner, has been comprised of 78 whites and 84 blacks. Their offenses have included 145 for murder, 11 for rape, 5 for armed robbery, and one for aiding and abetting rape.

Only fifty of Kentucky's 120 counties have sent men to their death at Eddyville, with Jefferson County—not surprisingly—leading the list at forty-four.

It was a solemn and sobering procedure—putting a man to death in the electric chair.

The law required the fateful time to be immediately after midnight on the designated day.

A grim procession began from the warden's office, as he, the prison physician, chaplains, and reporters made their way through the hushed cellhouses to the place of execution. The warden read the final death warrant to the prisoner earlier in the evening.

A hushed sense of dreadful anticipation fell upon the entire prison population—even upon the small city of Eddyville—on the night of an execution. To this eerie atmosphere was added the melancholy sounds of gospel songs and hymns being sung in chorus by the blacks in three cellhouse.

As emotionally charged as the procedure was, the execution itself is reduced to the cold science of electrocution.

Proctor-Tingels, the Consulting Engineers of Lexington,

Kentucky, outlined precisely how the deed was to be performed:

1. Prepare the "elephant ear" sponges by soaking in strong solution of sal-a-moniac and water for at least one (1) hour before time of execution.

2. In preparing the prisoner for execution, shave hair from crown of head, sufficiently large enough to receive the sponge.

3. Place sponge in the football helmet next to the electrode, retaining all the moisture it will hold. Place football helmet with sponge and electrode on prisoner's head, pulling down and fastening helmet under chin, so sponge fits firmly to crown of head.

4. Fasten other electrode to caf (sic) of right leg, retaining all moisture possible in sponge. As further precaution, wet a towel and place above electrode, so as to give additional moisture at this point.

5. Connect lead wires to electrodes at chair.

6. Set time control relay on control board to number of seconds desired to operate the 2600 volts and also the 600 volts. The time to operate the 2600 volts is 5 seconds. The time to operate the 600 volts is 10 seconds. This is based upon a person weighting up to 140 pounds.

Persons above 140 pounds, increase the setting of the relays one (1) second for each 10 pounds over 140 pounds.

7. Close the 2600 volt breaker. When this is done a buzzer will sound for duration of seconds, which the time control relay is set. When buzzer stops, open the 2600 volt breaker and close the 600 volt breaker.

8. When this is done the buzzer will sound for duration of seconds the time control relay is set. When buzzer stops, open the 600 volt breaker and reclose the 2600 volt breaker.

9. When this is done the buzzer will sound for duration of seconds the time control relay is set. When buzzer stops, open the 2600 volt breaker and reclose the 600 volt breaker.

10. When this is done a buzzer will sound for duration of seconds the time control relay is set. When buzzer stops, open the 600 volt breaker.

11. When this is done notify the attending physician to examine the executed person to see that no life exists.

12. If life does exist, repeat the above operation, after replenishing moisture to the electrodes in the football helmet and at calf of the right leg.

Moisture at the electrodes are to cause sufficient electrical contact to body, thereby preventing arching and burning at point of contact.

Clean and efficient. Within a minute, the state's ultimate claim is extracted.

Each of the 162 lives taken by the electric chair at Eddyville represents a story of tragedy and woe. This small corner of the prison, consisting of stone and steel, has housed a human compendium of suffering.

But there have been those who have been condemned to these corridors of death and have survived.

Bill Elliot was one of these fortunate souls. He was convicted and sentenced to death for the murder of a turnkey in a county jail. After he had exhausted his court appeals, he tried another tactic.

He played insane, knowing that the law will not allow anyone to be executed who is not mentally competent—a peculiar notion when one thinks upon it deeply, as though it makes a great deal of difference. This ploy did not work, as the likable prisoner was a terrible actor.

Next he turned to religion, and enlisted the support and affection of several members of the clergy. He was baptized, and became a very good Bible student.

Ministers enlisted church people to Bill's cause. One preacher went on the radio seeking funds to help carry his case from court to court. An unprecedented ground swell of community support developed. Even people on the streets of Eddyville stopped the prison chaplain and voiced their concern. Letters and telegrams poured into the prison. But Bill Elliot's execution date nevertheless arrived.

When the chaplain paid the condemned man a visit in the afternoon, he was met with a cheery assurance, "I can't explain it, but I have prayed, and somehow, the Lord has revealed to me the word that I will never be executed."

He was the only one convinced.

The usual routine was commenced—black prisoners singing, and ministers praying. A hearse containing an empty casket ominously pulled up and parked in front of the prison.

Arriving on the scene was a preacher from Owensboro, Kentucky, who had great plans of conducting a flourishing funeral for the well-publicized corpse. The huckster entered the death house and proceeded to enthusiastically describe—to Elliot's disgust—his upcoming funeral. He even showed him a picture of his casket.

Just before it was time for the condemned to step out of his cell the warden arrived, presumably with his final farewell. Instead he read to Bill Elliot a stay of execution.

The cellhouse and entire prison broke out in celebration. Only the funeral preacher was nonplused. Disappointed, he silently stole away and drove the empty casket back to Owensboro.

Elliot was finally given a life term, and was eventually paroled.

He had cheated death. And he left behind a chilling account of what it is like to live daily within the shadows of the chair.

From his diary of March 26-27, 1942:

> This is the date for the execution of Eugene B., age eighteen, colored, of Lexington, Kentucky. This boy has been tried and sentenced to die in the electric chair three times by Fayette County Circuit Court, Lexington, Kentucky. His lawyers are trying to get relief through a *habeas corpus* writ, but apparently they have failed. It is about two P.M. on the eve of Eugene's execution. He and his mother and those interested in his welfare are awaiting word, as is usually the setup on such occasion. Our Chaplain, Brother Chandler, was just here and prayed with us. Eugene's mother has just left to resume the vigil at a neighbor's house.
>
> It is 5:00 P.M. Reverend Davis has arrived to

be with Gene the last few hours. Our colored choir has just assembled for prayer and songs. They have sung "Near the Cross" and three spirituals I am not familiar with. One of the men who once was in the death cell himself is now sending up the most humble and earnest prayer while the Chaplain is reading from Isaiah. Reverend Waters has arrived. On his way he stopped to console Eugene's mother. The choir is singing "Well Done." Now, Brother Chandler is reading the 23rd Psalm.

7:30—We all joined in the singing of "Leaning on the Everlasting Arms." Brother Waters and Brother Davis quoted scripture, and Brother Chandler is now reading the 46th Psalm—now a prayer by one of the inmate choir followed with a song, "Lord Lead Me On." Then they sang "All Along."

The warden has come to read the "mandate" to Eugene, which is an unpleasant duty of the warden.

Here is what Eugene wrote in regard to the mandate: 'The warden just read the death warrant to me, and I felt fine, because I know God was with me. Reverend Waters has just had prayer with Otis Peter Smith, my cellmate, and I felt the spirit in my heart, and I thank God.'

A prayer followed, then a song, "Remember Me."

9:30—Our good brother and inmate preacher has delivered a wonderful message, and we are singing, "Must Jesus Bear the Cross Alone?" Prayer followed by the reading of St. John 17:1-14 inclusive, and St. John 14:1-9 inclusive, by Reverend Waters.

10:15—Holy Communion followed with the song, "He Is The One."

10:40 P.M.—Brother Clark has just arrived. Song, "He Will Remember Me."

11:00 P.M.—Some have gone with Brother Chandler for a cup of coffee and a breath of fresh air. Brother Clark and the guard and us boys in the death house are carrying on.

11:30 P.M.—All are back and all are singing again, "Leaning on the Everlasting Arms." Then "He Is The One." Brother Davis is now praying. Now,

Brother Waters is leading us in songs. It is but twenty minutes until Eugene takes his last departure, and as is customary, the ministers are leaving Eugene to be alone with Jesus these last few minutes. The Chaplain is saying his last prayer with Eugene at the cell door. The ministers, the guards, doctor, wardens and visitors are assembling at the death chamber.

Now they are taking Eugene out of his cell. While they are relocking the door, Eugene said "So long" to each of us other men and said for deathmen to keep the good work going.

He is being placed in the chair by now—and I can hear him bidding "adieu" to the people in there. There goes the switch, and the motors are singing their weird song of death as the electricity violently flows through his body—may God be merciful unto him. By now, Eugene is out of his agony, I pray.

All have gone, and here come the men carrying the still form of our late friend and brother in Christ. It is a sad ending, but now that the torture is over, it has an altogether different aspect to Eugene, I presume. The reward that is awaiting him in heaven is not to be compared to the suffering he went through here. "Death is like sleep; and sleep shuts down our lids . . . ." Byron.

(Signed) Bill Elliot

Sylvester Warner became known as "The Forgotten Man of Eddyville."

In the fall of 1933, he and two other youths got tanked up on moonshine and paid a terrible visit upon an old man and his son living in the hills of Casey County. Their purpose was robbery, and after calling them out into the yard, they bludgeoned them to death.

Their attempts at doing away with the bodies by anchoring them down in the Green River failed. The three were apprehended, indicted and convicted for murder.

Warner claimed he was just along for the ride, with no intention of killing anyone. His buddies of course said otherwise, and that they, not Warner were the least culpable.

One of the trio was given life. The other two, including Warner, were sentenced to death. They arrived at the Castle on the Cumberland, February 18, 1934. The execution date was set for

October 26. Only hours before the death march was scheduled to begin, Warner's rap partner had his death sentence commuted by Governor Ruby Lafoon to life imprisonment. Warner received an "indefinite" stay of execution.

Over a year later, in December, 1935, A. B. Chandler became governor. During this time Warner languished in the sunless and cribbed confines of the Eddyville death house.

The new governor took no action on Warner's case. No further commutation. No new date set for execution. Patiently, and proud to be alive, he simply hung in limbo. Weeks and months passed, and the new administration wasn't so new anymore.

The tension of the uncertainty was incredible. Each night as he lay in his solitary cell, he knew that the very next day he might receive that dreadful summons which would strike him from the roll of the living.

Months turned into years. He witnessed 25 kindred souls shuffle past his cell on the way to their deaths.

Like most death row residents, Warner turned to religion. It sustained him, and his cheerful and undaunted personality was an inspiration to his doomed neighbors.

Eventually, after he had corresponded with spiritual advisors and ministers around the country, his plight became well known. He became known as "The Forgotten Man of Eddyville."

People, to include a state senator from his home county, took an active interest in his case. Letters and petitions on his behalf began to flow into the governor's office. From time to time there would be a splash of publicity in the paper, and then his fortunes would recede to the dreary and timeless oblivion of death row.

Finally, Sylvester Warner had enough. In January, 1939, he asked a newspaper reporter to bring the matter to a head—for better or for worse. He was tired of the unbearable suspense. He requested, through the reporter, that the governor take action—either commute his sentence to life, or execute him. He asked for a decision, fateful and final—one way or another.

A brief history of the case appeared in the magazine section of the Sunday *Courier-Journal.* Correspondence and petitions flowed in to the governor's office.

Governor Chandler was on the spot. He had been highly critical in his campaign of the liberal pardoning and commutation record of his predecessor, Ruby Lafoon. He had made a promise that he would be much tougher.

But Warner's supporters had strong arguments for leniency. The subject of their attention—now pasty white and hollow eyed from lack of sun and fresh air—had spent almost five long years in penal purgatory. His accomplices in the terrible crime had long ago had their penalties reduced to life. And perhaps most importantly for a politician such as Chandler, public opinion seemed to be in Warner's favor.

The governor sent the case to the attorney general and the assistant commissioner of the State Welfare Department—under which the prisons were then administered. He solicited their recommendations. That move resulted in a split decision.

As one might expect, the state's chief prosecutor advised the chief executive that after reviewing the record, he could find no legal reason why the extreme punishment should not be extracted. On the other hand, the Welfare Department recommended that Warner's sentence be commuted to life.

So Chandler pondered. At the end of January, 1939, the governor came to what must be assumed a painful decision.

"Before sunrise," the executive order read, "Friday morning, February 10, 1939, the warden shall, in a manner and place prescribed by law, cause a current of electricity to pass into Warner's body, of sufficient intensity to produce death, and that application of said current shall continue until Warner is dead. And may God have mercy upon his soul."

This devastating development must have stunned Warner. But by all reports, he took the terrible news philosophically.

"Well, I asked the governor for definite action and I got it. . . ." was his stoic response to the fate which had befallen him.

His upbeat and affable manner continued unchanged, as he faced his final days with good cheer and courage.

On the day before the execution the governor announced that he would not waiver from his decision. He did order that a sanity hearing be held at the prison to make sure Warner was competent.

This, of course, was a farce. Perhaps no man to ever occupy death row has been more rational and in full possession of his wits, than the likable inmate from Casey County.

Warner was led from his cell across the prison yard to the hospital where a team composed of the prison physician and two psychiatrists from Western State Hospital at nearby Hopkinsville examined him.

Calmly and with great poise he visited with the panel, awing them with his great composure only a few brief hours away from his execution. He was the most cheerful person at the hearing. After he returned to his cell, his father, sister and other members of his family paid him a last visit. He tried his best to comfort and console them. Then with apparent gusto and appreciation he received his last meal—

a sumptuous selection of his own choosing.

Darkness fell against the old death house, and the hours remaining dwindled away. The prison chaplain remained with him throughout the night. The sympathetic guards checked on him periodically. Near midnight, one of them handed him a cardboard box for his personal belongings. He packed his pitiful stock with written instructions.

The chorus of three cellhouse began their haunting hymns.

Shortly after midnight his cell door swung open and he began the last walk. He bid farewell to his fellow condemned as he passed by their cells.

"So long Ves," they solemnly responded.

He was strapped in the chair and made ready for his final moment. His countenance remained steady to the end.

Reverend Chandler place a hand upon his arm and began the Lord's prayer. As he concluded, "for Thine is the power and the glory forever. . . ." he stepped back from the lethal charge.

The Warden dropped his hand and the switch in the small anteroom was thrown. Motors whined, and lights throughout the prison dimmed. Warner's body leaped and strained against the leather thongs binding him to the chair. A bit of smoke curled from his leg. The charge receded and his limp body fell back in the chair. The prison physician stepped forward to examine the remains.

In less than five minutes from the time he left his cell, he was pronounced dead. The "forgotten man" had been remembered.

Friday the 13th—July 13, 1928.

The National Democratic Convention had just wrapped up its business and the country readied itself for the presidential campaign between Republican Herbert Hoover and the Democrat's choice, Al Smith. The Prohibition Party—whose main thrust was to defeat the Catholic Smith—nominated William F. Varney as its candidate.

Germany had just accepted the American draft for a renunciation of war treaty—a deception of all deceptions.

Ohio was hit with heavy damage from storms, as heavy rains caused rivers and streams to overflow.

The captain of the steamer *Chris Greene* vehemently denied that his packet was beaten in a race up the Ohio River by arch rival the *Betsy Ann.*

The Kentucky State Penitentiary prepared for a grisly smorgasbord of death.

Through a hellish quirk in scheduling, seven men from varying backgrounds and crime stories, were to die in Eddyville's electric chair during the first dark moments of Friday the 13th.

Milford "Red" Lawson, age 35 of Corbin, Kentucky, convicted of murdering a mountain neighbor in Whitley County, was slated to be the first to be put to death.

Twenty-one-year-old Orlando "Red" Seymour's last-ditch legal effort to escape the chair failed. At 9:30 on the night of the execution, his lawyers were able to arrange a habeas corpus hearing on his sanity and competency to be executed. Seymour's belief that he would get one last trip outside of the walls of the Castle was dashed when County Judge A. J. Boughter of Lyon County opted to hear the petition in the prison chapel. The slayer of a Louisville coal yard manager appeared weak and needed assistance as he was led into the hearing. After hearing arguments from the lawyers for both the condemned and the Commonwealth, Judge Boughter declined jurisdiction, effectively sealing Seymour's fate.

Haskey Dockery, convicted and sentenced to death for killing a woman at her home in Harlan County, was also guilty of killing two other people. He was marginally mentally retarded.

Of all those mandated to die in the early minutes of the fateful 13th, Charles Mitra was considered to have the best chance for a stay of execution. He received the supreme penalty for the murder of a Louisville grocer. Subsequent to his own trial, Mitra had been a key witness in the successful prosecution of his co-defendant, Carl Hord. The prosecutor requested the governor to postpone Mitra's execution until Hord's conviction and death sentence had been upheld on appeal. Otherwise if Hord's case was reversed for retrial and Mitra was dead, the state's case might well go down the tubes.

Governor Flem Sampson was unmoved.

"There is no reason to presume that the trial court committed such grievous error as to require a reversal of the judgment in the Hord case. This plea, is, therefore, one more in the contingent expectancy than in substance."

James Howard, and William Moore, both convicted out of Jefferson County, and Clarence McQueen from Harrison County, were all black, and sentenced to death for murder. Typical of the time, their appeals for executive clemency were given short thrift. In passing on the Moore case the governor wrote, "The brutality of the crime could not be adequately matched by anything less than the death penalty."

So the stage was set for the execution night of all execution nights.

The afternoon was filled with crying and distraught relatives saying their farewells to their doomed kinsmen. Fathers, mothers, brothers and sisters—a parade of pain and agony. It was unsettling, even to hardened and seasoned correctional officers and staff. Families and news reporters jammed the administration building. It bordered on chaos.

At 4 p.m. the men were given their last meal of regular prison fare. None had requested anything special.

As the long summer day turned to dusk, most of the relatives had departed. Some stood vigil on the prison grounds outside the walls. Forlorn and in knotted groups of grief, they silently waited.

For many years there stood on private property, just off the prison boundary, a huge oak, twenty-four feet in circumference at its base. The tree was ancient, and dominated the landscape. It was located just a short distance from the death house.

Under the shelter of its bough, loved ones of the condemned would often gather at the hour of execution. It was as close as they could get to their beloved, soon to be departed. From there they could hear the dynamo groan, and see the cell block lights dim as the life was being taken. It became known as the "Vigil Tree," an outdoor shrine of remembrances and tearful farewells.

At 7 p.m. Warden John Chilton arrived in the death house and read the four white men their death warrants. They displayed little outward sign of emotion.

Dockery, killer of three, lit a cigarette, sneered and turned away.

A little later that night the three blacks were moved to death row from their cells in another cellhouse.

The night wore down. Although no clock sounded a doleful knell as the hours crept by, the death house grew solemnly quiet as the midnight hour approached.

A reporter later noted, "With heads supported in cupped hands, they sat silent, their bodies shaken by chills despite the intense heat in the squat stone house that had been their home in the prison. In plain view was the execution chamber and the chair. There was no somber darkness in the place, however, instead there was a brilliant light and shadow and polished steel."

Then at 12:15 a.m. the solemn death walk began. Whites first, even in death.

First was Lawson, and then Seymour.

Haskey Dockery, who had seemed the least affected by the ghastly ordeal, was next. He was originally scheduled to go first. However, at the last minute his bravado broke down. Just as the hum of the death chair dynamo filled the cell block, he asked for a priest, explaining that he wished to become a Roman Catholic. One was summoned and he was received into the church. Silently and shaken, he made his way slowly into the chair chamber. As the hood was adjusted he began mumbling prayers. Just four hours before when the death warrants were read, he had smiled disdainfully and contemptuously flicked ashes from his cigarette.

Twenty-three-year-old St. Louisian, Charles Mitra, was the fourth man and last white to go. He had shown little remorse during his stay on death row and had been rather disdainful in his attitude toward the guards. He made no closing statement.

Next were the three blacks.

Seemingly crushed and fearful during the first part of the awful evening, they recovered their spirits as their time drew near. They departed with notable grace and dignity.

First was William Moore, the oldest of the entire group at 45. He went to meet his Maker without a whimper.

James Howard entered the chamber singing "Sweet Lily of the Valley." As he slowly sat down in the large wooden chair, he casually waved to the spectators gathered. "Gentlemen, how are you all feeling tonight?" he asked in a warm and friendly tone.

Then finally, Clarence McQueen from Cynthiana, Kentucky, hummed an old spiritual and watched with great interest as the straps and electrodes were adjusted. At 2:22 a.m., he became the last to die.

"One by one," to paraphrase Ella Wilcox, "they had all filed on, through the narrow aisles of pain."

As the whining of the dynamo wound down at last, an eerie quiet fell over the entire death house. Seven cells stood poignantly empty. Guards spoke in low tones, as if not to reawaken the nightmare they had just endured.

The bodies of all seven were taken to the prison morgue and embalmed by a licensed mortician. Then they were placed in wooden coffins, to await any claim by family or next of kin. Some went unwanted, and were buried in the prison cemetery, "Vinegar Hill," located in the woods about a half a mile from the prison walls.

This night of death at Eddyville still stands as a record in the United States for the most legal executions in one day.

※ ※ ※

Time has a tremendous transforming quality. Time and place.

The death house at Eddyville has a way of reducing men to humble and docile human beings. In most instances they become monkish pilgrims, seeking out salvation for their own souls. In their religious revival they also seek to leave behind—as if to redeem in part the terrible strife and heartache their lives have sown—instruction and admonitions for others, especially the young. In "Death Cell Meditations," Sylvester Warner wrote for posterity,

> "Young folks please take my council,
> as on through life you go;
> Be very careful of the seed that bury where you sow."

Most all become repentant and make affable and well-behaved prisoners. Because of the transformation—this kindly and well-mannered behavior—it becomes easy for guards, wardens, and all those who attend to the needs of those fated for execution, to develop a bond with their captives.

Over time, it creates a terrific strain. Many of the death house guards who repeatedly worked with the condemned and took part in their demise developed close relationships with their hopeless wards. Tough and grizzled old officers have been known to shed a tear or two after the death of an inmate.

One can't help but wonder what the old timers would think of today's highly honed and antiseptic methods of executions. Special training in death house methods, rotating teams to bring in an "unattached" crew for the final 48 hours, professional, psychological counseling for employees affected, briefings and debriefings for those who are a part of the execution team, are all part of modern day death work which attempts to lend a cool and professional sheen to this gruesome and untidy business.

Yesterday's sentinels of doom had to grind it out alone, day by day, death by death. Asking no quarter, they took these dark experiences home, vanquishing the awful sounds, the smells, the youthful faces, in their winter fires.

Captain John "Buck" Rankin was a death house officer who had nurtured and coddled over one hundred men to their deaths. Naturally there were many to which he grew attached.

William Buchanan, in his riveting book, *Execution Eve*, captures some of the interesting recollections of Captain Rankin:

> "Well they were an odd lot, they were. Let's see. Black Texas—now there's a story for you. Been a soldier. He went on a fourteen-day robbery and shooting spree between Dallas and Louisville. Killed eight men and three women. He had a teenage nephew doing time in the reformatory up in Frankfort. Smart-

alecky kid, sour on the world, vowed to avenge his uncle as soon as he got out. Black Texas heard about the boy's bragging and asked to have him brought down here to witness the execution. Kid swaggered in here cocky as a banty rooster. Fifteen minutes later he stumbled out meek as a lamb. Instant rehabilitation, I tell you. . . .

"Whispering Dan. Had the most beautiful singing voice I ever heard on a man—Irish tenor, I guess you'd call it. Sang gospel songs day and night. Started singing while they were strapping him into the chair. Was singing 'Rock of Ages' when the shock hit him. 'Let me hide myself in Thee. . . .' Those were his last words.

"Pegleg Pete. Pete loved to dance. Could tap out a tune on that wooden leg better than most tappers do with two feet. They took away his peg when they strapped him in. Last thing he said was, 'Looks like this gonna be old Pete's last dance.' When the shock hit him that stump began to jump up and down, just like it was keeping time with the dynamo.

"Showboat. Now there was a puzzling case. Found him drunk one day, right down there in that end cell that Tom Penney's in now. We searched every nook and cranny of it, couldn't find a thing. All his mail and packages were censored. No one could get close enough to that high window in his cell to slip him anything. He just smiled at our questions, said he had no intention of dying sober. All we could do was scratch our heads. Few weeks later, there he was again, higher than a Chinese kite. Same search. Same result. Well, I started keeping a closer eye on him. I'd sneak into the dynamo room across the hall where I could see into his cell but he couldn't see me. He always saved a bit of bread from his meal to feed the pigeons that came to roost on his cell window. Nothing wrong with that. Now, those pigeons used to feed all day down at the prison farm before coming back here to roost. Well, sir, one night I saw Showboat grab one of those birds and start squeezing it's craw. Sure enough, that bird coughed up a few grains of corn. And that's how he was doing it. When he'd collect enough corn, he'd add some of the sugar I'd let him have for his morning coffee, mash it all up and mix it with water. After a while it got just ripe enough to give him a buzz. We put a screen over his window and that ended that. He died sober, by the way. . . .

"The names go on and on—Pope Leo, Bad Bill, Big Yellow, Three-finger John. If they hadn't brought a nickname with them when they came here, they usually acquired one in here. . . ."

As their crimes and victims are left behind, the personalities of these brutal criminals are transcended into subjects of morbid curiosity and even sometimes public sympathy. In their tranquil death house demeanor and pale, almost ghost-like complexions, they have successfully camouflaged the horrid evils of their crimes. Their impending doom has taken center stage while the suffering, heartache and pain of their victims are relegated to the past.

And while the reviewing authorities have not always been without fault, they have in most cases at least, tried to bring the awesome tragedy of the entire picture back into focus.

Governor Sampson eloquently spoke to the matter when considering the ill-starred seven:

"The execution of a human being is a serious thing. So much so that it makes one shudder, but it is hardly more serious than the menace to society from those so criminally inclined as to be willing to take the life of an innocent person. The punishment for crime must be sure, certain and speedy if we would break down the disregard for law which seems now to be so prevalent. So long as I am Governor of the Commonwealth I propose to look well to the protection and safety of the innocent, but shall let the law take its course with those who deliberately violate its plain mandates."

Thus the death house and the state house have historically made their own case in regard to capital punishment—a battle which still wages today.

❊❊❊

In the history of the Kentucky State Penitentiary there have been many inmates murdered by fellow prisoners.

Any prison, especially a maximum security institution, has a strong penchant for violence.

The methods have included stabbing, bludgeoning, incineration, and a myriad of other cruel ways and devices. Out of all of these atrocities—convicts killing convicts—only one of the guilty has had to pay with his life.

At about 5:30 on the evening of June 13, 1938, the prison population had been locked up for the evening. In four cellhouse an inmate water boy, known as "Sissy," was making his routine round of the cells. Moving down the inside walk on the third tier, he arrived at the cell of Clayton Sloan and Charles H. Smith.

What he saw was such a terrifying spectacle that it caused him to scream and throw his water bucket and dipper over the rail. The frightful yell and water bucket soaring through the air caught the attention of the inmates who, due to overcrowded conditions at the time, were bunking outside the cells on the main floor. When they looked up they, too, saw the grisly sight.

Standing at his cell door and growling like a wild animal was inmate Charles Smith. He was holding high, for all to see, the decapitated head of his cellmate Clayton Sloan. The deranged killer was proudly holding his trophy by its long blond hair, with blood dripping from its trunk. A front gold tooth of his victim glittered grotesquely in the light.

Sloan, age 22, was serving a three-year sentence out of Owsley County for horse stealing. His cellmate Smith, had decapitated him with the blade of a butcher knife, apparently stolen from the kitchen.

Smith, who at 42 was almost twice the age of his cellmate, had a long criminal record including two previous murders. The two should not have even been serving time in the same prison, let alone in the same cell.

Smith had killed a railroad detective at Ashland on July 15, 1918, and was convicted for murder. He escaped from the Frankfort jail but was recaptured.

He escaped again in September of 1921, and was out for ten years before being recaptured and returned April 26, 1931. On March 2, 1935, he killed a fellow prisoner at Eddyville and was given another 21 years.

At his trial for killing Sloan he simply stated he didn't remember what had led to the killing of his cellmate. In truth, the atrocity had been incited by a fit of homosexual jealously as Smith had repeatedly accused his young "lover" of "running around on him."

After wolfing down a hearty meal of fried chicken, biscuits, tomatoes and mayonnaise, oranges, and coffee on his last evening, he spoke freely with Warden Jess Buchanan, but could give only vague details of Sloan's murder.

A few minutes after midnight on July 14, 1939, he was electrocuted. He has the dubious distinction of being the only convict ever put to death at Eddyville for killing another prisoner.

⚏ ⚏ ⚏

Sadly, crime is too often a family affair. "Like father, like son" often carries over into the world of wrongdoing. So it was with Roy Tarrence and his son Leonard.

On February 28, 1952, they bludgeoned Louisville lawyer Frances McCormack to death and dumped his battered body in Harrods Creek. McCormack had represented Leonard's wife in legal action against him. They were both convicted in April 1952, and sentenced to death.

The father and son arrived at Eddyville in May of 1952. Extended appeals followed, but their execution date was finally set for March 17, 1955.

At 3 p.m. they were both moved from one cellhouse to death row, where they were put in adjoining cells. After eating most of the last meal brought to them, they spent most of the night with various ministers. Toward the end, both men assured them that they were "ready to go."

The father, Roy, was led to his death first. As he passed Leonard's cell, his son called out, "Goodbye dad, so long old pal. I'll see you up there."

Roy made a short statement, recited the Lord's Prayer, thanked the prison guards for their decency and kindness, and received the lethal charge at 12:07 a.m.

Leonard read verses from the Bible and also commended the prison staff for their treatment. The son then read a lengthy prepared statement. He excoriated his wife, and accused her and McCormack of conspiring to harm him. "They will reap their rewards," he concluded. Calmly, he shook hands with Deputy Warden Lloyd Armstrong who accompanied him to the chair. By 12:27 a.m., he was gone.

⚏ ⚏ ⚏

There is no evidence that any of the men executed at Eddyville were innocent of the crimes for which they were executed. Most all admitted their wrongs and meekly surrendered to their fate. Records and recollections do not recall a single man who in his last moments fought his executioners.

Many of those sent to the prison mortuary by electrocution were mean and vicious human beings, humbled only by death. If allowed to live, they would probably have killed again. Victims were vindicated. Society was protected. One can easily argue that they deserved to die.

But there are other names on this roll call of death, who may well have merited a better fate.

Reflecting upon this long line of cases, and reviewing background information about them, one comes away with the unsettling feeling that maybe all was not just.

There are far too many blacks—over fifty percent. We know in our heart of hearts that blacks did not commit fifty percent of all the crimes deserving of death. Of those eleven sent to their deaths for rape, only one was white. It is a safe bet that none were electrocuted for raping a black woman.

Youthful offenders of both races fill up the list. A large number were executed for their first offense.

Sixteen were put to death for a crime which did not take a human life. In other words, it was not an eye for an eye, but life for an eye. This disproportionate punishment is illegal today.

And there were some, who—unlike their co-defendants—turned down life sentences and instead pled "not guilty" with a jury trial. It was a deadly gamble with a deadly result.

On April 6, 1939, Eugene Burnam, a 15-year-old black boy, allegedly raped a white, Lexington, Kentucky, woman. He pled "not guilty" and went through four trials. The first trial resulted in a hung jury. A conviction was obtained in the second trial but it was reversed by the Court of Appeals. On the third try, there was another guilty verdict. It, too, was overturned by the appellate court. Finally, on the fourth trial, the state nailed down a conviction which stuck. On February 17, 1942—almost three years after the crime was claimed to have been committed—Eugene Burnam was electrocuted. He had just turned 18.

The next to last man to be executed at the Kentucky State Penitentiary was Robert Lee Sheckles. He was convicted of rape out of Jefferson County. His two co-defendants were also convicted, but were given life sentences. The execution was set for November 30, 1956.

Governor A. B. Chandler was out of state, and Lieutenant Governor Harry Waterfield was left in charge.

The condemned man's mother sat for most of the day in Waterfield's office in Frankfort. When finally given her chance, she begged for her son's life.

Even the victim of Sheckles' assault, an employee at General Hospital in Louisville, pleaded with Waterfield to commute the condemned man's death sentence. She contended that it was not right for him to be put to death, since his two companions in crime had been given life terms.

Waterfield, no doubt carrying out Chandler's orders, turned a deaf ear. At midnight, Sheckles, along with two murderers, was electrocuted. He was only 20 years of age and had no previous convictions. And, of course, he was black. His victim was white.

Kelly Moss did not go quietly into the night. Before he was executed on March 2, 1962, he railed against the prison officials, sued them, fought with his mother, and was swearing to his last breath.

Forty-eight-year-old Moss cut a menacing figure at six-feet-two-inches tall and over 250 pounds. He possessed a glowering demeanor which exuded contempt, and a broad face which most times supported a stubble of gray beard.

After four previous convictions, he was found guilty of the November 7, 1957, fatal beating of his step-father, Charles Abbitt of Henderson, Kentucky, and was sentenced to death.

Correctional officer Andrew Sills and another guard were sent to the Henderson County jail to bring the convicted killer to the prison for execution. Moss was placed in the back seat of the car, with Sills driving and the other officer riding shotgun.

On a lonely back road between Henderson and Eddyville, Moss—who was handcuffed—suddenly lunged over the back of the front seat and grabbed the steering wheel. He then attempted to pull the car off of the road. The massive Moss and the astonished Sills proceeded to play tug o'war with the wheel as the car careened wildly down the road. The other guard, panic stricken, simply looked on in a frozen stupor.

Finally, the alert Sills spotted an alfalfa field without a fence and managed to get the errant automobile safely off the road and to a stop. He immediately jumped out, pulled his gun and leveled it down on his rebellious prisoner. "Okay Kelly," Sills warned. "Get back there! I don't want to kill you, but I will kill you if I have to."

By that time, the other officer had come back to life and bravely offered to do violence to Moss if he didn't behave. The remainder of the scenic ride to the Castle on the Cumberland was uneventful.

After Moss was safely tucked away, a curious crowd of guards and other prison employees gathered in the prison parking lot to inspect the newly modified and egg-shaped steering wheel.

Upon arrival at the death house in Eddyville March 30, 1960, Kelly Moss proceeded to launch a desperate fight for his life.

After exhausting his appeals through state court, he was granted a stay of execution while the U. S. Supreme Court considered a writ of certiorari filed by his attorney. Finally the land's highest court upheld the conviction and his execution was reset for January 6, 1961.

In the meantime Moss—always belligerent toward the prison officials—filed a $100,000 lawsuit charging that the penitentiary guards twice shot him with tear gas in his cell. The hulking convict claimed that the shots knocked him unconscious and he lay for several days in the corrosive liquid, causing him to suffer burns on his back and legs.

He sued everybody—Warden Thomas, former Governor Chandler and a bunch of correctional officers.

Again he obtained a stay of execution while this lawsuit went to trial. On April 25, 1961, a Federal Court took only thirty minutes to find for the defendants.

When his lawyers jumped ship, Moss filed a motion for a new trial in his own handwriting. It was denied.

Finally, in early 1962, Governor Bert Combs set the last execution day—before sunrise on March 2.

As a last-ditch effort, Moss sent off a letter of appeal to Governor Combs to save his life. Fifteen minutes before the scheduled execution, the office of the state's attorney general called Warden Luther Thomas to inform him that Combs would not commute the sentence.

Moss' mother visited him frequently while he was on death row. At seventy years of age, she was still a pretty tough old lady in her own right. Almost every time they came together, they argued violently and almost came to blows. They fought "like a couple of cats," one guard commented.

It was no different when she showed up at the prison on the day before his execution.

Gary Kettler, reporter for the *Paducah Sun-Democrat*, gave a vivid description of the old woman as she appeared on that fateful day:

> "She was clad respectably in a brown satin
> dress with a white collar and gold symbols. Mrs. Moss
> wore an old black coat with what looked like a sheep-
> skin lining in it. On top of that coat was another
> lightweight black rayon coat to protect her feeble body

from the cold weather.

Mrs. Moss' legs were covered with a too-large pair of stockings. She wore a pair of black shoes with a good solid heel. Her left ankle was swollen twice the normal size.

The mother of the condemned convict wore a pair of black rimmed glasses. She also wore a hair-net with hair pins—a red one and a brown one—in it over her gray head.

Her long fingers were worn black in some places from many years of labor. Through the entire night-long vigil she kept tissue clutched in her worn hands, occasionally wiping her face.

Mrs. Moss carried a large red pocketbook containing some of her personal belongings. A big red scarf hung out over the side of the purse."

When she visited Kelly on death row for the last time, between six and seven in the evening, they proceeded to get into a knock-down, drag-out argument. In a plethora of swearing and cursing, Kelly blamed her for his predicament, having brought him into the world, and then marrying his step-father who he was convicted of murdering. "You brought me into this world," he exclaimed, "now you can watch me go out of it." In this heated exchange, Moss was not the only one throwing out the four-letter words.

When she finally left his cell, the condemned man slammed his supper dishes up against the prison wall, shattering them to pieces.

His mother then provided an extra bit of drama by saying that it was her, not her son, who had done in her husband. She claimed that she had killed Abbitt with an ironing board to protect herself. In spite of her frantic assertion, no one took her seriously.

Around 9 p.m., the distraught mother became very agitated and wanted to return to the death house to see her son again. The officials barred the way however. The last visit had been enough for everyone.

She was then relegated to the basement of the administration building where there was a couch on which she could rest. Instead of relaxing however, she proceeded to walk about in an agitated state. Once she stopped at one of the windows in the basement and screamed, "Kelly is not guilty!"

As the last minutes ticked away, Moss became loud and abusive. He unloaded on Governor Combs, calling him a "brutal vicious governor." Moss also attacked Warden Luther Thomas and other prison officials. Raising his shirt, he showed to reporters scars he claimed were tear gas burns inflicted by penitentiary authorities.

"They are trying to kill me twice!" he raved.

Only moments away from his final walk, he still proclaimed his innocence, alleging that he had been framed.

Warden Thomas, anticipating that the burly and ranting murderer might give them trouble, assigned a "goon squad" of three of his biggest and toughest guards to help escort him to the chair if necessary. But when Deputy Warden Armstrong arrived at his cell just past midnight, Moss gave no resistance.

Over in the basement of the administration building where his mother sat on the edge of the sofa, her hands clinched to a tissue, the time was only 10:45. A smart prison guard had pulled the clock's plug out of the socket.

Dressed in prison garb and house shoes, his shirt unbuttoned, Moss shuffled down the aisle of pain to the death chamber. The chaplain prayed as the condemned was strapped into the chair.

It was reported in the newspapers the next morning that just before the switch was thrown, tears rolled down his face—which was hidden by the black mask—and fell upon his massive bare chest. This report gave a certain melancholy closure of remorse to the whole turbulent episode. But the account was inaccurate and short-changed the subject's primal defiance.

In accordance to standard operating procedure, the "elephant ear" sponge, having been soaked in saltwater solution, had been placed in the football helmet next to the electrode. As always, the helmet had then been pulled down snugly so that the sponge and electrode were pressed firmly to the shaven crown of the head.

The sponge is supposed to be sufficiently damp to prevent arching and burning of the flesh. But on this occasion it was overly saturated with moisture. So it was saltwater from the sponge that was streaming down his face and onto his chest—not tears of regret.

"Where's that damn water coming from?" a voice growled from under the mask.

And, with those last words, Kelly Moss and this world parted company.

✲ ✲ ✲

The electric chair still sits waiting at the Kentucky State Penitentiary for its next victim. It has not been used since the death of Kelly Moss.

All of the cells on old death row are empty. But they are kept ready.

There are between 25 and 35 men on death row, and they are now housed in a newer cellhouse. The number changes almost weekly—new candidates arrive, while other residents have their cases reversed for new trials. In Kentucky, the death penalty is alive, but not well. The appeals are endless, and subject to meticulous reviews. Several have been under the gun for over ten years. Under today's judicial standards, the old list of eight score and two would have been reduced to a dozen.

But the same old oaken chair that's outlived 162 tenants stands brooding and waiting in the basement of three cellhouse. Part of its mystique is the haunting uncertainty of its future.

❈ ❈ ❈

On March 24, 1994, four youngsters—three blacks and one white—file, one by one into the death chamber. They are wearing green jumpsuits, their heads freshly shaven, inmate style. Their legs are shackled, their hands cuffed behind their backs.

The street swagger and macho cockiness are gone. There's a look of bewilderment and concern in their callow faces. Fear—mind numbing fear—lies just below the surface.

Convicted of minor crimes, they are on probation and being escorted on their court-ordered tour of the penitentiary. "Scared Straight" is the name of the program.

One of the delinqquents is directed to have a seat in the electric chair. Visibly affected, his eyes flash to those of the officials gathered there. Convinced he will survive, the adolescent awkwardly eases down upon the seat.

"Where you are now sitting, 162 men have died," one of his escorts advises in a solemn tone.

"The next time you sit down in that chair," warns Warden Phil Parker, "you will not get up."

You can cut the tomb-like silence with a knife.

A few moments later he is led out of the chamber, through the anteroom and the two deadly gray levers, and back down the aisle of pain. He finally manages to utter a response.

"I won't be back," he calls over his shoulder.

So say they all.

Chapter 10

The dawn came slowly to the prison yard on Friday, October 5, 1923. Warden John Chilton, who was diabetic anyway, had finally given way to exhaustion and was sleeping deeply for the first time since the siege began.

A circle of tired soldiers cradled their rifles in their arms. Gallantly they tried to keep their heads steady as they stared out toward the dining hall, still aglow from the gas lamps. Many of their comrades and guards curled up at various locations within the stone bastille, catching valuable minutes of sleep. Machine guns were silent, their operators asleep at the switch.

Every soldier knows, it is the toughest time of the watch—shortly before dawn. The whole tiresome night of watching and waiting comes tumbling down upon the body like a leaden mace. Eyes burn with the sensation of two burnt holes in an army blanket—the eyelids like giant wooden shutters. Limbs are numb, and do not want to move when the brain screams to move. One's mind tries to think, and finds that the only thought is: trying to think. Noises are magnified, silence is deadening.

One cannot help but believe that at least some of these young troops who peered out from the chapel, cellhouses, hospital and wall stands that night reflected upon the nature of their quarry. As solid, exemplary citizens serving their country, these upstanding warriors must have wondered about the murderous criminals holding them at bay—none of which they had ever met, and some of which their own age.

"Two roads diverged in a yellow wood," and the men ranked with honor took one, and Tex Walters, Harry Ferland and Lawrence Griffith took another. While some were slogging through the mud at St. Mihiel, others were running from the law. Down the meandering road of chance and happenstance, choice and moral ambiguities, these divergent and circuitous paths came back together at this fateful cross-road.

The captors had made wise and noble choices, the captives had taken calloused and foolish chances. Choices and chances become blurred when life and death are at stake.

So the epoch confrontation continued, as the darkness began to rise, and the gray messenger of day stole upon the scene. The sky lightened and the hissing gas lights lost their power.

Shortly after breakfast, a fresh pack of soldiers came streaming through the front gate. Thirty members of Company L, 149th Infantry, of Mayfield, Kentucky, under the command of Captain Fred A. Crawford had arrived.

Most of the young grunts, seeing their state's only maximum security prison for the first time, fell to silence as they lifted their heads in awe to survey the lofty, stone works of the medieval fortress.

The reinforcements were received with an elated but weary welcome. Most of the entrenched forces were too near collapse to show much emotion. At least one guard passed out from exhaustion before the Mayfield unit arrived, and had to be hauled to the guard quarters on the third floor.

The additional troops gave ranking officer Captain Radford much needed flexibility in working shifts. Two hours on and three hours off became the routine on Friday within the military ranks. Some of the guards who had not been out of the prison since the out-break were sent home. Others dragged their weary bodies up to the third floor and crashed.

A certain stillness pervaded the prison on that Friday. It was not without the persistent intermittent firing upon the mess hall. But compared to the prolonged and thunderous blanket of firepower the day before, it seemed tame.

Fresh from a few hours of sleep, Warden Chilton was on the phone that morning with both the governor and Chairman Tachau. Orders of the day from the state capital were to keep things just as they were. Chairman Tachau and the entire three-member Board of Charities and Corrections were taking a late morning train to

Eddyville. They would be there for an important conference in the early evening.

In the relative respite from the vicious attack upon the building, and with the knowledge that Tachau and company were on their way, there was a feeling that something pivotal was going to happen within the next 24 hours. Pressure continued to mount to storm the walls of the barricade. Crowds of curious spectators and volunteers increased upon the prison grounds outside the front gate. Still dead serious inside, it was almost carnival-like outside. Some of the uniformed guards patrolled the grassy front yard of the prison, where local citizens and visitors alike bantered with them good naturedly.

All but the absolutely necessary functions of the prison operation had been suspended. Mail for the prisoners, including packages, were piling up in the front corridor. One prison guard, sauntering around the crowded hallway on a break, made an interesting discovery. Casually looking over the heap of undelivered parcels, a familiar name jumped off one of the bundles. It was addressed to Lawrence Griffith.

The observant officer slipped the neatly wrapped box from the pile and took it to the warden's office. There they carefully unwrapped the item. Inside was a .38 caliber revolver with ammunition. It had come from a Princeton, Kentucky, address—probably fictitious. The investigation would have to be set aside for another day. In truth, it was cast aside for good.

The eager boys from Mayfield were ready for action. Not long after they had arrived, Captain Crawford, along with an expert marksman, went outside the prison and climbed high into the belfry of a nearby church. There, with field glasses, he peered across the stone prison walls into the windows of the dining hall. He reported to his companion that he saw two people lying prone upon the floor. The rifleman leveled his Winchester and took a series of long distance shots.

After the smoke cleared, Crawford raised the binoculars and checked the target.

"They've moved out of sight," he reported.

Some of the bullets fired into the prison from the church steeple banked around the stone masonry of the inner yard like a ballistic game of eight ball. The soldiers and guards on the opposite side of the dining hall thought they were being fired upon from the upper floor. This caused a fiery eruption of hot lead upon the lair of the three convicts.

Later in the day, one soldier thought he saw a face peeping out through one of the long windows. Another barrage of firepower fell upon the spot. Later, an outside observer reported that two of the convicts had been spotted out on the expansive roof of the building. More concentrated firing from rifles and machine guns into the aerial and rambling cover of the structure followed.

With this revelation, some of the guards who knew the inside of the dining hall began to speculate that the three may well have climbed up the pulleys and chains of the central elevator into the cupola skylight. There they would be escaping the devastating fire being leveled toward the main part of the upper floor.

For several minutes, Thursday was revisited, as a constant stream of bullets poured out from rifles, pistols, and machine guns toward the cupola windows high upon the roof. There was no sign that anyone was hit, but the glass from the windows came shattering down through the upper reaches of the ceiling and onto the dining room floor. It was highly doubtful that anyone could have survived the onslaught up in the cupola. The attackers also took pride in remarking that the jagged glass showering down upon the large room would surely wreak a bloody toll.

With this activity, day three of the "Battle of Eddyville" entered another October twilight.

Early that evening, the inmates confined to their cells received their first hot meal since the siege began on Wednesday morning. The fare, which included liver and onions was cooked up in the warden's kitchen and the galley in the hospital. Food supplies had been coming in for the past two days from Paducah, Louisville and even as far away as Cincinnati.

At about 6:00 p.m. on Friday night, October 5, members of the state Board of Charities and Corrections arrived at the penitentiary. Chairman E. S. Tachau, of Louisville, Judge Alex P. Humphrey of Louisville, and Henry Barrett from Henderson made their way up the crowded front steps after a long, six-hour train ride from Frankfort. Tagging along with the board members was Colonel Charles Morrow, instructor and advisor to the state National Guard units, and a twin brother of the governor. His appearance was significant, and certainly not lost on the astute news reporters covering the arrival of the Frankfort delegation.

After freshening up, and grabbing a bite to eat, the board went into conference with Warden Chilton and Captain Allan Radford. Before closing the door to the media, Judge Humphrey assured them that the members of the board had come to Eddyville only to obtain information and not to advise Chilton as to future action.

This of course was simply a smoke screen. They were there, along with the governor's brother, to carry out the governor's instruction.

It was time to get the matter out of the headlines and off dead center. An election for governor was only a month away. Tex Walters and company had captured the fancy of the press in their defiant stand against all odds. It was time for them to go. Although the meeting was conducted with gracious civility and a sensitivity to Warden Chilton's burdensome plight, the underlying message relayed by the board was clear. Three convicts were making monkeys out of the state correctional system, the National Guard, and ultimately the governor. Enough was enough.

As a result of the short but meaningful meeting, drastic steps were taken.

First, martial law was declared in the penitentiary. This executive directive by the governor as relayed by the Board of Charities and Corrections placed the operation of the siege under the control of military commander Captain Radford. He would receive his marching orders no doubt from the Morrow brothers—Governor Morrow from a distance, and Colonel Morrow at the scene.

The first order of business by Colonel Radford was to expel all news reporters from the penitentiary.

It was a surprised covey of newsmen when a gruff National Guard sergeant strode into the various offices of the administration building and barked, "All employees of the penitentiary stand up!"

After the employees present complied, he added, "Okay, everybody else out of the building immediately."

Startled reporters, along with all other camp followers, were herded out the front gate. Guardsmen then cleared the steps and outside penitentiary grounds of all onlookers, and the crowd dispersed to the town and homes. Military patrols stationed outside the main entrance were given instructions to permit no one to stop, whether walking or driving.

Within a short time the entire penitentiary seemed to have lost weight. The constant roar and bedlam of crowded corridors and offices disappeared and the place actually became quiet, almost lonesome.

It was a fuming, cigar-chomping group of news reporters parading back to the Lester Hotel down the hill a block away. Their ejection from the prison was a shocking change from the cordial and accommodating treatment they had been receiving from Warden Chilton.

A reporter from the *Paducah News-Democrat* had previously written, "Every courtesy has been extended to the staff of correspondents of the newspapers by Warden Chilton and whenever possible has divulged his plans well in advance of their execution."

Martial law had changed all of that.

Upon exiting the penitentiary, the members of the media had been advised by Captain Radford that he would provide them with daily dispatches at 11 o'clock each night for the morning dailies and 9 o'clock in the morning for the evening papers. They would have to show up outside the main gate to receive their daily quota. Of course, this type of censorship was not acceptable to members of the press—many of which had been on site through most of the dramatic ordeal.

It was a boisterous, smoke-filled hotel lobby on that Friday evening as veterans and cub reporters alike railed against what they perceived to be a blatant attack upon freedom of the press.

Finally, some of those on a first-name relationship with the governor took charge. They tracked down the chief executive in Paducah, where he was wrapping up his west Kentucky campaign swing.

Ever the politician and sensitive to the havoc which an aggravated news media can wreak in an election, Governor Morrow feigned surprise. He then proceeded to pour oil upon the troubled waters. "Don't worry boys" he reassured them by telephone, "I'll do anything I can for you."

Within a half hour, the news correspondents were back inside the penitentiary. The only face-saving gesture given to the military regime was the requirement that they present their credentials and receive official passes.

Another major decision was made at that Friday night meeting between Warden Chilton and the Board of Charities and Corrections. The next day, Saturday, October 6, 1923, Tex Walters, Harry Ferland and Lawrence Griffith—or what was left of them—were coming out of the dining hall. Conceding once again that dynamiting the kitchen building would be too destructive, an alternative plan was devised by the ruling junta.

Three hundred pounds of compressed ammonia was immediately placed on order with the Paducah Ice Company to be shipped to the prison on the 2:15 train the following morning. Under heavy fire, and behind metal shields, pipes would be laid to the bullet-riddled fortress and the interior flushed with the deadly gas. Afterward, troops would storm the place and finish the job. Meanwhile, constant fire would continue throughout the night in order to harass and keep the defenders sleepless.

The rest of the evening was spent preparing for the push the following morning. Once again, prison engineer and maintenance supervisor, Charlie Collier provided invaluable assistance. He, along with his crew, began to assemble the one-inch pipe that would be necessary for the ammonia gas the next morning. Also, work frantically began on the construction of the several shields which would be used to protect the workers laying the pipe line to the dining hall. Sheet metal bucklers were welded to the front of small trucks which could be wheeled ahead of the pipe fitters. Most of the steel bulwarks came from the capping off the newly-constructed dam below the prison.

This preparation took most of the night. Meanwhile, the troops and guards maintained their vigil surrounding the prison yard. Beginning at 11 p.m., a steady fire was maintained upon the target. There was a more relaxed atmosphere among the forces, as it had been some time since they had been fired upon. Also, with the decision made to charge the dining hall the following day, a certain sense of finality could be felt. There was light at the end of the tunnel.

Close to 6 a.m. on Saturday morning, just as it was beginning to turn light, the entire penitentiary went black. The main electrical power line providing current, not only for the penitentiary but the entire town of Eddyville ran atop the prison yard. It finally fell victim to the steady flow of lead, and had been severed by bullets. The break was at a point where the cable ran along the dining hall roof.

Only the dependable acetylene lamps pierced the gloom. To many of the besiegers it seemed that the gods were indeed on the side of the Walters gang.

The ammonia had arrived in the early morning hours and the tanks positioned in the chapel. Pipelines and armor dollies were at the ready. The long awaited final blitz was now only waiting for the command to begin. Guards and soldiers were poised for the attack. Now, with the power failure, attention was diverted to meeting essential needs of the prison.

Lanterns were placed in the dark cellhouses, where inmates were still being locked down.

A substantial number of the best behaved prisoners had now been released from their cells and were assisting the administration, not only in the operation of their penal facility, but also in getting ready for the final push upon the dining hall.

By this time, any support which Tex Walters and his confederates may have had within the prison population had long since evaporated. The remaining inmates had been cribbed now for over seventy straight hours in their cages, dining for most of that time on bologna, cheese and bread. The air was stale and tepid, and a faint odor of sweat and urine hovered in the cell blocks. They were without mail, visits and fresh air. And now they were about to be cast into daylight darkness. What was worse was the prospect of having to go back to a cold-cut-and-beans cuisine.

Virtually to a man, the prisoners of the Kentucky State

Penitentiary were rooting for the soldiers and guards to retake the dining hall and get their lives back to normal.

Without electricity to run the pumps, water now became a problem. Trusties were herded out front to the pump station reservoir from which they hauled buckets of water back to the cellhouses.

Physically and mentally exhausted, with his days and nights becoming blurred, John Chilton must have thought he was living a warden's nightmare. But he maintained his poise and gracious manner.

His wife, Lula, and their sixteen-year-old daughter, Sara, had won the respect and admiration of all by continuing to live in the warden's residence during the upheaval. The newspapers even commented about the courage with which they went about their daily lives inside their prison quarters, even though they could not venture into the hazardous back part of the apartment.

If they had given out medals after the "Battle of Eddyville," surely chief engineer, Charlie Collier, would have been awarded a Bronze Star.

He, like Chilton, had slept very little since the siege began. Being the most familiar with each nook and cranny of the mammoth fortress, the knowledgeable maintenance chief was not only called upon to hold the essential services of the facility together, but was constantly called upon for consultation concerning the siege. The army was well represented in firepower. But they did not have an engineer detachment. Collier and his devoted crew, consisting mostly of inmates, served that need.

After being up all night making ready the pipe and armor carts for the ammonia assault, he was now called upon to repair the electrical outage. The lack of electricity would not have postponed the final run on the dining hall if only the prison had been affected. But with the dousing of all lights, came instant suspension of the water supply for both prison and town. The entire village was clamoring for it to be repaired.

Consequently, Chief Collier and his crew went to work, while the fighting men waited.

The work was slow going and dangerous. New cables had to be laid to circumvent the breaking point. Although most of this was done through the cellhouses, the task required Collier and his men to be exposed at times to the free fire zone of the prison yard.

The day dragged on and the sun climbed to its perch directly overhead. Guards and soldiers grew restless and edgy. They pitched in here and there to assist the maintenance men in their arduous and pressure-packed efforts.

Finally, close to two in the afternoon, the power to the prison and the town was back on. A sense of relief surged through the penitentiary with the blinking light bulbs. People began to scrambled excitedly, as they prepared for the climatic charge.

It was a simple three-step plan which Captain Radford—with advice and consent from Colonel Morrow—adopted. Warden Chilton nodded his approval.

Behind the steel-plated dollies, the one-inch line would be laid by inmates from the ammonia tanks in the hospital—a last minute switch away from the chapel—to the main door of the dining hall. This would be done under heavy fire cover laid down by the surrounding troops. The second step called for the pumping of the lethal gas—a small amount of which could choke a human being to death—into the cavernous confines of the building. Lastly, after full fumigation, the infantry would charge the barricade.

At this stage, in the opinion of Warden Chilton, there would be only three possible places of refuge for the beleaguered three. These were a small, brick meat house adjoining the kitchen, the steel drying closet in the laundry, and three, 95-gallon stainless steel, steam cookers in the kitchen. These huge vats would repel any kind of bullets or grenades.

The anticipation of the three embattled prisoners—after days of unrelenting firepower—retreating to the inside of the prison pots from which they would hold at bay the oncoming legion of troops, graphically demonstrates what mythical giants the convicts had become.

Nevertheless, the plan called for shooting out holes in the meat house through which grenades would be thrown. Then the same would be done to the laundry drying room.

If, once inside the dining hall, it was discovered that their prey had escaped down the elevator, dining room officer Lewis Hill would point the soldiers to directly above the cooking vats. From that vantage point they would fire through the wooden floors, making the huge steam cookers cauldrons of death.

After the electrical power was restored, Sergeant James Hawkins and Lieutenant Joseph Kelly of the National Guard, assisted by three prisoners, moved out onto the yard behind the armor plates. They proceeded to lay the pipe from the hospital across the one hundred fifty feet or so of open territory. Toward the building they went as a steady stream of lead was poured out to protect them. Quickly and boldly, the pipe line progressed right up the steps to the top floor dining room. Two inmates, Otho Lance and George Eastman, performed the heroic duties of taking the line the rest of the way. Lance knocked panes of glass from the doors with a wrench and then inserted the nozzle of the pipe. Incredibly, Eastman then entered the building and from the main hall warned them to surrender or be gassed.

Just around the corner from where he was standing was Lawrence Griffith. A couple more steps into the huge room and he would have been staring right at him.

There was no response from any of the men in the dining hall. Quickly the intrepid Eastman retreated.

Since the pipe had been laid to the hazardous front door without rejoinder, it was decided to run a line around the side of the building to the bottom floor kitchen and laundry. This advance was also without incident.

With the line now snaked into the building at three different entries, the daring pipe fitters returned to the safety of the hospital. As a precautionary step to protect inmates in four cellhouse—the housing unit closest to the target—from drifting fumes, they were moved out to the foundry located in the extreme southeast corner of the premises. For the same reason, the administration building was also evacuated. A few seconds of quiet fell upon the scene as the soldiers poised for the final rush. The huge bullet-riddled dining facility stood silently waiting.

Then the assault began. A volley of rifle bullets and hand grenades were fired into the mess hall. Immediately thereafter, Chief Collier ordered the petcock on the ammonia tank opened.

Deadly gas began to pour through the pipes and into both levels of the building. Soldiers resting on their arms watched with fascination. For one solid hour, the fumes permeated every nook and cranny. There was no sign of any other movement inside.

Finally, at 4:30 p.m., the scene of operation shifted to the prison chapel. From there, rapid fire tore an opening in the meat house and hand grenades were thrown inside by guardsmen Hawkins and McCollum. That took care of one possible protective enclave.

With this done, attention was given to the other side of the building and machine gun bullets made an aperture in the steel drying closet in the laundry. Through the opening, hand grenades were thrown.

This left only the steel kettles in the kitchen where refuge could be taken. And that possibility would be addressed once the troops had invaded the dining room.

As if storming a German gun emplacement, the first wave of soldiers yelled, "Over the top!" and charged out of the hospital toward the dining room steps. They were led by Sergeants McCollum and Hawkins along with Lieutenants Kelly and J. C. Hanberry.

Following close behind the infantry were some reporters,

including a photographer from the Louisville *Courier Journal*. Dining room officer Lewis Hill was in the pack.

When the leaders reached the steps, Sergeant Hawkins began hurling grenades toward the doorway. The first grenade was a direct hit. However, the second one struck the top step and rolled to the landing. It proved to be a dud.

His third missile missed the entrance, hit a step and bounced back into the charging squad of men. The group scattered as the grenade exploded, sending deadly shrapnel through the air. Miraculously, no one was wounded. After recovering their nerve from this near catastrophe, Sergeant McCollum dashed up the steps, through the double doors and into the bowels of the dining hall.

As he ran down the hallway and into the open eating area, he immediately crouched close to the floor and panned the room with his rifle. For a few brief seconds, he was there alone as his followers recovered from the grenade explosion and clumsily made their way up the front steps.

McCollum's throat was like cotton and it was so quiet he could hear his heart pounding against his chest. The veteran soldier's eyes watered and his lungs burned from the lingering gas. Slowly he surveyed the devastated room. Large chunks of plaster, mortar, glass shards, splintered wood, and thick dust covered the dining tables and overturned benches. Two gaping holes yawned from opposite walls. Pots and pans had been so perforated by bullets that they were soldered together. Large ceramic pitchers of molasses which had been sitting on the tables were shattered, the wooden floor veneered with the sticky syrup. Hardly anything in the large open room had been untouched by the relentless onslaught of lead and steel.

In the brief interlude of silence, Sergeant McCollum's ear caught the sound of a low metallic clicking. It sounded like a trigger mechanism of a pistol being repeatedly engaged. Frantically, he searched for the source of the ominous noise. Upon the wall, near the right side of the door, just above the wooden guard platform, he spotted the answer to the riddle. Amidst the bullet holes and shrapnel scars hung a wall clock. Unbelievably, it had escaped the thick barrage of firepower over the past four days. Its ticking pendulum claimed victory over the vanquished dining room. The time was 5:20 a.m.

Just below the clock was another item which had survived the siege unscathed. A small framed sign read, "Choose ye today whom ye will serve, as for me and my house, we will serve the Lord."

Quickly McCollum looked under the benches and tables. Lying under the wooden guard platform just below the clock he saw the bodies of Lawrence Griffith and Harry Ferland.

They were stretched out side by side on their backs as if they were sleeping. Griffith's shoes were off and he was stripped to the waist. Ferland, whose shirt was unbuttoned, had a newspaper lying across his face.

For some reason McCollum then looked up into the rafters of the cupola for a sight of Walters. Returning to his crouch once more his eyes scanned along the north wall underneath the tables.

Then, near the northwest corner of the building, about thirty-five feet from Griffith and Ferland, he saw the body of Tex Walters against the wall. He immediately ran to the front door.

"They're all dead!" he yelled to the others just entering the hall. The word was passed back through the lines.

Pandemonium broke loose and the dining room filled up immediately with yelling and celebrating soldiers and guards. Newspaper reporters swarmed in and cameras flashed like fireflies.

Captain Radford, arriving, tried to close the door to the onrushing mob in order to protect the crime scene. It was a futile effort as the euphoric and relieved victors stampeded the place.

Dr. Horace T. Rivers of Paducah crawled under the table and examined the bodies of Griffith and Ferland. He then revealed the first significant bit of information by proclaiming that their deaths were due to suicide.

In his right hand, Ferland gripped a revolver—the .38 caliber revolver wrestled away from guard T. R. Scoles on Wednesday morning. After having been wounded twice in the side, powder burns upon his cheek indicated that he had fired the fatal bullet into his own head.

Griffith's arms rested on his naked chest. A 32-20 police Colt special lay nearby. Five rounds of live ammunition still remained in the chamber. It was the same weapon smuggled into the prison by inmate Jim Hawkins. A single self-inflicted bullet hole ran through his heart. Powder burns encircled the entry wound.

On the back of a wooden bench, only a few feet away, Lawrence Griffith had scrawled several significant sentences with a pencil.

"Remember," the top note read, "you didn't kill us all. Killed ourselves. L.E.G."

Griffith had obviously enjoyed his moment in the sun. He wrote with bravado, "Lawrence Griffith, I killed the cellhouse fellow and Killihan. Tried my God damndest to kill the son of a bitch Miller as he wint in the hospital.

"Now, ha, ha, J. B. Chilton I guess you and some will keep me locked."

Then as his final epitaph, "If there ever was a game bunch tis

171

L.G., T.W., H.F."

Walters' body was a mess. His shoulder was mangled, and fatal bullet holes ran through his head and heart. Flames from either a rifle grenade or exploding gas canister had struck him after his death, burning off the clothes on his right side and severely singeing his face. The fire had blackened the wall behind him and incinerated some cloth kitchen towels hanging just over his head. A stream of dried blood ran on the floor for several feet from the wound to his head. Tex's gore-encrusted cap also lay beside him and his coat hung on a peg nearby.

The chaotic mess hall was ransacked for souvenirs by the marauding conquerors. It was not their finest hour. Even the bodies were ravished, as soldiers pilfered a watch, money, and the homemade knife found lying near Walters. The pistols were heisted.

In Tex's coat pocket was the letter he had written early that fateful Wednesday morning before he left his cell.

"My darling wife," the letter began.

"In reply to your last letter I shall answer that under no circumstance let my parents know that I am in a place of this kind. Yet if anything should ever arise where there is a demand for any large amount of money to use in my case or to bring results if anything should happen to me, while then notify my father and have him get my uncle, for he is in a position to pull any political strings that are necessary.

How is your health? Be sure to tell me. As for myself I am all to the good. That is physically, but mentally I am always blue. That yearning and longing for you will always remain as long as I am kept from you.

Dear, you must excuse this short letter. I have answered your question and will close.

Yours forever,
MONTE WALTERS."

On the back of the letter, and written in pencil after the siege began, was his dying message, "Love to you beloved. I am wounded and surrounded by guards. Goodbye. I know you will be surprised."

His very last statement would one day prove to be her salvation.

After a prolonged frenzy of jubilation and pillaging, a second very important revelation began to sink in.

Dr. Rivers was joined at the scene by other doctors including prison physician Dr. D. J. Travis. After examining the bodies, they gave medical confirmation to what should have been obvious to all. The bodies were already decomposing. They had been dead for days.

While the troops were still celebrating their victory, and wandering back out onto the prison yard, prison officials began to move in and take over the scene. They examined the bodies and, totally mystified by their discovery, huddled with the physicians. Deputy Warden Miller was of the opinion that the men had been dead since Wednesday night.

Captain Radford and his officers first tried to ignore the significance of the time of death of the convicts. Then they disagreed, by pointing out that Tex Walters had bled from the head wound sustained by the gas canister, proclaiming that dead men do not bleed. They failed to point out that the bleeding had most likely been from the bullet hole through the cranium. Also, no one lies in one spot while their clothes are going up in flames.

Finally, inmate orderlies from the hospital arrived with stretchers to remove the bodies. The surface underneath their lifeless forms was clean of any debris or dust which littered the remainder of the dining room floor. This was further proof that they had been lying lifeless through most of the bombardment.

It was inescapably clear that the company of soldiers and a host of other besiegers had been held at bay for days by three dead men.

The death of Tex Walters, like his life, was shrouded in mystery. No one knows what went on in the upper floor dining room between the time he and his two friends arrived there early on Wednesday morning and when their bodies were discovered over three days later.

The invading soldiers bursting into the room on Saturday evening had no interest in knowing what had gone on there, or, for that matter, when their three enemies had died. Their total contamination of the crime scene would make it almost impossible for investigators to do more than venture educated guesses. The prison people didn't do much to help. The three bodies were taken to the hospital morgue. Efforts were made to notify the next of kin. Griffith's body was claimed and picked up by his family from Dresden, Tennessee. Unsuccessful efforts were made to locate the next of kin of Harry Ferland.

Lillian Walters, located in Louisville, first advised the prison administration that she wanted to claim her beloved husband's remains and transport him to that city for burial. However, as it turned out, she was unable to do so.

On Sunday morning, the corpses of Tex Walters and Harry Ferland were embalmed on the prison yard. Plain wooden coffins were prepared. One by one, they were placed on a bier and pulled by a solitary mule to Vinegar Hill, the prison cemetery. There, without any services or benediction, they were buried by convicts in unmarked graves.

There were no meaningful autopsies, no inquests. It was a rush to burial, as if to wait longer might result in the two desperados leaping from their caskets and dashing back to the dining hall. Enough evidence remains, however, to provide a reasonably reliable account of what happened in the brick fortress after the three rebels captured it on Wednesday morning.

Tex had undoubtedly been wounded by the firefight before entering the dining hall. As the prisoners inside were fleeing the building, one wasn't as anxious to leave as the rest. Harry Leslie, a trusty employed in the mess hall, saw the exchange of lead on the prison yard and thought it might be safer remaining inside. As Walters burst through the door, he gave the terrified inmate some kindly advice, "If you're going, you'd better go now." Wisely as it turned out, Leslie lit out across the prison yard to safety. He later reported that Walters was holding a bleeding right shoulder when he entered the dining room. Harry Ferland had also entered the building wounded twice in the side.

Griffith had climbed up to his deadly outpost totally unscathed and pouring out lead while yelping with delight.

Once inside, Walters and Ferland were in pain and probably little help to Griffith. With the temperature climbing to almost 70 on the outside, it became considerably warmer than that in the upstairs room as the day wore on. It also took a while for the rising heat from the downstairs cookers to dissipate.

The sills of the elongated windows were only about three feet off the floor. This meant the convicts had to virtually crawl about on their hands and knees at all times to avoid the incoming bullets.

Griffith was getting a workout. As things warmed up, he removed his shirt and took off the large, prison-made brogans which impeded his movements. Tex hung his denim jacket above his head.

The defiant, Tennessee uncle-killer returned most, if not all, of the fire that morning, yelping and crowing like a rooster as he did so. Most of the singing and yelling heard by Lewis Hill who was caught in the nearby coal shed was coming from Griffith.

Sometime in the afternoon, the occupants became quiet.

Roscoe Gumm, one of the crack shots among the guards, reported to his companions on Wednesday that he was sure that he had shot Walters through the head. He told the prison officials that Tex's body would be found at approximately the place it was discovered on Saturday evening. Most veterans of the siege-especially among the guard force—went away believing that Tex Walters was shot and killed by Gumm on Wednesday.

After the death of their leader, Griffith and Ferland—the latter in physical agony—no doubt recognized the futility of the situation. Their prospects were darkened further by the arrival of the National Guard in the late afternoon. They entered into a suicide pact. The Californian shot himself first through the heart, or may have had Lawrence to do it for him. The surviving rebel laid out his friend in almost funeral parlor form, folding his arms across his chest, the pistol placed in his hand. Out of respect for his dead comrade, a newspaper was placed across his face. They were both under the wooden guard platform located near the doorway.

Some time, perhaps hours, passed before Griffith completed the pact. He took time to write out his farewell messages with pencil on the back of the wooden bench. Sometime on Wednesday night, one of the shots believed by the soldiers to be coming from the dining room, was actually entering Lawrence Griffith's heart.

The temperatures dropped into the low 50s on that autumn night. If Griffith had survived the evening, he would have most likely reshirted. Perhaps the most convincing evidence that they were all three dead, at least by noon on Thursday, is not what was said, but what was left unsaid. When the army lieutenant took to the megaphone on that day and offered the three a chance to surrender, the warning was met with only silence from the dining hall. Those knowing the bellicose and belligerent Griffith also know that he would not have let that pregnant moment slip by without a loud and profane rejoinder. Prison guards know convicts. Had they—the guards—been in charge, not the prison administration nor the military—they would have most likely, at that time, stacked arms and casually strolled into the dining hall.

When the dining room was captured on Saturday, the conquering army found that the three had not run short of ammunition. Not only were both pistols loaded—excepting the suicide shots—but a full box was also found. In addition, numerous live rounds were found scattered all over the floor. They did not even stick around long enough to use up all their fun.

Near the body of Tex Walters were a few slices of bread and bologna. There was also a small bag of tobacco. Some of the Army officers pointed this out to support their claim that Tex had lasted long enough to become hungry and descend down the dumb waiter to the kitchen for food.

It was a weak supposition. Climbing down the open elevator to the lower level, some fifteen feet below would not have been an easy task—virtually impossible for someone who was wounded. Also, to have been lowered to the kitchen area by the crank, would have required at least two able-bodied people. Most likely the bread and bologna had either been left by the exiting dining room help on Wednesday morning, or Griffith climbed down into the kitchen for food sometime on that same day.

Considering all of the evidence which history has allowed into the case, there seems little doubt that by sunrise on Thursday morning, October 4, 1923, Tex Walters, Lawrence Griffith, and Harry Ferland were all dead.

But the resolution of that inquiry opens up a much stranger and confounding mystery. Who held the dining hall for three days and nights? What gunman constantly returned the fire in defense of the dining room? Who shot three times at Guthrie Ladd on Thursday night? What were the forms seen in the window, on the floor, on the roof, and at the front door? Who doused the laundry flames with water?

The answer lies in magic—the production of baffling effects and illusions by things seeming instead of being.

This show of sorcery played to a highly-wired and stressed-out crowd. Three prison guards had been killed and a fourth wounded. Adrenalin and emotion raced at a fever pitch as the murderers took to the high ground. A deadly siege ensued, and soon the army arrived on the scene. They raced onto the battlefield, pumped up and ready to kick butts and take names. Instead, they were required to pull up short and settle into a shooting gallery siege. Over 25,000 rounds of machine gun and rifle fire was unleashed during the four-day ordeal. That's not to mention the grenades and gas. There was little sleep for anyone within the prison walls. Nights and days ran together. They were doing battle in a strange, almost dream-like, medieval castle. And there at center stage—they thought at least—holding the spotlight, was Tex Walters, whose reputation grew legendary with each passing hour. Perfect chemistry for magic to take its toll.

The reporting of return fire by the convicts is probably the easiest to understand. When the soldiers on the yard mistook Captain Crawford's shots from the church steeple as coming from the dining hall, it only illustrated how vulnerable they were to deception. Their target was encircled by armed cadres of troops who were firing pretty much at will. There was no communication between the outposts except by sight and runners. At night they became almost totally in the dark as to what the others were doing. Consequently, most of the bullets they perceived coming from their enemy, were in reality some of their own—or from their own—coming back. It serves as the only explanation.

When the laundry was closely examined after the battle, another interesting revelation was discovered. A water cooler had been positioned on the window sill. The bullets had exploded the huge glass reservoir and that had been the source of the water dousing the fire.

Of course, no one can fully explain the forms in the windows, at the door and on the roof. Prison officials did point out that coats and aprons of dining room attendants hung at various places on the wall inside the gunmen's roost. They moved when fanned by the winds that entered through the bullet-shattered windows.

"Or in the night," Shakespeare wrote, "imagining some fear, how easy is a bush suppos'd a bear!"

Again, it's an explanation. At least good enough, perhaps, to describe the illusion.

In truth, not much time was spent attempting to solve the incredible riddle.

The nightmare was over. Soldiers packed their gear, joked and laughed to relieve days of tension. Then, happily, they smartly exited the front gate, where flatbed trucks waited to haul them to the depot and departing trains. Newspapers herald the heroics of the troops as if they had just conquered a heavily defended German city. Only passing mention was made of the ghost defenders.

Prison officials and employees mused over the matter of dead defenders for only a little while. Some found it funny, since it had been mostly a military affair. They thought the old, seasoned doughboys had been duped. Primarily, the correctional warriors left behind were relieved that it was over and their warden had been pretty much vindicated in his conservative tactics. No more of their men had been lost. Valiantly, they began to put their prison back together.

The last inscription which Lawrence Griffith had scrawled on the back of the bleached-out wooden bench proclaimed proudly, "Defiants from the dead. (signed) Tex, Harry, L.E.G."

It turned out to be an eerie and uncanny prophecy.

⚞ ⚟ ⚞

Governor Edwin Morrow arrived in Eddyville the following Tuesday night to make a political speech at the town's opera house. He reverently eulogized the fallen prison guards Hodge Cunningham, V. B. Mattingly and William Gilbert.

Then, to the joyous applause of the entire Commonwealth, he

177

announced that he was going to pardon Daddy Warner for his heroic deed during the siege.

"I don't deserve no credit, but when that pardon comes, they ain't going to have a bit of trouble of getting me to leave," Warner said when hearing the good news.

"I've already got my pardon from the other side, and that means even more to me than the governor's," added the born-again Christian.

A few days later, after Morrow returned to Frankfort, the necessary paperwork was prepared and executed for the old convict's release. When it arrived at Eddyville, Warden Chilton happily gave word to process him out.

Daddy cleaned out his meager belongings from three cellhouse, and stuffed them into his battered, old suitcase. He went around the cellhouses and prison yard, shaking hands and saying his farewell to his many friends. Convicts and guards alike grabbed his large hand and hugged his old shoulders. His last but most important goodbye was at the prison library in the old, brick chapel.

From inside its doors he had viewed the carnage going on during the Tex Walters shootout and had anguished at the sight of the suffering guard on the yard. It was also where he had worked as librarian and as assistant to Reverend Adolphus Hanberry. Tears came to the eyes of both of them as they embraced and said good-bye.

Then the large, gray-haired man, with the dark, leathery skin, left the church and headed for the front gate. He walked down the sidewalk past the dining hall. Carpenters and masons were still busily repairing the wounds to the old, embattled landmark. Just in front of the kitchen, he stopped near the steps which would lead him into the administration building and freedom. There, the 70-year-old soon-to-be ex-convict turned and surveyed the scene one last time.

A few convicts, in familiar pressed denim and cloth hats moved casually around the hill. Up near the pool, beside the chapel, two blacks sat on a bench playing dominoes under two large maples. It could have been a scene straight from any city park in the land.

The trees on the prison yard—with their characteristic white washed trunks—were beginning to change colors. They blended beautifully against the October sky. There were the familiar sounds of convicts yelling, the distant throbbing of machinery in the factories, black smoke billowing out of the tall smokestack anchored at the boiler room. A faint smell of green beans and corn bread being prepared in the kitchen reached his nostrils. He thrilled to the knowledge that he would not be around for dinner.

It was a familiar but yet peculiar scene to Daddy Warner—the prison yard with a peaceful, almost pastoral look.

His eyes fell upon the nearby slope where V. B. Mattingly lay dying only a few short days before. The massive dining hall looming over him now seemed friendly, even inviting.

As he took this last look, a strange and troublesome feeling stirred within him.

He reached down and gripped his valise and headed down the steps.

As Daddy Warner would later report, "You could feel Tex Walters' presence on the prison yard, even after he was dead and gone."

Chapter 11

The Kentucky Penal Code defines a riot as "a public disturbance involving an assemblage of five or more persons which by tumultuous and violent conduct creates grave danger or injury to property or persons or substantially obstructs law enforcement or other government functions."

Neatly said. But it can get messy.

Prisons and riots go together like summer and baseball.

Considering its long history, the prison at Eddyville has been relatively free of major inmate uprisings. One must understand that any maximum security penitentiary is one of constant upheaval and turmoil. There are daily occurrences of disorderly behavior ranging from possession of contraband, escape plots, and minor assaults to the more serious offenses of inmate stabbings and attacks upon correctional staff. The place is a bubbling cauldron of perpetual discontent and danger. Even when tension is at the lowest, someone—somewhere—in the commodious and rambling stone castle is up to no good. Penalties are imposed weekly by the prison disciplinary committee upon prisoners breaking the rules. Sometimes "outside charges" are taken to be tried in the Lyon County Circuit Court.

There have been sit-down strikes, hunger strikes, and "water tank" protests. Prisoners in lockup have been known to cut their wrist, stop up their commodes, rip apart the plumbing and otherwise cause havoc just for the sake of raising hell.

No correctional officer has ever had to apologize for the size of his check—except to the wife and kids.

Every prison warden, especially in the south, is wary of summer. As the blazing heat raises the temperatures in the cellhouses and on the prison yard, the propensity for violence and discord also rises.

The Kentucky State Penitentiary is one hot place to be in July. Perched above the Cumberland River valley, the seething humidity from the bottom land—now the lake itself—combines with the searing sun to envelop the prison in a steamy haze.

The desolate prison yard is now bereft of trees and shade. Also the old cooling pool for the boiler room, which was converted into a popular swimming hole, has been covered. But at least the prisoners can now retreat from the simmering hill to the air-conditioned cellhouses. Only a few short years ago, convicts were not so fortunate. In the summertime the stone caverns were like giant saunas. Large fans along the walks could not dissipate the heat. Temperatures on the upper tiers were unbearable.

It was hot and humid on June 25, 1952—temperatures knocking at the 100 degree mark.

Harry Truman was president, but not for long. General Dwight Eisenhower and Senator Robert Taft were lining up support for the upcoming Republican Convention. Adlai Stevenson was disgruntling fellow Democrats by his procrastination. Kentuckian Vice-President Alben Barkley proclaimed that, if nominated, he would run.

American boys were dying in Korea to the rate of 640 casualties that very week. Television was just coming in, but most all homes were still without. Instead they tuned in to radio. Teenagers were jitterbugging to Woody Herman's "Woodcutter's Ball."

Firestone tires were selling for $11.95 each.

Little Bobby Shantz, pitcher for the Philadelphia Athletics, just had his eleven-game winning streak brought to an end, losing to Cleveland 2-1. But the big sports item of the day was the upcoming Light Heavyweight Championship bout between Sugar Ray Robinson and Joey Maxim. The much ballyhooed prize fight was scheduled for that Wednesday night in Yankee Stadium.

On that evening there were over 1,000 inmates housed at the Kentucky State Penitentiary. They were double bunking in the narrow cells of the three older cellhouses. The sweltering heat—which had topped out that day at ninety-eight degrees—had not subsided as the prisoners in four cellhouse settled in. Scantily dressed, some in the nude, most were looking forward to listening to the Robinson-Maxim fight on their radios. Much discussion, debate and even betting had surrounded the boxing matchup.

Summer darkness fell upon the castle as the captive audience tuned in to the Gillette Cavalcade of Sports.

The blast furnace heat of Yankee Stadium that night almost equaled the hugging humidity of four cellhouse at Eddyville. Sugar Ray and Pal Joey battled gamely through the hot night before almost 48,000 perspiring spectators, with Robinson easily outscoring his opponent.

Midway through the affray, a terrible thing happened on the banks of the Cumberland River, a half continent away from the Big Apple. At about 10 p.m., the electrical power went off in four cellhouse at the Kentucky State Penitentiary. The radios went dead, and the Sugar Ray Robinson and Joey Maxim prize fight was no more.

It was too much for the edgy and heat-frayed convicts. They began to shout and rake their bars. Soon the entire cellhouse was caught up in the sounds of rioting prisoners, which could be heard in downtown Eddyville. There was nothing that the meager night shift of guards could do to quell the discord.

Not until well after two in the morning did the racket finally die down. Long before that time, and unknown to the enraged convicts, Sugar Ray had succumbed to the heat himself and had failed to answer the bell for the thirteenth round.

The Wednesday night outburst was simply the manifestation of discontent which had been simmering for several months. In prisons, torrid summer weather has a way of boiling problems to the surface. The sources of irritation were varied. Overcrowding placed convicts virtually on top of each other in an ancient prison which had, over the years, received far too little attention from Frankfort. There were still no toilet facilities in the old cellhouses and inmates used buckets for their needs.

Food was poor. Whether in the military or in corrections, the stomach determines morale. Daily drill of inmates upon the baseball field had been instituted in the 30's when the private industry was removed from the yard, causing idleness among a portion of the prisoners. Now, in the scorching Kentucky summer, they had requested that it be suspended. After all, two soldiers at Ft. Knox had just that week died from heat exhaustion while on maneuvers. The request had been bluntly denied. As in many instances of prison unrest, their frustration focused on an unpopular administrator, in this case, Deputy Warden Walter Stephens. They blamed most of their woes on Stephens, who had a reputation among inmates and staff alike as being overbearing and insensitive. They wanted him removed.

All of this came together with the miserable heat, and the news of outbreaks at other prisons throughout the country. It was dry tender for a prison riot.

A sulking and ill-tempered bunch of felons moved out onto the prison yard for breakfast and their daily assignments on Thursday, June 26, 1952. By mid-morning they began to congregate in bunches around the hill. Some refused to report to work.

By 10:30 a.m., a mass of almost three hundred prisoners had gathered on the baseball field—or recreation area, as it was called, located toward the back of the quad. They were getting in a nasty mood—hollering, booing and cursing. They refused to obey the orders of the guards to disband.

The warden was notified.

Big Jess Buchanan is one of the central figures in the history of the castle on the Cumberland.

The former lawman from Union County, Kentucky, stood six-feet-eight-inches tall and weighed three hundred pounds. He was the biggest prison warden in the United States. Not only was Buchanan massive, but he was also tough and totally fearless. He carried a cane and prisoners would never approach him closer than the length of the stick.

"He was rough", said an old con years later. "He could knock a man down like he was swatting a fly."

Needless to say, "Big Jess" was revered and respected by inmates and employees alike.

But through the center of this mean-looking giant ran a stream of human kindness. He was inscrutably fair in all of his dealings with both convicts and staff. Inmate brutality—a it was defined in that era—was not tolerated. Warden Buchanan agonized intensely with each execution over which he presided, making sure the rights of the condemned were protected all the way up to the end. He treated their families with compassion and respect. The warden's wife, Margaret, made curtains for the death house windows in an effort to lighten up their dreary existence.

As big and intimidating as he was, Jess Buchanan still had his limitations. Like wardens everywhere, he had to contend with the politicians in the state capital. It was even worse then than it is today. He had to work those people sent to him by local political patronage, who were without training or skills, sometimes of questionable character, and always poorly paid. "Big Jess" had to survive—run a maximum security prison of 1,000 prisoners and the state's death house—on what money Frankfort decided to dole out. And in those days, that wasn't much. For instance, he was provided only one hundred dollars a day to supplement produce from the prison farm in feeding over 1,000 mouths. The soup got mighty thin. Breakfast consisted of water gravy, rice or oats, three slices of bread and black coffee. Dinner was usually cabbage, green beans, tomatoes, bread and ice water. Supper was the same as dinner with some potatoes thrown in. On Sunday, they got a small piece of meat.

Buchanan once joked to a guard, "If they cut my budget any more, I'm gonna riot."

But Jess was a good soldier. As he worked for better conditions, expanded vocational schools, and a larger prison farm, he also had to live within his means and keep a tough rein on the inmate population—even though he knew in his heart that some of their frustrations were justified.

So he was not completely surprised when hearing of the unrest on the yard that June morning. Having just returned to work from a minor illness, he dispatched Deputy Warden Stephens and Captain Thus Duncan to check out the problem.

Stephens was the wrong man to send. In their particularly testy mood, he was not the one the inmates preferred to see. There were discussions between the deputy warden and the prisoners. After a short while the dialogue broke down and things turned nasty. The angry mob headed toward the dining hall, which was located in the bottom floor of five cellhouse.

"Take the dining room! Take the commissary!" they yelled almost in unison and began to charge in that direction.

Stephens, backing away, yelled at guard Ollie Williamson, who was in number six wall stand located just to the rear of five cellhouse. He ordered him to fire into the mutineers. With some hesitation, Williamson finally fired his shotgun into the crowd. Four or five convicts fell to the ground, wounded by the buckshot. The others began to retreat across the prison yard. They proceeded to wreck the inmate commissary and the recreation hall. Two helpless guards were swept up by the wave of rioting convicts. One was slightly injured by a blow to the head. A few moments later, they were both released.

Moving around the hill, about three hundred convicts entered the garment factory. This was the same old four-story brick building in which Tex Walters had worked and Daddy Scoles had been bound and robbed of his pistol. The basement was now a machine shop for the prison maintenance department. On the main floor was the "shop"—a recreational area where prisoners loafed and shot pool, played checkers and chess, even played some clandestine poker. Inmates worked on the top two levels manufacturing shirts, socks, pants, underwear, and mattresses for other state agencies.

The entire building was captured by the marauding prisoners.

Supervisor Fred McChesney was taken hostage. After causing a great deal of damage to the recreation hall, most of the convicts moved to the upper floors. Many had armed themselves with homemade knives and clubs. At first, the younger convicts roughed up their hostage. Older cons intervened, however, to protect the likable McChesney. By noon, the garment factory belonged fully to the convicts and, with their hostage, they were holding the prison officials at bay. By this time approximately thirty state troopers, under the command of Captain Estill "Buck" Jones, had arrived on the yard to supplement the guard force. They were armed with tommy guns and riot equipment. State Corrections Commissioner Dr. W. E. Watson had been summoned from Frankfort.

The revolt was led primarily by convict Benny Rayborn of Louisville, Arthur E. Ringsberger of New Castle, Indiana, and Tony Caprinegro from New Jersey. All were serving life sentences for armed robbery and had been a source of irritation to the prison keepers during their stay at Eddyville. While in the Jefferson County jail, Rayborn had led a riot when he was separated from members of his gang. He and many of his confederates hung out of the open windows overlooking the prison yard, yelling and taunting the guards and troopers. At one time Rayburn brought McChesney to a third floor window Pointing at the bewildered subject, he yelled to the troopers below, "If you guys try and come up here, we are going to drop him out of here on his head!"

Warden Buchanan moved to secure the rest of the penitentiary. The large number of prisoners not participating in the outbreak were locked up. Those inmates wounded by the shotgun blast of Ollie Williamson were taken to the prison infirmary for treatment. None were seriously hurt, although one had to be removed to an outside hospital. Troopers moved in to protect the boiler room and light plant located next to the garment factory.

Then the confrontation between the barricaded prisoners and the rest of the world quietened down into a war of nerves. The prisoners demanded to voice their complaints directly to the warden.

That suited Jess Buchanan just fine. Alone and unarmed, Big Jess strolled over the prison yard and across the rioters' own threshold. There, in the garment factory, the intrepid warden conferred with the leaders of the uprising. They gave him a list of demands, including the firing of Deputy Warden Walter Stephens. There were nine others including better food, improved hospital facilities, upgrading the sanitary conditions in the old cellhouses, and the ending of drill.

"Upon granting these conditions" the neatly typed petition concluded, "we agree to go back to regular prison routine. We will accept nobody's word but insist upon a written statement to us and a like statement to the public."

The young felons—including "Benny Denny" Rayborn—intoxicated with their sudden charge of power, were loud, demanding, and impatient. Older cons, seasoned with a lot of time behind bars, calmed the waters. They knew that when it was all over they would still be there. Big Jess would still be there. The problems would still be there. And in the end they would lose. But they also knew their warden. He would listen. And somewhere down the road, if he was convinced, he would remember. That—in the real world of prisons and convicts—was the most they could expect.

Buchanan returned to the administration building and reported the results of the meeting. He also announced to the reporters swarming the halls that he did not have the authority to grant any of the demands. "I wouldn't anyway," he added, "with a knife at my back."

Dr. W. E. Watson, State Director of Corrections, arrived from Frankfort and told the rioters they would have to surrender unconditionally. But negotiations continued with the hostage-holding convicts, who had now formed their own grievance committee.

"Time and talk." That is the basic strategy of all hostage-holding situations. "Time and talk" in most instances work toward defusing the tension and bringing about a resolution. There would be "time and talk" on this day, but Warden Buchanan made it clear that there were limits.

"I'll not allow prisoners out of their cells after dark," he declared sternly. "If they have not surrendered by the end of the day, we'll go in after them."

During the long, hot afternoon, newspaper reporters were allowed to roam the yard at will. They yelled back and forth with the hooting men in the garment factory.

"Hey, why don't you newspaper people print our side of this thing?" they complained.

Dix Winston, reporter for the *Paducah Sun Democrat,* challenged them to send out a spokesman. Incredibly, the leaders themselves, Benny Rayborn and Tony Caprinegro, came out of the building and across the roadway and began "letting their hair down."

They retold old problems.

"We gotta have better sanitation in the old cellblocks. . . .It's terrible there. . .no modern facilities at all," said Caprinegro.

"Look at that recreation room in there," chimed in Rayborn. "Nothing but pool tables and poker tables. They are supposed to be rehabilitating us. There's better poker played on those tables than in

Reno. . . .deuces wild and everything goes."

They spoke of poor food, and the high costs of living.

Said Caprinegro, "They are selling us smokes at 21 cents a pack. . .charging us 62 cents per month to run a radio. . . .25 cents for a haircut. . .15 cents for a shave, 50 cents to a dollar for clothes pressing, and. . .80 to 100 dollars for a set of false teeth."

At that time a toothless old convict in an upper window peeled his lips back and yelled, "Yeah, and I ain't got 100 dollars!"

The others laughed.

But the most rousing and emotional topic of all was Deputy Warden Walter Stephens.

"That guy has to go," insisted Rayborn. "As long as he is around there is going to be trouble and plenty of it!"

He then peered up at the third floor windows and hollered, "What do we think of Deputy Stephens?"

A loud roar of profanity and booing came from the building.

As the day wore down, and the heat diminished a little, many citizens of Eddyville began to congregate on Pea Ridge—a series of hills overlooking the penitentiary. From there they watched the activities on the prison yard and could hear the yelling and hooting of the convicts in the garment factory. There was no sense of dread or apprehension, only an abiding curiosity. Too much had come to pass at the foot of the castle for the locals to become unglued about anything which happened there. Some of them had stood there thirty years before to gawk at the Tex Walters siege.

At about 6 p.m., gutsy little Dr. Watson went into the barricaded building. Forty-five minutes later he emerged with three prisoners including Tony Caprinegro. It was "the committee."

They went into conference with Warden Buchanan. The prison administration, through the straight talk of their warden, laid down the final surrender terms. The nature of this final ultimatum was not disclosed. But the consequences were made quite clear: if the terms were not accepted by 7:15, the troopers and guards would storm the building.

The prison yard, especially the area around the garment factory, grew silent and tense as the committee brought back the message. They knew that Big Jess was not one to bluff. The jig was up.

At almost the appointed time, the prisoners began to quietly file out of the building with their hands clasped behind their heads. Troopers immediately moved in to take them into custody. In an orderly fashion, the inmates were stripped, searched for weapons and ushered toward the cellhouses. An eerie hush hovered over the yard. The barking commands of the troopers pierced the humid stillness as the erstwhile rioters shuffled meekly across the hill.

A flurry of interest congregated around 41-year-old Fred McChesney as he emerged from the building bedraggled but unharmed.

"They treated me pretty good," he reassured the prison officials as they descended upon him. "They offered me cigarettes, cigars, Kool-aid, ice cream, and other things."

Then with a thin smile he added, "But, of course, I couldn't eat at a time like that."

The riot was not over.

On the very next morning thirty inmates bunched together and ransacked the inmate commissary. Lieutenant Lloyd Armstrong— one of the best prison men to ever walk the yard at Eddyville—proceeded to knock heads and take names. Armed with a machine gun, he rounded up the misbehaving convicts and made them return every single item to the store. Warden Buchanan then locked down. He had seen enough. The prison population was still seething and on the edge of revolt. Tension rose even more when they learned they would not be allowed to go to the dining hall for supper, but would be fed in their cells instead. One group of mutinous prisoners tried to break out.

On Saturday morning they remained locked down. It was not a happy group of campers confined to their stifling cells. They tore apart their beds and mattresses. Some, in the porous five cellhouse, began to hammer away at the walls with the legs off their beds. Covers were removed from the locks. The whole place sounded like a shipyard.

The National Guard was put on alert. A sizable number of state policemen remained at the prison, trying to screen out the trouble makers and have them isolated. It was a sweaty, grueling ordeal of one interrogation after another. A beleaguered and weary warden— aided by his boss Dr. Watson and prison chaplain Paul Jaggers—continued to talk to inmates in an effort to cool down the simmering unrest. Buchanan authorized the establishment of a permanent prisoner grievance committee and assured the prisoners that their current complaints would be investigated. Rumors began to circulate that Stephens was being transferred to another institution.

All of this pleased the committee and the tension began to thaw.

For the evening meal, the warden authorized the release of the prisoners in bunches to eat in the dining room. As a creative means of control, they were required to eat naked. Almost 1,100 nude men were herded in groups of 150 into the mess hall under the guns of guards and state policemen.

Slowly things began to return to normal. Many guards, fatigued and nervous, failed to report for duty. The state police stayed on for several days and patrolled the yard.

On Monday, Buchanan mercifully let the prisoners out of their cells. The garment factory and machine shop, which had been torn to pieces, were cleaned up and repaired. Over $3000 worth of damage had been inflicted.

On Tuesday, the first day of July, there was still no relief from the scorching weather. Nevertheless, most of the general population returned to their normal routine and the garment factory was back in operation.

"I think the heat has had as much to do with all this as anything," reflected the warden as he finally relaxed in his office. "It must be 150 degrees out there on the yard."

The riot of 1952 came to a close. It moved off the front pages as the scores of newspaper and radio reporters packed up their gear and left. The state police, after turning in a superb performance, departed. Headlines, shrinking with the dying crisis, gave the prison administration the victory. But the wise prison warden knew that one does not talk about winning and losing in the arena of human tragedy. When the glare of the spotlight had vanished, when "the tumult and the shouting" died, it was just him and them again in the castle. What had been released to the world was one thing. What had been understood between desperate men was another. As the old cons had hoped, big tough Jess had listened.

By the end of the summer, Governor Lawrence Wetherby announced the allocation of a half million dollars toward improving conditions at Eddyville. Money was earmarked for specific improvements to include a new hospital, expanded educational facilities, installation of commodes and lavatories in all cells, a new recreation building, exhaust fans in the cellhouses, and a new meat packing and cold storage plant.

Walter Stephens was quietly and unceremoniously transferred to a reform school for boys. None of the rioters were prosecuted in outside court. The bureaucrats in Frankfort finally realized that prisoners could not live off the prison farm alone. Slowly, almost imperceptibly, things got better.

"The village belongs to the castle, and whoever lives here or passes the night here does so, in a manner of speaking, in the castle itself." So said the melancholy Czech writer Franz Kafka.

The marriage between the little town of Eddyville and the Kentucky State Penitentiary has been a good one, lasting for more than one hundred years.

The castle and the community are so intertwined that most people associate one with the other. From the time that General Lyon ushered the first convicts into town—all decked out in stripes—and set up construction shacks on top of the conical hill overlooking the town and the river, prisons and prisoners have been a part of the Lyon County culture. Generations have come and gone under the shadows of the Gothic house of corrections. There is hardly a family native to the area that has not had a relative to be employed behind the gray stone walls.

Before the relocation of most of Eddyville for the impoundment of Barkley Lake, the prison sat smack-dab in the middle of town—right on the main drag to Louisville and Nashville. The town was greeted each morning by the resounding moan of the five o'clock whistle emitted from the prison's boiler room. It blew again at noon, and at one and at four in the afternoon. Children playing after school would began to make their meandering way home after the last whistle. They lived, "in a manner of speaking, in the castle itself."

For many years, the town's source of electricity was from the prison's coal-operated generators. Convicts and citizens alike drank from the same water tank. During the devastating 1937 flood which covered most of the village, furniture from the homes evacuated was stored in the penitentiary factory buildings.

In the early days of the penitentiary, young boys of the town would romp and play through the gates and porticoes, literally at the feet of the convicts themselves. Later, when rules became more strict, local baseball teams still went behind the walls to play the homestanding lifers. Prisoners thrilled to outside attention and always extended a warm and enthusiastic welcome to the visiting squads, to include rooting for their guests. Trusties selling leather goods and other convict crafts on the sidewalk in front of the prison spent much of their time joking and jousting with the barefoot boys of town. Occasionally a baseball, stolen from the inside team, would come out of the trusty's blue denim shirt and into the eager hands of the young lads.

Children were especially welcomed by the leathery-faced old cons. They congregated around them on their rare visits to the hill. Warden Chuck Thomas reassured an anxious father whose small son wanted to accompany a local ball team inside as bat boy. "That boy is safer on the prison yard than he would be out on the street. If one of those prisoners harmed a hair on his head, that convict would be dead in a matter of minutes. Inmate code."

Since the time of "Highball's" indiscretions in the weeds near the big spring, convicts have moved in and about the community. In the early days, trusties hauled water from the river, made trips to the depot, and shopped in town. To this day, minimum security inmates labor in the community at public works in both Eddyville and its sister town of Kuttawa. Many are skilled and have participated in running city water plants, and restoring historic buildings. They are even assigned to the recreational complex in the summer to maintain the playing fields, work in the concession stands, and have on occasion umpired ball games. Convicts have provided emergency manpower in times of crisis. More than once prisoners have been rushed to the nearby town of Smithland to assist in battling flood waters from the Cumberland and Ohio rivers. Convict musical groups have performed for outside charity drives. Inmate clubs have repaired toys to be given to needy children and conducted their own fund-raisers for special community needs. Unquestionably, over the years the felons of Eddyville have done much good.

The attitude of the people of Eddyville and Kuttawa toward these convicted felons running free around them and even those behind the walls has been a mix of benevolence and caution. "Behave yourself and we will treat you right. If you don't—there will be hell to pay." That has been the collective sentiment of these decent and conwise Lyon Countians. On public projects the trusties are often working along side—sometimes even supervised by—citizen volunteers. These upstanding and reputable pillars of the community will many times go to bat for their inmate friends by assisting them with the parole board or in some other fashion. Friendships develop that last a lifetime. As the prisoners contribute to the community, the community—through ordinary people—exert a positive influence upon the prisoners.

Some of the convict-citizen relationships have been highly unusual—even bordering on the bizarre. Lyon Countian Benny Pinnegar has a story which will enthrall his listeners as long as he lives.

Just past midnight on a July night in 1975, Benny was traveling home after completing the evening shift at a plant in Calvert City. His car-pooling friend let him out at his truck which was parked in the Chevron parking lot at Suwanee—a little settlement just west of Kuttawa. At that time of night it was dark and deserted.

As he opened the door to get into his vehicle, two escaped convicts jumped him. They had been attempting to hot wire his truck.

"Don't think about running," one of them warned in a rough voice as he pointed inside of his shirt to what Benny thought was a gun. They told him they needed his truck, and proceeded to march him up into some lonely woods away from the road. There, near an old pond, one of the convicts threatened to cut his throat and throw him in the lagoon. The other one intervened on his behalf and convinced his partner to take their hostage farther up the hill to an abandoned and secluded old house. There, he insisted, they could tie him up and leave him. Benny's mind was racing. There was no rope, no bindings. He was afraid that once he was inside the hovel, he would be killed.

"You can't leave me up there," he finally blurted out. "That house is haunted."

One could not have created more shock if ice water had been thrown into the face of the two culprits. They immediately went into a huddle.

"Okay", they turned back to their terrified captive. "We can't leave you in a haunted house. We'll have to take you with us."

They then proceeded back to the truck, hot-wired it and took off with Pinnegar caught in the middle. One of them laid a menacing homemade dirk on the dashboard. The point was not lost on their hostage.

His kidnappers talked gruffly with him at first as they headed east on the West Kentucky Parkway. It was in the middle of the night and little traffic. Once they pulled over at a rest stop and the motor died. With the starter fouled, all three had to get out and push to get it going. After that, their tough guy demeanor began to thaw and Benny was treated well.

The escapees had money for the tolls and gas, and the three rolled on into central Kentucky. By the afternoon, the trio had made it to Clark County, apparently the home territory of one of the escapees. Sticking to the back roads, they made their way into some pretty remote countryside. Pinnegar constantly looked for a chance to escape. But they were in the middle of nowhere, and he grew more confident all along that they would eventually release him. Once they stopped at a country store and the two fugitives bought him a drink and a candy bar.

Finally, after arriving in familiar surroundings, the convicts purchased some moonshine whiskey from a bootlegger. They proceeded to tie one on. As they became more intoxicated, the two felons grew even friendlier to Benny and began to share with him stories of their criminal past.

One of them wanted their new friend's address. "I've got over $10,000 from a bank robbery and I want to send you some of it," he explained.

But Benny didn't want any part of their money, and he sure didn't want them to know where he lived.

Late in the afternoon, one of them left and after a while came back with a car which he had hot-wired and stolen. They no longer needed Benny or his truck. So they gave him ten dollars for gas money, and sent him on his way.

"You take off for home now, and don't look back," one of them instructed him, and he cheerfully obliged.

On the way home a state trooper, recognizing the truck which had been reported stolen, pulled him over. After extensive questioning Benny about his ordeal and relieved that he was alright, the trooper allowed Pinnegar to proceed home. But not until he loaned him another $5 to help him buy gas for the trip. All the time the trooper had been questioning him, Benny was not able to shut off the truck.

So Benny Pinnegar made it home to his greatly relieved family, on money given to him by both the criminals and the law.

Most wardens down through the years have—even while serving relatively short terms—made great efforts to accommodate the needs and concerns of the local citizens. Incredibly, of the twenty-five prison masters to rule at the Kentucky State Penitentiary over a hundred years, not a single one has been from the prison town—although neighboring Trigg County has supplied two penitentiary leaders. Yet, for the most part, they have blended in well with the natives, realizing that the prison and the town are in many ways interdependent.

One warden survived a very close shave with one of his own inmates. In 1978, Warden Donald Bordenkircher's own trusty houseboy got into some liquor and grabbed one of the warden's loaded pistols. In his inebriated state he intended to take the whole family hostage. Bordenkircher jumped the convict and was able to wrestle the weapon away from him. In the struggle the pistol was discharged and Bordenkircher received a flesh wound in the thigh. Holding the gun on his assailant, the warden managed to radio for help and the inmate was brought under control.

The Kentucky State Penitentiary has not confined itself to the conical hill overlooking the hamlet of Eddyville, and later Barkley Lake. It has actually reproduced additional institutions.

Up until the late 1930s, the prison farm consisted of approximately twenty acres immediately behind the back walls. It was convenient but overburdened. The land was located within a draw between two sharp hills. During Jess Buchanan's first stint as warden the state purchased several acres about six miles away. Then, in 1942, an additional 432 acres was purchased four miles east of Kuttawa. In 1949, during Buchanan's second and last term as superintendent, another large tract was purchased in the fertile Fredonia valley, some eight miles away from the prison. Another parcel was added in 1962. Altogether, the total farming operation finally reached over 2,400 acres. The farms produced vegetables, beef, pork, poultry and eggs. A cannery was also constructed.

Inmate workers were trucked back and forth, daily, between the prison and the farms. Not only did the enterprise provide fresh produce for the prison and other institutions in Kentucky, it also provided much needed work for idle convicts.

In 1968, dormitories were constructed at the big farm near Fredonia under the supervision of Captain R. P. Parker. About 200 minimum security inmates were then assigned from Eddyville to the prison farm. The satellite correctional facility was managed by the prison administration at Eddyville through a farm manager who lived on site.

In 1977, the farm center became a totally independent prison with its own warden and staff. It was named the West Kentucky Farm Center. On July 13, 1990, that facility was converted into a medium security prison with 330 beds and named the West Kentucky Correctional Complex. Barracks for approximately 80 minimum security inmates were retained outside the razor-wire perimeter for those prisoners assigned to the farm and community work details. So today, three separate penitentiaries—maximum, medium, and minimum— give even more of a penal legacy to this small community.

Like most good marriages of long duration, the prison and the community have had their share of arguments and spats. Ever since the complaints of the townspeople to the 1899 Senate investigation about prisoners making a nuisance of themselves, there have been periodic outcries of protest.

Most times the disputes are resolved at the warden's office. Sometimes they filter through all the way to Frankfort. One such probe was that of 1945 concerning the administration of Warden Dewey Ward. In addition to allegations of graft, the Lyon County citizens complained that convicts were running "free as foxes, frightening women and children." Witnesses at the public hearing conducted at the court house gave rather mixed accounts. Most of the allegations involved the inmates assigned to the prison farm as neighboring farmers voiced concern about prisoners wandering on and about their land. According to them, the practice was getting worse.

Town people, however, seemed to have accepted the regular presence of prisoners in their midst as business as usual, and no matter for alarm. L. B. Fuqua, operator of the town's motion picture theater, testified that prisoners attended his shows in the company of a guard and sat in the balcony. But he said their conduct had always been good and he was glad to have them as a favor to the warden.

Some of their outings obviously got out of hand. A guard took one prisoner to Paducah for eye treatment and they didn't come back for two days. When they did return, the official was drunk and the convict had been drinking. They enjoyed a good time in the big city. The guard was fired and the prisoner punished.

But an episode occurred on July 4, 1953, which generated a bitter uprising in the community. It almost caused a riot outside of the prison walls.

John and Viola Glass ran a country store about four miles north of Kuttawa at the intersection of two highways, one of which led to the prison farm a short distance away. In the early afternoon of the hot summer holiday, Mr. Glass went down the road a short distance to do some farm work. He left his wife, age 44, and their two-year-old daughter at the store.

Meanwhile, two inmates working at the prison farm that day gave fellow convict Bobby Jordan $11 to go out and purchase some beer and tobacco for them. Jordan, age 22, got in a prison truck and drove toward town. He stopped at the Glass store around 2 o'clock in the afternoon. He had been in the little grocery several times and there was nothing unusual about his visit. He asked for a Coke, and they engaged in casual conversation as Mrs. Glass got it from the drink box and gave it to him. The drink was almost gone when suddenly, and totally unexpected, Jordan pulled a jack handle from out of nowhere and proceeded to attack the defenseless store keeper.

She was beaten savagely about the head, and knocked back against the shelves behind the counter. After approximately sixteen bloody blows, he left his victim for dead on the floor and took $60 from the cash register. Jordan also dashed into the back part of the store where the Glasses lived and took more money. He then fled, as the little tot cried hysterically at the horrible crime that had taken place. Her screaming caught the attention of the first people to stop and, incredibly, they found Viola on her feet staggering about the store. The alarm was sounded and she was rushed to the hospital in Paducah. There she lingered near death, with multiple fractures and a large number of bone fragments were removed from her skull. Her body was a mass of bruises, and her right arm broken.

John Glass, who was in poor health, went into shock when he learned of the terrible assault upon his wife. He, too, had to be hospitalized.

In spite of her critical condition, Mrs. Glass was able to give the authorities enough information about her assailant to lead them to questioning Jordan. After a short amount of interrogation, he admitted being at the store, but implicated another individual as the one actually doing the beating. The story did not check out and, over the next two days, other inconsistencies were found in his story. Finally, he made a full confession admitting that he was the sole perpetrator.

At the time of the assault, Bobby Jordan was only thirty days from going home.

The vicious attack upon Viola Glass took place on Saturday afternoon. By Sunday morning, news of the crime was the talk at every church service in the county. Members of the little Fairview Methodist church, located just across the road from the Glass store, were especially distraught. Not only did one of their own lay battered and near death, but all of them felt threatened. The mood of this farming community became ugly. Over the long history of the penitentiary, the convicts running "like foxes" among them had been mostly just a bothersome, if somewhat unsettling, nuisance. Now the danger had struck home with the dreadful hand of violence. What these good, law-abiding people had feared had actually come to pass.

By 1:30 on that Sunday afternoon between 300 and 400 people gathered at a mass meeting under the oaks and maples of the Fairview Church lawn. Most of the people there were from the surrounding community with local political officials laced into the mix. The angry citizens were giving vent to their smoldering resentment of the management of convict labor at the prison farm. Complaints spewed from the group that prisoners were allowed to roam about the farm and adjacent countryside without guards—even stay at the farm overnight without supervision.

It was not a mob without rational thought, however. Two committees consisting of top-notch people were appointed at the meeting. One was to confer with Warden Jess Buchanan and request major changes in the farm's operation. The other was to circulate a petition in the community to be delivered to the governor.

During the course of that turbulent Sunday, public sentiment was raging against Bobby Jordan. Once word got out that he had confessed to the crime, the people wanted quick justice. The fact that he was continually changing his story to falsely implicate other people only angered the community more. It was a good thing for Jordan that he was tucked away in the impregnable fortress of the Kentucky State Penitentiary.

The situation became so tense, and resentment ran so high, that Director of Corrections, Dr. W. E. Watson, and the department's psychologist, Harold Black, rushed to Lyon County to investigate and assist the beleaguered prison administration.

Just as he had adroitly dealt with the prison riot just twelve short months before, big Jess Buchanan again shouldered this crisis masterfully. First of all, he cooled the passions by not running from or denying the citizen allegations.

"This neighborhood is one of the most substantial, respectable and decent ones in western Kentucky," he announced to the press. "I'm going to do my best to see that there is no recurrence of this brutal, vicious crime. I have no fear that I can get along with the citizens here and work out a solution."

Next, he did what all good leaders do when things go wrong. He accepted full responsibility upon his own massive back.

"I just picked the wrong man for a trusty," he boldly declared, although some underling no doubt made the decision to put Bobby Jordan on trusty status.

The people of Lyon County knew Jess Buchanan—and just like the inmates—they respected and trusted him. These calming assurances, along with the good news that Viola Glass was going to make it, helped mightily to defuse the volatile situation.

By Tuesday, the citizens' committee and the Department of Corrections had hammered out an agreement providing stricter supervision and control of prison trusties working on the penitentiary farms. The provisions of the accord included the prohibition against farm inmates traveling off state property without being accompanied by at least one guard.

As Mrs. Glass recovered, things returned to normal in Lyon County. Convicts continued to be trucked to the farms each morning and returned to prison in the evening until dormitories were constructed for the farm help and correctional officers moved to the country.

In January, 1954, Bobby Jordan was tried in the Lyon Circuit Court for the brutal beating and robbery of Viola Glass. His punishment was fixed by the jury at life imprisonment.

※※※

To a prisoner doing time, maintaining an established routine is important. Because such a small slice of place is allocated for a long period of time, inmates become persnickety over everything. Small privileges loom big. Slight interruption in the norm are major irritations. There is a certain rhythm—a pitch and roll of daily tedium—in doing time. It helps to deaden the senses to life's vast wasteland. Things which disrupt this rhythm—trifles which are meaningless on the street—will irritate and provoke convicts. Slight variations in visiting hours, mail call, visits to the weight pile, shower time, are all monumental happenings. That's why many wardens use the "carrot and stick" approach in making major changes in prison operations. That rule states that no standing privilege is ever taken away from general population inmates without replacing it with another. If the Christmas party is done away with, there will be a Fourth of July cookout on the yard.

It's the rhythm of things. The ebb and flow.

This reality was reflected in the old inmate code. There was a time—when the prison was populated by older, more seasoned convicts—when, to a large extent, they policed themselves. If one prisoner began to abuse a privilege, jeopardizing it for the rest, he would be paid a visit by the "committee." Stop the nonsense, or else. They could make a convincing case. It usually ceased.

In 1979, a battery of phones was placed on the prison yard for the use of the general population. They were programmed so only collect calls could be made. Most of the inmates used them to keep in touch with families and friends. A sagacious white-collar criminal from Louisville named Keith Phillips saw them as an opportunity to continue his trade. Through ingenious manipulations he was able to use the telephones to rip off thousands of dollars in cash and property from various credit card companies and merchandising stores. The local Grand Jury and prosecutor went to war attempting to have the telephones removed from the hill. The legal battle raged for months and finally ended in a compromise whereby the phone conversations would be subject to monitoring. The inmates came within an eyelash of losing the phones. That would not have happened thirty years ago. Mr. Phillips would have stopped his shenanigans or had to check in to protective custody.

What happened to the so called, "inmate code"?

Traces of it still exist. Through the "rat system" an inmate may still be marked for punishment, even death, if he is known to be an informer for the administration.

But like the value system on the outside, it has lost its ardor, its driving force. In a day of written rules, regulations, and directives, the inner unwritten code of human behavior has weakened.

Times have changed the nature of the convict. During the first two thirds of this century, most criminals sprung from conventional parenting. They were taught the difference between right and wrong. Many, like Tex Walters, received religious training. They learned of a value system, even if they rejected it. As the mournful country song laments, it left "only me to blame, for mamma tried." Bad company, whiskey, greed, poverty, and sometimes a fickle woman, were their undoing. Once in prison, these convicts of yore were stripped of their vices and reduced to a brutal world of surviving with people as bad, vile and criminal as they.

Faced with a baseline existence, these outcasts revisited one important, if unarticulated, lesson of their youth—the need for community. And in their rough-hewn ways they knew that for a community to exist, there had to be some form of value system—some structure. To survive—they had learned—required some order amidst the chaos.

"In a savage kraal," historian H. G. Wells wrote in 1920, "a savage knows that he belongs to a community, and lives and acts accordingly."

So a code evolved, not anchored necessarily in morality or religion, though it might have inklings of virtue. But it was rooted in the primal need of survivorship. So, there was in a manner of speaking, "honor among thieves"—as that word was defined by thieves.

Most young convicts of today, however, come from the much too familiar dysfunctional family. Fathers—the natural role model for boys growing to manhood—are dead, absconded, unknown, or all of the above. Single mothers, demoralized by numbing poverty, hopelessly entangled with numerous offspring, are uneducated, unskilled and dependent on welfare. Most struggle to survive, without moral moorings of their own. Therefore, their children are cast to the wind like tumbleweed—without discipline, nurturing, or any semblance of moral instruction. Once churches urged us to "take your children to Sunday School—don't send them." Now, it's a good parent that sends them. Far too many of the young offenders going to prison these days are bereft of any meaningful notion of right and wrong. For most, their past is a moral wasteland barren of tenets, standards, or duties—totally devoid of any value system. They are raised in moral slums in which, again in the words of Wells, "the individual neither knows of nor acts in relation to any greater being."

In essence, the inmate code has followed the deterioration of moral standards on the outside.

By June 1986, the inmate code was not the only thing which had changed at Eddyville. Life in the castle will never be considered a walk in the park. But compared to the sweltering conditions of the riot torn summer of 1952, things were pretty good.

Needless to say, a lot had transpired during the thirty-four years between the days of Jess Buchanan and Benny Rayborn and the summer of '86. The Korean War wore down to a truce, and the '50s became the years of peace, Elvis Presley, and the Yankees. Toward the end of the decade, the U.S. Corps of Engineers began to buy up most of old Eddyville for the impoundment of Barkley Lake. The business district and most of the residents relocated to higher ground to what was known as the Fairview area of the county. By the summer of 1965 the river bottom, to include the old town site, had been leveled. Barkley Dam, located only five miles downstream, was completed. In the late fall of that year, the entire valley began to fill up with water. The castle now stood almost surrounded by the lake—resolute and defiant.

The turbulent battle of civil rights waged throughout the country. Assassinations, Vietnam, hard rock, drugs, and the shifting values and awful venom of the '60s spilled out upon the American landscape. Neil Armstrong landed on the moon. Watergate came and went and the flower children gave birth to Yuppies. A movie star was elected president. Microwaves, cablevision, computer games, and fax machines came upon the scene.

In the face of all of this transition, the stone demeanor of the Castle on the Cumberland remained unchanged. The social and cultural revolution on the outside did, however, affect the inside world of the Eddyville prison.

Over a period of three decades the status of the death penalty in the United States became uncertain. With the expansion of the constitutional rights afforded persons charged with crimes by the U. S. Supreme Court in the '60s, speculation began to rise that the death penalty might be declared unconstitutional as cruel and unusual punishment. Various state legislatures were taking it off the books, and lower courts were taking a hard second look. Several cases, which would be determinative of the matter, began to make their slow and laborious way up the appellate ladder. Most governors went into a holding pattern, either commuting all death sentences or granting indefinite stays. The criminal justice system, as well as the entire citizenry of this country waited for the nation's august court to make the call.

This stalemate on death was evident at Eddyville. There were five executions in 1955, four in 1956, and then a six-year respite until the execution of Kelly Moss in March of 1962. Then the lethal trickle came to a stop. Kentucky also waited.

There were eleven men on death row in 1972 when the U. S. Supreme Court handed down the case of *Furman v. Georgia.* That landmark decision held that the death penalty itself was not cruel and unusual punishment. However, the way people were charged, tried, convicted and sentenced could be unconstitutional. The decision effectively invalidated the death sentences of those awaiting execution at Eddyville. Their penalties were reduced to straight life, with possibility of parole.

By the summer of 1986, all of those condemned prior to

Furman were gone from the Kentucky State Penitentiary. All but Henry Anderson.

Anderson arrived on death row March 1, 1960 after being convicted of murdering a a Louisville physician. He was from Paducah, Kentucky, and graduated from Notre Dame law school. Henry never practiced law, but instead ventured into numerous labor causes and became known as somewhat of an eccentric. He was released from his employment at the General Electric plant in Louisville as having psychiatric problems. There were serious questions raised about his mental state during his trial. Anderson insisted that he was both sane and innocent.

When the *Furman* decision offered the convict lawyer an exchange of his death penalty for a life sentence, he incredibly refused the offer.

"Either free me or execute me," was his plea.

His intransigent stand on this matter threw the entire legal system a curve. So he remained on death row down through the years, fighting his legal battle by the filing of numerous writs, always insisting that he was innocent and that he should be freed. All of the other convicts whose sentences were reduced to life by the Supreme Court edict had been paroled. In 1992, then an old man with gray hair, Anderson was transferred to the geriatrics ward at the Kentucky State Reformatory at LaGrange. He died there on April 6, 1994, at eighty years of age—technically still a death row inmate.

After *Furman*, Kentucky went back to the drawing boards and fashioned a death penalty statute modeled after Georgia's law, and which has passed constitutional muster. Beginning in 1976, prisoners condemned under the new law began arriving at the Kentucky State Penitentiary. In the summer of 1986, there were approximately 30 inmates on death row at Eddyville, housed in the new and air-conditioned six cellhouse and outfitted in red jumpsuits.

Classification has been a critical part of modern penology. Over the last twenty years, the general population at Eddyville has reflected a drastic change in prison demographics. Kentucky has built new medium and minimum security penitentiaries and camps, allowing for a more sensible distribution of convicted felons throughout the system. Eddyville has always been a maximum security prison. But up until recent times the mix has been varied, with serious offenders serving long sentences with lesser criminals. By 1986, most of the convicts serving time at Eddyville were truly maximum security convicts loaded down with heavy sentences. Also, the population was and is today much younger. The older convicts have been mostly weeded out of Eddyville and moved on to less restrictive institutions. In 1976,

Kentucky's new persistent offender law went into effect. It was an updated version of the old habitual offender act, or the "bitch" as convicts termed it. Under the new law a criminal having two or more previous convictions could be sentenced up to life in prison. The main kicker, as far as the prisoners are concerned, is that under that law one could not become eligible for parole for at least ten years.

So, over the past twenty years, the general population at the Kentucky State Penitentiary has become younger—average age in the early 20s. And they are also looking at longer terms to serve. This makes for a volatile and troublesome combination for correctional officers and staff.

If the nature of inmates has changed over the last two decades, so have the conditions. Mostly for the better for those pulling time. Guards, in spite of remaining grossly underpaid, have become more professional. Living facilities have become more comfortable with the enlargement of cells and installation of air conditioning in all of the housing units. Each cell has access to cable television. Professional dietitians plan and supervise food services. Vocational training and schools have been expanded to the enclosed back lot and have included masonry, auto body repairs, and carpentry. Inmate punishment is administered through a disciplinary committee which is required to afford procedural due process to the inmate charged, to include the assistance of an inmate legal aid. Convicts have almost unlimited access to the courts, facilitated by a fully serviced law library.

A Federal Consent Decree issued out of the United States District Court of West Kentucky in 1980 precipitated much of the change. It culminated several years of litigation between the inmates and the Department of Corrections. The controversial decree revolutionized the Kentucky State Penitentiary.

It mandated a total revamping of the operation of the prison, to include new capital construction. A population cap set at one inmate per cell outlawed double celling. The ancient structure had to be brought up to building and electrical codes. Old cellhouses one and two were to be renovated into facilities for inmate programs such as caseworker offices, a new chapel, and visitation areas. As a result of converting two of the old cellhouses into other uses, a brand new number six cellhouse was constructed which houses 189 prisoners.

The Consent Decree placed new restrictions upon the classification system, expanded educational and vocational requirements, improved recreational facilities, and implemented new procedures to insure inmates greater access to the courts. The latter provision included the increasing and training of legal aides.

But the edict did not provide only for inmates. It imposed new standards for correctional officers and staff, to include a more sophisticated employment process and increased pay.

For the next several years after the order was entered, the operation of the Kentucky State Penitentiary was monitored by the Federal Court and in accordance to the Consent Decree. The Department of Corrections worked diligently to comply with its terms and, by the summer of 1986, had earned full accreditation by the American Correctional Association. This is the coveted housekeeping seal of approval for penology.

Finally, the Substantial Compliance Hearing on the Consent Decree was scheduled for July of 1986. If the U. S. District Judge determined the prison to be in full compliance with the 1980 blueprint for change, the order would be lifted and the Kentucky State Penitentiary would once again be on its own and free of Federal rule.

Anticipation and excitement began to build as corrections' lawyers and the prison administration prepared for the July showdown. The inmate committee also prepared. Naturally, the prison administration wanted out. The prisoners wanted the penitentiary to stay under the court's supervision. Tension on the yard began to rise with the heat as June pushed toward July.

On June 21, 1986, there was a boycott of the inmate kitchen— a hunger strike if you will. "Food conditions" were blamed for the protest. Only eleven inmates ate the noon meal there. Only 16 inmates from general population ate supper.

The weather was clear, dry and hot. But Warden Gene Scroggy was warned by his officers to brace for the storm. Informants and the yard barometer told them that something was coming down.

On Sunday, the 22nd of June, the strike continued. Only a handful from the yard ate in the dining room. Threats began to circulate against those prisoners defying the kitchen ban. By nightfall, the war of nerves had escalated to the kindling point.

That evening a list of grievances were given to the warden. They had to do with food, phones, use of inmate showers, access to the legal office, the grievance committee for the pending litigation, and television. Much of it was Consent Decree stuff. Other than the food complaint, it would have been like language from outer space to the rioters of 1953.

Warden Scroggy waste-canned the complaints.

Early on the Monday morning of June 23, 1986, some of the kitchen help refused to come out of their cells to go to work. Once again, as the sun rose in the pale blue sky, only fourteen inmates went to the kitchen for breakfast. The rest of the general population—about three hundred strong—gathered on top of the hill near the water tank.

Fights began to break out on the yard as those prisoners eating in the dining hall were attacked by those who didn't. Guards were thrown into the bubbling cauldron as they rushed in to rescue the inmates being assaulted. Wall stand officers observing the mob scene enveloping the yard, fired warning shots above the heads of convicts involved in the fights. Some of the guards attempting to break up the encounters were struck by inmates.

At 7:03 a.m., Major Robert Hendricks radioed to "lock up the hill" and to ring the bell. Instead of moving to their cellhouses, the prisoners started sitting down on the yard. Yard officers moved to relative safety underneath wall stands.

The hill belonged to the convicts.

There was no Benny Rayborn here—no Robert Benewitz or Tex Walters. The mob was essentially leaderless. There was a group of about thirty inmates, however, who were the most vocal. With the exception of a handful of cheerleaders and primary agitators, the gang milled about at random without direction. There was no planned agenda, no primary objectives to be taken. In a flash, the disorganized swarm broke loose in a frenzy of destruction.

At first they began hurling rocks at the wall stands and yard officers. A group moved into "number one shop"—a long metal recreation building. There they proceeded to demolish the place, destroying the toilets and water cooler and setting fire to a pool table. The large screen television was pulverized and the barber shop ransacked. Windows were broken out. Pool sticks were broken in half, and the ivory balls were taken from the shop and hurled at the guard stands.

Pool balls and rocks went crashing through the window of number ten stand, a tall, newly constructed tower erected on top of the hill next to the water tank. The guards inside were unable to react with weapons because of the flying glass and deadly ballistics raining down upon them.

Several inmates headed for the legal office, a square building just to the south of the decimated number one shop. A filing cabinet was dragged outside and left about ten feet from the entrance. Then smoke began to rise from inside. Their much-cherished access to the courts began to go up in flames.

While most of the guards—unarmed and at great risk—had retreated to within the protection of the wall stands, there were officers and staff still trapped in the middle of the melee.

Behind the legal office and number one shop were two separate buildings housing the yard office and the laundry. There were guards inside of each. Needless to say, it was a terrifying situation. They were sitting ducks as the mass of screaming and raging convicts swarmed toward them. Many of the prisoners were now armed with broken cue sticks, pipes, rocks, and pieces of furniture. Officers Marie Harper and George Aldridge locked themselves in the yard office and hoped for the best.

Veteran guard Jack Smith bolted himself in the laundry just in time. A large group of inmates began breaking through the back window of the building. "Let's kill the old son of a bitch!" some of them chanted. Smith radioed for help.

Meanwhile, Warden Scroggy and his leading officers were observing the riot and giving directions from his office which overlooked the yard. This command post had once been the dining room for the warden's residence when convict bands gave Sunday afternoon concerts just below the windows. On this day, it was a hectic command post of grim-faced and anxious correctional officers determined to keep their prison.

When the warden saw his caged officers on the yard seriously threatened, he ordered number six wall stand to fire warning shots into the laundry area. Numerous shots were fired over the heads of the rampaging inmates and into a bank directly in front of the laundry. The rioters got the message, and began retreating from that building and the yard office.

Meanwhile, inmates had smashed their way into the unoccupied caseworkers' office located off to the north of the recreation shop. They tried setting it afire.

By now the center of the prison yard looked like it had been struck by a series of mortar rounds. Three buildings were either aflame or smoldering. Black smoke billowed into the powder blue sky.

While the inmates were having their fun, the keepers of the prison had not been standing by biting their nails. Neither had they been caught unprepared.

Just as the yellow flames punched through the roof of the legal office, the highly-trained and well-armed prison Emergency Squad was entering the yard through the sally port near number six stand and out of sight of most of the prisoners. The thirteen member team, dressed in riot gear and led by Lt. Rick Pershing moved around toward the back of the yard. They then lined up on the lower ground behind five cellhouse, facing the top of the hill where all of the destruction was taking place. Slowly the column began to sweep the yard. An officer in number six wall stand armed with a .37 millimeter grenade launcher was directed to volley ten rounds of tear gas into the area underneath the water tank, where most of the rampaging inmates had clustered. The E-Squad fired several warning shots above the heads of the prisoners from .12 gauge shotguns.

As the E-Squad moved up onto the hill, they first rescued their fellow officers from the laundry and yard office. Then Lt. Pershing used a bullhorn to order all prisoners to lay down on the ground or risk being shot. One convict charged Lt. David Ezell and was knocked away with the butt of his gun. Slowly, through the haze of acrid smoke and gas, the prisoners began to lay down. Pliable plexi-cuffs were used by E-Squad officers to bind their hands behind them. There were patches of resistance on the yard, but nothing the capable troubleshooters couldn't handle. All of the rioters were finally herded into their respective cellhouses. Some inside six cellhouse attempted to jam cell doors with pillows and sheets. They also threw debris and set some fires while screaming profanities and threats. After some effort, the rowdy and destructive bunch was brought under control.

By 10:00 a.m. all inmates were in their appropriate cells. A few minutes later, the count cleared. The riot had been quashed.

Out on the yard it still looked like a battle zone. The Eddyville Fire Department was there assisting prison personnel in fighting the fires. The state police had arrived to offer assistance.

Nine employees were treated by the medical staff, but none were seriously hurt. Twenty-three inmates received only minor injuries.

Damage to property, however, was heavy. The legal office and its contents were completely destroyed by fire. Other buildings, including fixtures and furnishings, were substantially damaged, as were two of the guard towers.

Due to the stellar performance of the prison administration, correctional officers and staff—especially the E-Squad—lives had been miraculously spared.

The riot of '86 differed in many ways from the bash of 1952. In 1986, its purpose was vague and, in reality, vented no legitimate complaint. It was largely aimless, leaderless, and wasted havoc. It cost the state a lot of money—close to a half million dollars. And it cost some inmates a lot of time. Several of the prisoners were indicted and convicted for their involvement and received substantial sentences tacked on to what they were already serving.

Chapter 12

After Lillian Walters embraced her husband for the last time on Monday, October 4, 1923, she departed the prison and returned to the Lester Hotel a couple of blocks away.

She hurriedly checked out of the inn and took a taxi cab to the train station, crossing over the narrow Depot Bridge, under which she and Jim Sparks had planted the seeds of revolt, a few nights before.

The savvy gangster's wife then caught a train to Louisville. Upon arriving at the state's largest city she went to stay at her sister Lorena's house.

There she waited.

The tension was unbearable. No doubt she received commiseration from her sister who had previously supported and even aided the criminal marauding of the Walters couple.

Lillian knew that news would soon be coming from the western end of the state. Tidings would be either good or bad—there would be no in between.

On Wednesday evening word began to trickle into Louisville about a major disturbance at the state's maximum security prison down in Eddyville. Rumors and counter rumors circulated wildly. Chilling reports of people being killed reached the anxious ears of the waiting wife.

Any suspense as to what was going on at the Kentucky State

Penitentiary was removed on Thursday morning when the headlines of the *Louisville Courier Journal* screamed, "GAS BOMBS ARE ORDERED FOR DRIVE TO KILL CONVICTS WHO SHOT 4 EDDYVILLE GUARDS." The picture of her handsome husband looked out at her from the front page.

She learned of the shooting death of Hodge Cunningham, as well as the wounding of the other guards. As bad as the news was, she was nevertheless relieved to know that Tex was still alive, even if under siege. Where there was life, there was hope.

To her consternation, she also learned for the first time that she was being sought by the local police for questioning.

On that Thursday while the dining hall at the penitentiary was being riddled by a maelstrom of lead, and her husband most likely lay dead on the littered floor, she turned herself in to the county jailer, Thomas Dover. He directed her to the city detectives working the case.

In answering their questions, Lillian assumed the winsome role of a devoted but totally innocent wife.

"I was in Eddyville Monday and saw Monte," she related softly with just the right amount of bewilderment in her voice, "I talked to him for two hours within sight of the guards. He told me 'I am not going to stand this any longer.' I asked him what he meant by that but he said that he was not going to tell me."

Dabbing her eyes with her handkerchief, she continued, "I tried my best to get something out of him but he would not say any more. So I left for Louisville that afternoon to go to my sister's."

They were taken in by her sweet and innocent ways and let her go.

After a telephone call to Warden Chilton he in turn told the press, "We do not believe she was involved."

Other people at the prison were not so easily fooled. Chilton's comment to the press may have been just a cover. He had to maintain a strong suspicion of her guilt. Not only had Roscoe Gumm and Hodge Cunningham approached him some time before that fateful Wednesday with the information gleaned from their inmate sources, but he had closely censored her letters to Tex. He had also placed two guards in attendance at their last meeting. Most of the guards and prison officials were convinced that Lillian was some way involved with the bloody revolt. Wounded officer William Gillihan, from his hospital bed, zeroed in on the young beauty. "She's been spending entirely too much time hanging around the prison," he complained as he recounted his harrowing experience.

But they needed evidence.

Even with the volcanic eruption of blood shed and violence at the penitentiary and the consuming battle of the siege which ensued, an investigation was at the same time being conducted as to how the deadly weapon got in to the Walters gang.

The critical information which would prime the evidentiary pump came out of Paducah and Lillian's finances there. She had worked at the Settlement House—a charity shelter established for the purpose of teaching life skills to children and women. In addition to being friendly and pretty, she was also a good worker. This combination of virtues won her many friends, to include Miss Nannie Boyd, resident head of the Settlement House, and Mrs. J. R. Crawford, the chairperson of the Settlement House Committee of the Woman's Club. Although her five years of marriage to a convicted murderer had made her one tough lady, she gave the outward appearance of being somewhat vulnerable. No doubt her reputable friends also felt sorry for her in having a husband in the penitentiary.

"She did her work very nicely, and we were all very fond of her," stated Miss Boyd. "She had a sweet disposition and I am sorry to hear about her trouble."

The head lady also observed, "All the time Mrs. Walters worked here she evidenced the deepest devotion to her husband. She wrote to him a letter every night. She never retired without first writing to him. Her love was so deep and her life was wrapped up in his welfare."

Lillian's life in Paducah was also shrouded in mystery, even to her friends. On several occasions she received telephone calls from unknown men, to whom she would speak in a low, whispered tone. Also, time and again the enigmatic spouse would leave the Settlement House to secretly rendezvous with unidentified people. Undoubtedly this all tied into the conspiracy, as Tex would send messages out through convicts being released from prison.

While at the charity home she kept a pistol, with which she once ran off a would-be burglar. With a devilish grin, she would boast that the gun belonged to her husband, and each of the three notches on the handle represented his dead victims.

Underneath the soft frills and sweet demeanor ran a vein of cold steel.

During these Paducah days however, her finances continued to be a problem—primarily because she channeled most of meager earnings into supporting her confined husband. On her frequent trips to the prison she took food, clothing and books. "She never wanted anything for self," said matron Boyd. "It was all for him."

The devoted wife would not even allow him to have his clothes washed in the prison laundry. Instead she paid for them to be sent out to be washed and ironed in town.

Because of her affection for Lillian, Mrs. Crawford made arrangements for her to enroll in night classes at a private school. For a young girl who was forced to quit her formal education at age eleven in order to help support her family, this opportunity was greatly appreciated. However, she finally gave up this pursuit because it took away from the attention she wanted to give to her husband.

In June 1923, in spite of being a good worker, her job was in jeopardy because of all the time she was taking off to tend to Tex. In April, for instance, she was given a few days off to go to Frankfort and plead with Governor Morrow for a pardon. She overstayed her leave, disappearing for almost 10 days. When her employer informed her in June that she would have to stop going to Eddyville more than once a month, she refused such a proposal. Lillian was then given the opportunity to resign, which she sadly did on June 8.

From that time forward Mrs. Walters struggled financially, relying on sporadic part-time work, support from her many friends, and at last—the money of Jim Sparks.

It was during the siege that prison officials, working with the Paducah police, learned that she was receiving financial assistance from suspicious sources. After resigning from the Settlement House she moved into the residence of Mrs. Minnie Sweeny at 611 Willie Street. Shortly thereafter her landlady received a check from Sparks for thirty-five dollars with instructions to endorse it to Lillian. She did so without asking any questions.

In the midst of the dining hall shootout Richard Rudy, president of Citizens National Bank of Paducah arrived at the penitentiary to relate what he knew about Lillian Walters. He told them about the financial transaction of September 14 when she brought Sparks to the bank to cash a four hundred dollar check. The newly released ex-con was also being escorted around Paducah by Lillian and being introduced as her brother.

They began to put the pieces together.

She came to the penitentiary on Monday for a visit with Tex before she left on "a long trip." Then trusty Andrew Hawkins escaped on the same day and an empty ammunition box was found on his trail. Only two weeks before she cashed a check for and consorted with Jim Sparks, a friend of her husband's who had also provided her with money.

Although Warden Chilton insisted that it would have been impossible for her to have brought the gun into the prison herself, no one at Eddyville doubted that she had a hand in it.

Knowing it, and proving it were two different things. The

hard evidence was still pretty thin.

Nevertheless, afraid that Lillian might try to flee the jurisdiction of Kentucky, the Louisville police decided to make the pinch. Major Ben Griffin, assistant chief of police, awoke the sleeping suspect and arrested her at 2 a.m. on Saturday morning, October 6. She was charged with aiding a felon to escape and taken to the county jail. There she was grilled for hours by Griffin and other officers. Totally exhausted, she would only admit to the financial transaction with Hawkins in Paducah. No further explanation was given, and no other admissions were made at that time.

That was the day before Miranda rights and the scrupulous attention to due process. Anything short of the rubber hose was pretty much accepted as the norm. The policeman on the beat working a serious case did not give much heed to Kentucky's "anti-sweating" statute, which was then on the books.

Convinced that he could later squeeze more evidence out of this attractive container of information, Major Griffin locked her up.

That Saturday night, the anxious young wife of Tex Walters paced the corridor of the women's ward of the Jefferson County jail. Smartly dressed with a white shawl across her shoulders, this pretty inmate with the congenial disposition seemed strangely out of place in the bleak and dimly lit halls of steel and concrete.

It was then that jailer Tom Dover approached his unusual prisoner with the bad news.

"Mrs. Walters," he said solemnly, "a newspaper man has a message for you. It is all over."

She knew all too well what he meant.

A jail matron was immediately at her side as she crumpled in grief. Tenderly the mistress led the newly-made widow into a nearby room. Slowly Lillian sat down in a wooden chair, placed her head on a table and sobbed. Her face wet with tears, she finally raised her head. Appealing to the sympathetic jailer, the tortured young woman lamented softly, "It is so hard. So hard."

The next morning—Sunday, October 7—she was ready to talk.

Totally exhausted from a sleepless night of grief, and emotionally devastated by the loss of her beloved husband, she gave a full confession.

Yes, she was part of the conspiracy to smuggle in guns to Tex Walters.

Yes, Jim Sparks financed the plan and the two of them buried the guns under the Depot Bridge.

And yes, Andrew Hawkins was the trusty who was suppose to

take them in.

She finished the long, detailed written account by concluding, "I do not want anybody to think that I am shifting the responsibility to anyone else and am ready and willing to share my part of the burden. I feel that I have done no more than any wife would and should do toward their husband."

With her shining star fallen from the night sky, her purpose in life was gone, and she had no desire to carry on the deception.

Immediately the Louisville authorities telephoned Warden Chilton and read the written confession to him. It basically corroborated the bits and pieces of information he and his staff had put together.

On Monday morning warrants were taken against Lillian Walters, Cellond Henry Knudson a/k/a Jim Sparks, and Andrew Hawkins for aiding and abetting in the murder of the three prison guards.

Hawkins, after escaping, had simply vanished from the face of the earth.

Sparks had also disappeared. But he then did something which was incredibly stupid. He wrote Lillian a letter and also sent her a telegram at the Louisville jail. To the astonishment of all, the correspondence included his return address.

Sparks was hiding out in Guthrie Center, Iowa at the home of Tex Walters' mother.

After recovering from the initial surprise of their unbelievable good fortune, Kentucky law enforcement immediately sent warrants to the "Hawkeye State" and the fugitive was swept into the slammer. Tex had been right in not giving Knudson-Sparks much credit in the brains department.

The little town of Eddyville began to settle back to normal, glad to be out of the media spotlight and back to its bucolic existence of barking dogs and friendly neighbors. School resumed on Monday. But still very much on the minds of everyone, was the Tex Walters bloody ordeal. Citizens of this river town and its sister hamlet of Kuttawa, two miles away, followed closely the dramatic follow-up investigation.

For days after the epoch struggle came to an end, over six thousand people from the region were allowed to tour and view for themselves the war-torn dining hall. Young and old alike were escorted onto the prison yard, and up the broad steps to top floor where they viewed in wonder and amazement all of the devastation. This parade of fascinated visitors only served to lionize even more the already billowing legend of Tex Walters.

With Walters gone from life, if not fame, public attention concentrated on his beleaguered widow, now charged with being an accomplice to commit murder. People were captivated by the dramatic story of a pretty, young wife attempting to free her man from the penitentiary. Yet at the same time, the public conscience was seared by the tragic loss of three, good, family men as victims of the lethal conspiracy.

So there was a peculiar sense of both infatuation and rage hovering over the community as the Lillian Walters story unfolded. The murder charges leveled against her aroused even more both the public's interest and the demand for vengeance.

By the first Monday in December, people had finally begun to talk about other things. On that day almost a hundred solid citizens of Lyon County—all male of course—gathered at the court house in Eddyville to begin the term of circuit court.

Everyone knew what the big item on the docket would be. There was hardly a one of them who had not followed the October uprising closely in the weekly *Lyon County Herald*. While many would not admit to it, most believed that "the woman had something to do with it" and she should pay the piper.

A grand jury was impanelled by Circuit Judge Charles H. Bush. Commonwealth Attorney James H. Coleman of Murray, Kentucky, and local prosecutor Coleman Molloy, Sr. presented the rather intricate case against Lillian Walters to the grand jury. On December 4, three separate indictments were returned against her charging her with "accessory before the fact to willful murder" of each of the three prison guards. The maximum penalty was death. Indictments were also returned against Sparks and Hawkins.

The completion of the grand jury's work set the stage for a life and death struggle between the Commonwealth of Kentucky and Lillian Walters. This punishing bout of high drama would consist of three rounds.

ROUND ONE

The court system of rural Kentucky in 1923 was drastically different from what it is today.

It was a much simpler time. Dockets were not wallowing near the water line from an overload of civil cases. Most people who got married, stayed that way. No one sued the faithful family doctor. The lucrative and contentious litigation of products liability, negligence claims, and insurance battles was for the most part, still a ways down the road.

In most county court houses, criminal matters made up the lion's share of the action. Without the bulging dockets and critical need for calendar space, there was very little need for plea bargaining. The defendant was either guilty as charged, or not guilty, and a jury decided. Consequently most criminal cases were tried.

Also, when the circuit court came to town for a designated term, the lawyers tried cases one after the other. It was not unusual for the court to have one jury in deliberation, while seating another one for the next encounter.

Judge Charles Bush of Christian County presided over a circuit of Calloway, Christian, Lyon, and Trigg counties. While the automobile had come of age—honking and sputtering gamely in competition with the steam engine for transportation—trains were still the most dependable means of travel. Rural roads were poorly maintained, consisting mostly of dirt and gravel. These motoring avenues were reduced to mud bogs in the winter and trails of dust in the summer. And the automobile of 1923, although much improved, was still a mechanical throw of the dice. You expected trouble, and you got it. It might make it, and it might not. In far west Kentucky, highway bridges across the abundant supply of rivers and streams were few and far between.

All of this is to say, that when the circuit court came to town, it usually stayed. The circuit judge, commonwealth attorneys, and even some of the other lawyers would put up in the local hotel for the duration. They would only go home on weekends, and during unexpected lulls in the court's activities.

So it was not surprising nor unusual when the indictment charging Lillian Walters with aiding and abetting the murder of Hodge Cunningham was set for jury trial on Monday, December 10—within a week from when the grand jury returned the indictment.

Since Lillian was in jail, an early trial date was expected. Prosecutors, defense lawyers, judge, and witnesses were all ready to go.

But they were doubtful that a jury from Lyon County could be seated to hear the case. Most court officials believed that the sensational publicity given to the Tex Walters revolt and his wife's involvement, as well as the deaths of three guards, would make it impossible to find twelve men in the community who had not formulated an opinion as to the guilt of the defendant.

Nevertheless, Judge Bush decided to give it try and not move the case to another county until the jury panel was exhausted.

It was a mild winter morning on December 10, when the huge crowd of jurors, lawyers, reporters, witnesses and spectators began to swarm over the court house grounds. The day was sunny, and the temperature would edge up close to fifty degrees. Excitement ran at a fever pitch as the mass of people jostled through the two entrances and made their way upstairs to the court room.

The handsome two-story, brick court house hung onto the side of Penitentiary Hill. Less than eight years old, the building fronted the main drag—called Water Street—which fell off steeply into the business district of town. Most of the parking was on an adjoining side street from which a long and challenging flight of steps led up the side of the hill and into the building.

It was three doors down from the prison.

The court room was large. Like most trial arenas of that day—when legal battles were great entertainment—most of the room was taken up by seats for spectators. Fashionable wooden seats—theater type—provided for a large gallery, which was divided from the litigation area by a wooden rail. The well of the court was so small that both parties to the action and their lawyers sat at the same big wooden table.

Tall windows at the back of the court room, opposite from the bench, looked out over the diminutive skyline of downtown Eddyville and the gray Cumberland River which slid silently by.

At 9 a.m. Judge Bush called the case of *Commonwealth of Kentucky vs. Lillian Walters,* and both sides announced ready.

The sixty-seven year old jurist was a man of impeccable integrity and a pleasant personality. As a practicing attorney he had been one of the more respected stalwarts of his profession in the west Kentucky area. Bush was not new to highly visible and emotionally charged criminal cases. He had only been on the bench for a short time when his mettle was severely tested.

On December 9, 1916, a black man by the name of Lube Martin shot and killed the popular Murray city police chief, Guthrie Diuguid. The community was enraged, and when Martin was arrested in Tennessee he was taken to the Hopkinsville jail for safe keeping. Such turmoil was generated by the killing that Judge Bush called a special term of circuit court for January 8, 1917. After the defendant was indicted for murder, he was brought back to Murray for arraignment and a trial date set for February. Bush ordered Martin returned to Hopkinsville until the trial.

Feelings were running so high against the accused murderer that a mob of over 500 assembled outside the Calloway County court house demanding that the judge rescind the transfer order, and leave Martin in the local jail. Obviously a lynching was in the making.

The unruly crowd became loud and angry, hurling threats against Judge Bush that if Martin was moved out of town, they would hang the judge. As the elderly man bravely made his way from the court house to the New Murray Hotel where he was staying during the term of court, he was pushed and shoved by the jeering crowd.

But he stuck to his guns. Martin went back to Hopkinsville and Governor A. O. Stanley rode into town on a special train the next morning and addressed the large gathering which was still clamoring for blood.

Calm was restored and the crisis passed. Judge Bush decried that "this demonstration was a shame and disgrace to this community and is lamented by all thinking people."

Lube Martin was tried by a Christian County jury and found guilty of murder. On July 25, 1919, he was executed in the electric chair only a short walk up the hill from where Judge Charles Bush now opened up the case against Lillian Walters.

The court was called to order by the bailiff and the judge settled into his hefty chair behind the bench. Having stood with the entry of Judge Bush, the large crowd sat down and became quiet.

Then a noticeable stir rippled through the gathering as the one-armed Lyon County Sheriff, Nath Murray, entered through the side door with his prisoner—dazzling Lillian.

Necks craned, and bodies leaned to get a look at the star of the show and the one most of them had read so much about.

She did not disappoint them. Tastefully dressed in black, she was nevertheless adorned in the latest fashion. A ribbon around her neck held a pendant at the waist. Her resplendent brown hair was cut short and swirled to one side. A full-bodied wave fell down around her right eye, flapper style. The oval face was expertly made up, accentuating her high cheek bones and flashing brown eyes. Her tall, lithe figure glided gracefully across the floor.

She stood out in the drab court room and amidst the gray congregation of country folk like a sparkling light.

Young boys who were there would someday, as old men, shake their heads slowly, and with narrowing eyes softly remember, "She was a good looking woman." Young girls who were there would someday as old women recall, "she was beautiful and all dressed up in the finest fashion—like no one we had ever seen."

From the time the defendant appeared in the court room, trailed by her entourage of respectable friends from Paducah, the prosecution had a formidable problem. It would be extremely difficult to make the dastardly charge of murder match the appearance of Lillian Walters.

She appeared, as one newspaper reported, "a pretty young widow in mourning." Her good looks was the kind that appealed to the men, without offending the women. Older men saw her as the lovely daughter they never had. Younger males saw her as the stylish wife of their dreams. And it was the style, devoid of cheap volup-tuousness or pretense, which gained the respect of the hand full of women looking on that December morning.

She took her seat at the large wooden table along with her attorney, Charles C. Grassham of Paducah, retained and paid for by her friends and supporters there. Several of them—Rev. J. R. Crawford and his wife, Minnie Boyd, and social worker Alice Compton—were at her side for moral support. Lillian had been lodged in the Paducah jail because there were no accommodations for female prisoners in the rickety and grimy old Lyon County stockade.

Across the table from the widow of Tex Walters sat the prose-cutors, Commonwealth Attorney James Coleman and County Attorney Coleman Molloy, Sr. At their side sat Emma Cunningham. She too was in black, with a long dark coat and ebony hat.

If the defendant distracted the crowd from the grim business they were about, the wife of Hodge Cunningham reminded everyone that this was a murder trial and a life—father, husband—had been taken. Lillian Walters—still a few days short of her twenty-second birthday—had been the object of attention from her friends and keep-ers while awaiting trial. On the other hand, Emma Cunningham, the forty-three-year-old mother of two, had grappled with the hard and lonely reality of both grieving and making a life for herself and two small sons.

It had not been easy. Her clothes were old and worn. She wore no makeup and her appearance was that of a poor widow striving to survive, rather than to look good.

Emma's stare alternated from the table top into the eyes of the other widow a mere arm's reach away. The contrast between the two was dramatic, and the assemblage chose to avoid the messenger of death, and cast its gaze upon the vibrant beauty of young Lillian.

Also at the table that morning—following with wide eyes the strange and somber business about him—was little Mitch Cunningham, sitting in his mother's lap.

After each side announced ready the long tedious jury selection process began. A certain number was called for questioning. First the court, then the lawyers plied the panel with questions, attempting to ascertain if any harbored preconceived notions or opinions which would keep them from being fair and impartial.

It was during this stage when the Commonwealth conveyed the heavy news that it was seeking the death penalty for Mrs. Walters. A slight murmur passed through the crowd as the dreadful potential was made known. If the defense had a challenging chore of finding jurors without opinions as to their client's guilt, the prosecution had to find a "death qualified" dozen men to hear the case.

By mid-morning—and to most people's surprise—it appeared that they were going to get a Lyon County jury to try the case. Most of those being lost were being struck by the Commonwealth for either not believing in the death penalty, or being unable to sentence a woman to the penitentiary. Most of those having opinions about the guilt or innocence of the defendant, nevertheless cleared the hurdle by insisting they could put aside these feelings and give a verdict based solely on the evidence presented.

By 2:45 in the afternoon, a jury of 12 Lyon County farmers was accepted by both the Commonwealth and the defense. They were all married and averaged thirty-five years of age. After a short recess, the case began.

County Attorney Coleman Molloy, Sr. made the opening statement for the state, outlining the evidence he believed would make Lillian Walters guilty of accessory before the fact to commit the murder of Hodge Cunningham and deserving of being put to death.

It was never revealed, and it would forever puzzle lawyers and court followers, as to why the Commonwealth obtained three separate indictments against Lillian Walters. She could have been charged with three separate counts of murder on one indictment and tried in a single trial. It would have saved the state the extra expense and time of three separate prosecutions. Also with each trial and all of its accompanying publicity, it would be more and more difficult to seat a jury.

It's a puzzle, which time and study have not resolved.

The crowd became especially attentive when Lillian's lawyer stood to give his opening statement. That she had made a full confession to her involvement was public knowledge. All were curious as to what her defense could possibly be.

Charles Grassham was an impressive sight. Heavy set and round faced, he was graced with splendid white hair and a large silver moustache. He had been general counsel for the well known Ayer-Lloyd Tie Company of Chicago, one of the nation's premier makers of railroad ties. After leaving that prestigious position to return to his hometown of Paducah, he quickly established a reputation as an outstanding trial lawyer. Courtly, and dramatic, he was known as being short on the law, long on theatrics.

His personal life was also colorful. He was a heavy drinker. When he was not in court, he could usually be found in his office in the afternoon downing good Kentucky bourbon. By the close of the day his black butler would have to help him home. Although married, he was correctly labeled as an aggressive womanizer, quick to assess the looks of his female clients without much regard to the fee. Lillian filled the bill in this department, so it did not take much convincing by his friends at the Settlement House to take her case.

Lillian Walters was a fine woman, Grassham would contend, whose only fault was total devotion to her husband. He went on to paint Tex Walters as a brilliant devil, a hardened criminal with the wiles of a wizard. His weak-willed wife had been duped by him, and had suffered failing health through most of the marriage. This weakened her further until she became susceptible, not only to his art of hypnosis, but to his total control. In short, she was under his spelll and incapable of resisting his instructions.

Lillian looked on impassively.

Then the prosecution began to put on its case.

Inmate witnesses were called to tell of the activities leading up to the bloody revolt—-Hawkins bringing in the dirty shirts wrapped around something heavy; Walters and Ferland meeting in the laundry. Some told of seeing Lawrence Griffith fire the fatal bullets into Hodge Cunningham. Prison doctor D. J. Travis told the jury that Cunningham died from gunshot wounds to the chest. Emma dabbed at her tearful eyes as the account of her husband's murder was given.

Prison chief engineer Charlie Collier told of seeing Griffith and Walters together on the day of the killings in the prison barber shop. Next was officer R. L. "Daddy" Scoles who related being jumped and tied up in the basement of the shirt factory, his gun taken.

On and on went the damning evidence of the prosecution, to include the close relationship of Walters and his wife.

"He bragged that she would do anything he wanted her to do," reported inmate J. C. Willard.

Judge Bush recessed the court at 5:30 for supper, and began the night session at 7 o'clock. Not a seat was deserted, as the darkness settled in around the windows.

Captain Radford, commanding officer of the National Guard units, took the stand. It quickly became apparent—to his embarrassment—that his troops had made a total mess of collecting the evidence after the dining hall was taken.

During the course of ransacking the large dining room, soldiers had taken valuable evidence as souvenirs. For days after the siege was broken, the prison administration had hounded Radford to track down the guns which had been taken, and return them for future prosecution. Some of the items—such as Tex's watch—were never recovered. The pistols were finally recovered, and now they were introduced into evidence through the witness as being those found in the hands of the dead inmates when his troops arrived at their sides.

The two revolvers—the .38 caliber taken from Scoles, and the

32-20 police Colt brought into the prison laundry—were shown to the jury and then laid on the table.

Lillian ignored them, while Emma stared sadly at the instruments of death. Mitch reached out and touched the soft cloth in which they had been wrapped, and ran his small hand across the shiny surface of the revolvers.

A surge of anticipation ran through the crowd during the night session when the Commonwealth called Jim Sparks to the stand. Not surprising to the lawyers however, he took the Fifth Amendment on each and every question thrown at him by County Attorney Coleman Molloy. Finally the prosecutor waved him off the stand. It was an old prosecutorial trick employed in those days. Make the witness look guilty in front of the jury and some of his criminality will splatter onto the defendant.

Finishing up the evening of testimony were witnesses from Louisville telling about Lillian's arrest and interrogation. Police detective William Oeltjen read the confession made by Mrs. Walters at the Jefferson County jail.

With this climatic and incriminating statement falling upon the ears of the jurors, the curtain came down at 9:30 p.m. on the first day of trial. A sizable gathering which had swelled even more during the evening session, shuffled quietly out of the court room and into the night. It had been a good show, and the theater crowd eagerly anticipated the defense side of the case to begin the next day.

Judge Bush called the attorneys and Sheriff Murray to the bench. He directed that Mrs. Walters be put up in a local hotel for the night.

The prosecution's case had been damning and convincing. However there was a noticeable pattern which had developed during the first stage of the trial. Most all of Judge Bush's rulings had gone in favor of the defendant.

He sustained the defense motion to exclude any evidence coming in as to the killing of the other two guards. With the exception of recovery of the murder weapon, he even prohibited from jury consideration information about the siege. Only evidence leading up to and including the shooting of Hodge Cunningham was ruled admissible.

Also the circuit judge suppressed oral statements made by the defendant in the 2 a.m. interrogation in which she talked about her financial dealings with Jim Sparks. He declared that the admission was extracted in violation of the state's "anti-sweating" statute. This was merely a sop for the defense however, as that information was also included in the written statement taken later and which was admitted.

And there were other lessor objections to which Judge Bush

gave the nod to the defendant. At one time the judge warned the Commonwealth Attorney that he was attempting to introduce too much information that was irrelevant. The veteran prosecutors secretly hoped that his honor had not become another victim of the young lady's charm.

Undoubtedly the first day of the trial had been an agonizing twelve hours for the two widows at center stage. Both seared from the tragic developments which one of them had helped bring about; they confronted each other with only the width of the counsel table separating them. What thoughts were exchanged during this dramatic encounter is of course not known. Mrs. Cunningham—old enough to be the mother of the lovely girl across from her—stared often into the eyes of young Lillian as if searching for an answer to her torment. The younger showed no emotions and avoided locking eyes with the lonely mother.

At 10:30 the next morning the Commonwealth rested its case.

The first witness for the defense was Lillian Walters.

To a hushed crowd, she softly gave her name and began her testimony. Every head in the court room, including Judge Bush and the twelve men of the jury, bent forward to catch every word.

Attorney Grassham gently led her through her early years in New Castle, Indiana where she was raised by good parents in humble surroundings. She was forced to quit school at 11 in order to work as a waitress and contribute to the income of her family.

It was a story of poverty and hard work—a familiar topic for the twelve Lyon County farmers.

Bowing her head and lowering her voice even more, she told—with just the right amount of embarrassment—of her brief marriage to a soldier who left her the day after their marriage and ended up in Leavenworth prison.

At age 16, she met Monte Walters who was a mechanic, boarding in their home. They were married and lived together for three years and three months before he was sent to the penitentiary. Grassham gingerly avoided asking her about their rowdy and lawless lifestyle.

Then she began to describe the mystic personality of Tex Walters.

He was a student of hypnotism and had put her under a trance about six times. The first time under hypnosis, she was able to see their baby, which had died six days after it was born.

Grassham let the words hang in the air as a strange chill ran through the stuffy court room.

Lillian proceeded to calmly tell of her undying love and devotion for her husband. Grassham painfully extracted from her in bits and pieces the transcendental mind control her lover exercised over her will.

Finally, she got into her confession, which she generally repeated. She believed Tex when he told her that they intended to go up the drain pipe and over the death house and use the guns only for self-protection after they got out. Looking at last into the eyes of Emma Cunningham, she concluded her testimony by swearing that she never knew that the guns would be used to kill prison guards.

Commonwealth Attorney James Coleman could do very little with the witness on cross-examination. After all, she admitted everything. Everything but a culpable state of mind. After a while the state's lawyer gave up and sat down.

Court was recessed for lunch.

The most dramatic moments of the entire trial occurred over the noon break and by pure coincidence.

Lillian was being brought back to the court room by Sheriff Murray and several of her friends from Paducah. As they reached the top of the stairs leading to the second floor, Emma Cunningham walked out of the court room door. There at the top of the steps they met face to face. After a brief moment of awkward silence, Emma stepped forward and held out her hand.

"Mrs. Walters," she spoke somberly as the surrounding throng looked on breathlessly, "I want you to know that I forgive you for all that has happened. I do not think you knew what you were doing."

Lillian took her hand and sobbed.

Then, in a lowered voice, as if thinking to herself, Emma lamented, "But oh why did you do it?"

The women exchanged a few more words, and Lillian passed on into the court room. It had been a magnanimous gesture on the part of the prison guard's widow. In their own way and as far as was possible under the circumstances, the two embattled women came to terms with each other.

Throughout the afternoon Charles Grassham put on several witnesses who told of the close relationship between Lillian and Tex and of his charismatic and dominating personality. Character witnesses from Paducah testified as to both Lillian's good traits, and her "insane love" for Tex. Said Nannie Boyd, "she wrote to him every day even when he was in solitary confinement after his first attempt to escape from the penitentiary, when she could only send him two letters a month."

The twelve husbands in the jury box listened attentively. Before them as an exhibit they had the written confession wherein Lillian had proclaimed, "I only did what any wife would or should do for their husband."

One of the most interesting witnesses for the day was Dr. W. J. Bass of Paducah. He described hypnotism as an acknowledged, though feared, field of science by the medical profession. The physician gave the opinion that it would have been very possible for Walters to control his wife by the sheer strength of his will, even to the point of doing something she knew was wrong.

The prosecution objected to the testimony, and their protestation was overruled by Judge Bush. He was undoubtedly aware of a man from within his own hometown of Hopkinsville who was, during that very time, doing some amazing things while under hypnotic trance. The person's name was Edgar Cayce.

In the late afternoon the defense completed its case and the attorneys made their closing arguments.

Typical of such events of that time, both lawyers put on quite a show.

Here's the account the *Paducah News-Democrat* gave of Grassham's summation:

> "Silence fell over the court room as Mr. Grassham began his speech for the defense, and only once did Judge Bush rap for order. Occasionally a spectator would stand up in his seat to see the prisoner, and when the attorney scored a particular strong point every face in the room was turned toward the accused woman."

Bellowed the Paducah lawyer with a flourish, "Tex Walters was a criminal so black he would have been a Beelzebub in a crowd of demons and whose hypnotic influence over his wife made her as helpless in his hands as a child in the hands of its parents."

At one point the eloquent attorney referred to Lillian's work with needy children at the Settlement House in Paducah. He told of how she helped give these poor children a second chance. She now deserved a second chance. One of the leathery-faced and toughened farmers was seen wiping a tear from his eye.

It was, by all reports, a moving oration.

Prosecutor Jim Coleman was equally up to the challenge. He lashed into the pretty defendant, claiming that her attractive facade harbored a deliberate and sinister criminal. "Mrs. Walters is a criminal blacker than even Tex," the Commonwealth Attorney insisted, "and has more brains and will power than her husband ever had."

Then with an exaggerated snarl he pointed his finger at the willowy brunette and exclaimed, "there sits the greatest murderess in Kentucky today!"

For the first time during the closing arguments Lillian showed some response by simply dropping her eyes.

At 5:30 on Tuesday afternoon, the case went to the jury.

They took with them written instructions which had been read to them by Judge Bush just before the closing arguments.

Jury instructions are prepared by the judge, with input from the lawyers and are supposed to relate to the jury the law as it pertains to the case. The panel is sworn to comply with the legal precepts enunciated as they apply to the evidence submitted.

Judge Bush, over strenuous and prolonged objections by the Commonwealth, had given the defendant an early Christmas present.

First of all, realizing that the jury of good-hearted, country people might have trouble sending a pretty young woman to the electric chair or even life in the penitentiary, the prosecutors asked for a "lessor included." That is a legal term for a crime which is less serious than the one charged, but encompasses some of the same misconduct. And of course the penalty for a "lessor included" is not as harsh. The state requested an instruction by which the jury would have the option of finding the defendant guilty of a "lessor include"—in this case, accessory before the fact to the crime of escape. It carried a maximum of five years in the penitentiary.

Judge Bush declined the request, giving the jury only the choice between murder or not guilty. And if murder—death in the electric chair or life in prison. It is in many cases a roll of the dice. In this one, defense lawyer Charles Grassham looked like the cat that had swallowed the canary. They all knew it would make it doubly hard for the jury to convict.

The second bonus the normally astute jurist gave the defendant was that he clearly misstated the law.

Again over the Commonwealth's jumping-up-and-down objections, Judge Bush told the jury that in order for them to find Mrs. Walters guilty of accessory to commit murder, they had to believe beyond a reasonable doubt that she knew the weapons were going to be used for that crime. He totally ignored the principle of "felony murder." Lillian Walters did not have to know that murder was going to be committed with the gun she helped smuggle into the penitentiary. If it could have been reasonably anticipated that murder would be necessary in carrying out the escape, then she would be criminally responsible for the killing. It was no defense that murder was not a part of the original conspiracy.

It was an incredible ruling. It was made even more amazing by the realization that most judicial "errors" made in highly publicized trials where public sentiment runs against the accused, are usually made on behalf of the state. No one was saying that Lillian had once again cast her spell. But people thought it.

The jury began its deliberation with a prayer. They then elected preacher J. L. Wall as foreman. Throughout the evening they debated in the small room off to the side. At times their voices would rise loud enough to be heard by the crowd still assembled in the court room. One time, and to the astonishment of the gathering, there was a burst of laughter.

Close to 10 o'clock Judge Bush called them back in. After an admonition not to discuss the case with anyone, he sent them home for the night. He directed that the large gathering remain seated until the jury was out of the court house.

The second long day of the trial came to an end. Lillian Walter's fate now rested in the hands of twelve men asleep at home with their wives.

At 8:30 the next morning, Wednesday, December 12, the jury reconvened and continued their deliberation. By noon the crowd had thinned out considerably and the lawyers and judge began to talk regrettably of a possible hung jury.

The jury took a break at noon. After eating, they returned to their work. Into the afternoon they deliberated.

In the court room Lillian Walters sat calmly with great poise. At least one of her Paducah friends was at her side at all times. Emma's kin sat with her. Little Mitch and his older brother Perry grew restless and were finally taken home by a relative.

At four o'clock in the afternoon Judge Bush called the jury in. They appeared haggard and tired. In response to the judge's question, Foreman Wall announced that the jury was hopelessly hung. They were sent back for further deliberation. But after conferring with the attorneys, Judge Bush called them back in thirty minutes. The split was too wide. No chance for a verdict.

Reluctantly the judge declared a mistrial, thanked them and sent the jury home.

Charles Grassham immediately asked that a bond be set for his client. Judge Bush granted the request and set bail at $2,000 on each indictment. Lillian's friends were confident they could raise the amount when they returned to Paducah.

A May date was set for the retrial, and Sheriff Murray stepped up to escort his prisoner back to the Paducah jail. Lillian walked up to the bench and extended her hand to Judge Bush and thanked him for giving her a fair trial. A touch of class from the working girl.

Emma Cunningham, tired and exhausted, and faced with the dark prospects of doing it all again, gathered herself together, thanked the attorneys for the prosecution and stoically walked out of the court room, flanked by a bevy of kin.

Packaged in contrasting coverings—one in gold and the other in lead—the two widows of different worlds shared one common trait. Both women were hanging tough.

The first round had been a draw.

ROUND TWO

Western Kentucky is a soft and rolling land, supplied by an abundance of resourceful streams and rivers. Spring transforms it each year from hardwood skeletons and meadows of sear into lush foliage and meadow carpets of green. Neighbors, seemingly just beyond the curtilage disappear behind hedgerows and ballooning trees. Tobacco plant beds, with their canvas coverings, dot the countryside. Fields are laid open to the glorious sun.

It is a time of both renewal and change. It becomes almost unrecognizable from its drab winter dress.

As the trial date of May 8, 1924, arrived, the same parties returned to the Lyon County court house to retry the case of Lillian Walters. But just as the change in season had cloaked the surrounding country side with a different look, so would the second trial take on a personality of its own.

First of all, the prison guards at the penitentiary and the family of Emma Cunningham had hired a special prosecutor to head up the second round.

He was Denny Smith, former Commonwealth Attorney of the same judicial district.

Smith, who had lived in Cadiz, had a reputation as a tough prosecutor, but ran into a bramble bush politically during the days of the renown Night Riders between 1904-09. This violent and militant band of farmers had taken up arms against the strangling monopoly of the American Tobacco Company. Their clandestine activities had become so widespread that many reputable and upstanding citizens belonged to their order. These included the sheriff of Lyon County, and—Commonwealth Attorney Denny Smith. The district's leading law enforcer protected the Night Riders from prosecution. That is until their cause ran out of steam and they began losing their power.

Then Denny Smith, in an effort to buoy his chances for his candidacy for state's attorney general, turned on his former confederates and prosecuted their leader Dr. David Amoss in 1911. Amoss was acquitted, Smith's political fortunes plummeted, and he withdrew from the state-wide race.

Ironically the defense lawyer for Dr. Amoss in that celebrated trial was none other than the then sitting jurist—Charles H. Bush.

Now Smith was back, and three prosecutors would take on the dandy Charles Grassham.

May the 8th fell on a Thursday. A garden-variety embezzlement case started on Wednesday had continued over. So the court room was full, all the players were present, to sit by and watch the theft case wrap up. It was like a warm up feature performance prior to the main event. The lessor case and it's lawyers were even mentioned in the newspapers—a little extra for being on the same show bill.

Judge Bush also decided to take the time to summons extra jurors. He and the lawyers were again doubtful of securing a jury in Lyon County—especially after having already gone through one highly-publicized trial only five months before. Sheriff Murray and his deputies went out into the far reaches of the county to supplement the panel.

Lillian once again caused a stir as she arrived in the court room that morning from Paducah. She had not been able to make the bond, so she had remained in jail. It had not been wasted time. She had charmed her keepers, been given many special privileges, and had bagged Jailer S. B. Gott to add to her growing list of character witnesses.

She still wore black for the occasion, this time with a hat and veil. It partially concealed her pretty face, but also added to her enchantment.

While waiting for the arrival of more jurors, Judge Bush took up some minor whiskey cases.

At mid-morning a burst of excitement erupted in the court room. Louis Manger, father of Lillian Walters, and a car load of friends from New Castle, Indiana arrived on the scene. Lillian was ecstatic and overcome with emotion.

It had been a back-breaking journey. Manger, a Salvation Army captain, was accompanied by two other Salvation workers, and two children. They had made the twelve-hour trip by automobile, having slid over an embankment once, and experienced numerous break downs along muddy roads. The group was decked out in full Salvation Army regalia, lending a bizarre and colorful touch to the drab courtroom. Lillian's mother was ill and unable to make the trek to be by her daughter's side. The friends would begin their return trip later that day. Her father would remain by her side for the duration.

Jury selection began in the early afternoon. It was slow going.

One after another reported that they had already formed an opinion about the guilt or innocence of Lillian Walters. One got the feeling that this trial was going to be tougher and meaner. By late afternoon, eighty-four citizens of Lyon County had been examined and all but thirteen had been excused for cause. At least twenty-five jurors were required to be qualified from which both sides could make their peremptory strikes.

As the day drew to a weary close, the jury pool was depleted. Judge Bush then ordered that forty veniremen from adjoining Caldwell County be summoned into court the next morning to supplement those already tested. With that decree, court was adjourned. Lillian, with her father and Paducah friends, was allowed to retire to a local hotel. The court house emptied, as lawyers, witnesses, and spectators dispersed into the spring dusk.

Caldwell and Lyon counties were—and still are—more than just neighboring communities. They share a common origin. Up until 1854 they were one county with Eddyville as the capital. That year Lyon split off and Princeton became the county seat of Caldwell. The two towns were only 12 miles apart. Commerce of the two political subdivisions intermingled, farms crisscrossed county boundaries, and many Lyon Countians spent more time in Princeton than Eddyville or Kuttawa. A good number of Caldwell Countians worked at the penitentiary. Princeton had sent doctors to offer their assistance at the prison during the Tex Walters siege.

So when the forty men from Caldwell County—mostly young—arrived at the Lyon County court house that Friday morning, they did not feel like aliens. They were in well known surroundings and among friends and familiar faces. No doubt many of them were fully aware of the Tex Walters case.

That is why it came as a pleasant surprise when it took only an hour to get a jury. By 10 o'clock six Lyon countians and six Caldwell countians were in the box ready to go.

If any there in the overcrowded court room thought that this was going to be simply a rerun of the December contest, this notion was quickly doused when Cellond Knudson, now notoriously known as Jim Sparks, took the stand.

He looked entirely different. At the previous trial, he had appeared as a criminal—disheveled, and with a stubble of beard. Now he was all decked out in a nice suit of clothes, his face clean shaven and his hair neatly trimmed. Even though he had languished in the Lyon County jail since his arrest, the young 19 year old could have passed as some clean cut student off a college campus.

It was apparent to all that the Commonwealth had sharpened

up their knives for this rematch.

Unlike his first time on the stand, Sparks—who was represented by counsel—did not hide behind his Fifth Amendment rights. He testified candidly and openly. Casting his eyes periodically at the pretty widow who looked on without expression, the ex-con laid out the whole conspiracy. Under the guidance of Denny Smith he especially elaborated on the deep involvement of Mrs. Monte Walters.

Sparks spoke so low that ears in the back of the court room strained to hear over the sound of the spring rain which began to patter against the windows.

At about the time the court house crowd poured out of the building for the noon recess on one side of Penitentiary Hill, a truck bearing three rough boxes rambled down the other side, heading for the depot. The coffins contained the bodies of Frank Thomas, George Weick and Charles Miller—all executed in the electric chair at the prison just after midnight. Thomas, age 71, earned the dubious distinction of being the oldest man ever executed in Kentucky. The remains were on the way to the railway station to be shipped home to their families for burial.

The prosecution pushed on with their case in the Friday afternoon session. Incriminating evidence seeped into every nook and corner of the court room. Seemingly, beginning with Sparks, the government's presentation was much stronger than it was in December. It was as if the dress rehearsal had ironed out all the kinks.

Also unlike the first trial, Emma Cunningham took the stand. She had discarded her mourning clothes, but still cut a very sympathetic figure. Both of her young boys were in the court room with her, as she briefly told of her dead husband to a hushed gathering. Her testimony was genuine, straight forward and poignant, but without apparent rancor—very effective.

At last the Commonwealth closed out its case just after dark, and the court was adjourned until the next morning.

As if the avalanche of damning testimony was not enough for defense lawyer Grassham to contend with, Judge Bush made it even worse. He reversed his ruling in the previous trial and now held that evidence as to hypnotism as practiced upon Lillian would not be admissible. It, in the judge's opinion, was not a field of knowledge which had been commonly accepted in the scientific community.

The seasoned Paducah lawyer adeptly shifted gears, and beginning through his cross examination of prosecution witnesses, attempted to shift the blame from his client to the prison administration. Through his questioning, he was able to paint a picture of Tex Walters as a dangerous inmate and an extreme security risk. He tried to show that far too little attention was given to him and Andrew Hawkins by the prison authorities, and that this negligence by the state employees had contributed greatly to the introduction of the contraband weapon.

This road was blocked however, as Judge Bush sustained prosecution objections, and sternly reminded Grassham that his client—not the penitentiary officials—was on trial.

So Charles Grassham did what all good trial lawyers do when things are not going well. He kept his cool, showed no signs of distress, and pressed on, waiting hopefully for the breaks to come.

A steady rain which had been falling since dawn was just letting up when Judge Bush reconvened court on Saturday morning. The sun broke through when Lillian Walters rose from her chair and took the oath to testify in defense of her life.

Her lawyer hoped that it was an omen.

The widow in black seemed to speak with more emotion in her voice this time around. She repeated all of the personal background given in the first trial. Then looking at her father tenderly, she added that as a little girl she had played the tambourine in his Salvation Army band.

There is that warm feeling which comes to the heart of a trial lawyer when he first senses that his client is going to shine. Charles Grassham had that feeling.

While she was not allowed to report the hypnosis under which Tex placed her from time to time, Lillian did relate once again his indescribable charisma and the powerful sway he held over her. With the choking emotion of a concerned wife, she emphasized her trepidation upon his being wounded in his escape attempt at Eddyville, and how she begged him never to try it again. Squeezing the embroidered handkerchief between her hands, Mrs. Walters softly but solidly drove home the repeated assurances Tex made to her that the guns would not be used against prison guards. They were going up the drainage pipe and over the death house, Tex insisted.

When Charles Grassham passed the witness, an admiring murmur went through the crowd and the spectators shifted in their seats. She had been terrific.

But hard-nosed Denny Smith was not taken in. He tore into the lovely accused with a vengeance.

He began picking apart her background, especially her days with Tex—hinting strongly that she was a part of his criminal shenanigans. Finally he asked her point blank, "Did you take part in the murder of the Jefferson County milkman?"

Grassham leaped through the ceiling. He objected loudly, yelling and stomping around the table demanding a mistrial. Judge

Bush finally calmed the defense lawyer and angrily admonished the prosecutor not to pursue that line of questioning.

Undaunted, Smith turned to other matters. He pressed the witness on some weaknesses in her story. "What would he want with the pistols if he wasn't going to use them?" he inquired.

She answered by saying that Walters intended to use them when he got outside.

"What would he want to use them for when he got out?" the special prosecutor asked incredulously.

"I don't know," she replied and dropped her head.

The cross-examiner challenged every thing she had done in carrying out the conspiracy, to which she repeatedly responded, "Because Mr. Walters told me to."

On and on it went, for an hour and a half, the fiery lawyer badgered, and attacked her at every turn. She became visibly shaken and distraught—even trembling at times underneath her dark cloak. At last, as the skies blackened and rain once again began to pound against the windows, the punishment ended. Rising slowly to leave the witness stand she staggered and swooned into the arms of her father. There was a buzz of excitement in the court room as Judge Bush immediately called a recess to give her a chance to recover.

Smith joined his fellow prosecutors with a triumphant look upon his face.

But most eyes in the court room were turned to the young daughter being held and caressed by her loving father. It was a poignant scene, and there were many who felt that the mercenary prosecutor had overdone it.

In most fields of battle, the combatants know how they are doing. In war, objectives are won or lost. In sporting events scores are kept. But in a criminal trial, experienced lawyers know—that they do not know. The inscrutable faces of jurors do not often give way their feelings, and when they do, it may only be a passing thought. Cases seeming to be going well may actually be going bad. The dynamics of a criminal trial are such that as self-assured and confident trial lawyers may appear—they are always unsure as to how they are doing. Like walking through a lightless room at night. One may think they are near the door, but they are still in the dark.

So brazen and bellicose Charles Grassham, in spite of all his bluster, felt uneasy about the fate of Lillian Walters. He knew that his client had been hammered pretty well. He was deeply concerned, as the defendant's character witnesses began to take the stand.

The defense lawyer—like the prosecutors—was too much enmeshed in the emotional roller coaster ride of the trial to have been able to notice a change in atmosphere within the Lyon County court room. Little did he notice that Lillian Walters was becoming a star.

From her initial entrance into the court room at the first trial when sentiment was clearly against the perceived murderess, feelings had begun to change. She soon began to take on the role of a soft, vulnerable underdog, fighting against the odds. Spectators imperceptibly began to nod approvingly with the defense, smile at Grassham's antics, and follow her movements in and out of the court room.

The dignified and respected Judge Bush began to show more than the usual courtly respect for the lady defendant. On one occasion he called a halt to the day's proceedings because "Mrs. Walters is getting tired." Over the months, court officials—especially Sheriff Murray and the McCracken county jailers—had actually become her friends, giving her many privileges and special treatment. Perhaps there was no more accurate reflection of the public mood than that of the news coverage of the trial. The newspaper accounts began to stray from the middle and give the pretty defendant favorable billing. More and more she was appearing as another victim of the manipulative and deadly leadership of Tex Walters.

But even if her defense lawyer was aware of this transformation, he knew that the only people who really counted were the twelve tough men in the box. And they only showed serious and intense interest in the proceedings.

Coming down to the end of the trial, Grassham groped for one last volley to hurl in Lillian's defense.

The last boost came from an unexpected source.

He called Tex Walters from the grave.

At the first trial the Commonwealth had failed to produce the farewell letter to Lillian found on Tex's body. This time Grassham had it.

Lillian sobbed softly as the tender epistle was read into evidence, the ears of the crowd straining to catch every single word. Its effect was both haunting and mesmerizing, as the actual words of the central figure were being heard for the first time.

The main letter had been neatly penned out in his cell prior to his coming out on that fateful morning. But added at the end was his last farewell, scribbled out in pencil while bleeding and dying on the dining room floor.

"I am wounded and surrounded by guards. . . ." read the note.

And then the ringing defense of his widowed wife, ". . . .I know you will be surprised."

It fell upon the gathering like a thunderbolt. It was true, just as she had related. He had promised to escape without shooting anyone.

Closing arguments were once again filled with sound and fury. Both Smith and Commonwealth Attorney Coleman doubled up for the state.

Grassham rose to his usual eloquence for the defense.

Arguing hard for conviction Denny Smith proclaimed that Lillian Walters' "hands are as black as Lady Macbeth's." He traced her travels with Jim Hawkins, and scoffed at her plead of ignorance to the intended use of the pistols. Her fainting spell during the trial was labeled as "a piece of superb acting."

Charles Grassham insisted that the last note of Tex Walters proved that she knew nothing of a conspiracy between the men to shoot their way out of prison. Calling Tex a desperate and powerful personality he asserted that "if he was feared so much that he could hold at bay an entire company of militia for three days, this girl could not be expected to combat his personality."

Lillian showed no emotion through the closing arguments until her lawyer made a reference to her baby which died shortly after birth. Then she wept, and tears also streamed down her father's face.

Grassham closed his argument on an emotional pitch, "send this girl's mother her daughter's freedom for a Mother's Day gift tomorrow."

It was almost 2 p.m. on Saturday afternoon when the jury arose, in the midst of an overflow court room, and retired to deliberate. Lawyers milled about the court house, but most of the mass gathering remained in their coveted spaces.

Less than two hours later there was a knock on the jury room door. They had a verdict.

The tension was electric as the twelve poker-faced men of Caldwell and Lyon counties slowly moved back into the jury box.

"Do you have a verdict Mr. Foreman?" the judge inquired.

"Yes sir," came the response.

"Hand it to the bailiff," he was told.

The deputy sheriff took the piece of paper and handed it to the judge. He peered down at the writing for a long silent moment. A heavy hush hovered over the large room, with only the sound of a distant whistle from the river drifting in through the open windows.

Then Judge Bush read the verdict, "We the jury find the defendant not guilty."

Thunderous applause broke out wall to wall. Friends and family jubilantly hurried to the side of Lillian Walters who had buried her face in her hands.

Judge Bush gaveled the buzzing congregation back to order.

He then thanked the jury for their service and discharged them, directing that everyone else in the court room remain in their seats until the panel had exited the room.

One by one, each of the rough hewn jurors filed by the table where Lillian Walters cried happily. Each stopped to shake her hand and bowed ever so slightly in the mannerly fashion of a country gentleman. They then moved out the side door, and dissolved back into the land of flowering dogwoods and emerald meadows.

ROUND THREE

If public sentiment had swung dramatically and surprisingly over to the side of Lillian Walters, it had not influenced Warden John Chilton, and Commonwealth Attorney James Coleman.

They still wanted blood.

And Judge Bush had once again put the prosecutors in a fit of rage by not giving a "lessor included" instruction. Most importantly he had repeated his erroneous instruction which ignored the "felony murder" law.

After the acquittal on the Hodge Cunningham indictment, Lillian's bond was set at $500 on each of the remaining indictments. It was posted by her lawyer Charles Grassham and McCracken County Jailer Sam Gott.

For the first time in seven months she had her freedom. After some fond farewells she went back to Indiana to visit her ailing mother. She then returned to Louisville , got a job as a waitress, and awaited the next trial.

The state lawyers were scratching their heads. They were still convinced that with the proper instructions to the jury they could get their conviction. In their zest for nailing the female defendant and her wily lawyer they had ignored one ancient reality of jury trials: in highly emotional type cases, juries will do what they want to do regardless of the charge from the judge. Many times the only part of the instructions they take seriously is the verdict form.

Nevertheless, with three good prison men dead and another wounded, the Commonwealth was not going to give up. They struck upon a clever idea.

They would appeal Judge Bush's ruling on the instructions in the Cunningham case, and if they were successful it would enhance their chances on the remaining indictments.

It was decided to "certify the law" to what was then Kentucky's highest tribunal—the Court of Appeals. In criminal cases, the

Commonwealth cannot have acquittals reversed on appeal. Lower court decisions can be appealed, however, in order that the law can be "certified" for future cases.

The prosecution of the future indictments was put on hold, while the state went to the Court of Appeals. Even then, it was a rather long and time-consuming process.

Not until the following December did the high court rule on the matter. It was good news for the Commonwealth.

"It is no defense," Chief Justice and future governor Flem Sampson wrote for the court, "that the crime of murder was not a part of the original conspiracy if the conspiracy had for its object the commission of some other felony, and the commission of which murder should have been reasonably anticipated." One can almost see the august court in Frankfort shaking their collective heads in holding that the instructions were erroneous. "The admitted facts are overwhelming against her. She confesses of the stint that she knew all about the conspiracy of her husband and other prisoners to break out and that her husband wanted the pistols brought to him before he attempted to make his escape. We examined the instruction with great care and have reached the conclusion that the facts upon which it is hypotheticated, if accepted, do not constitute a defense, but serve only as mitigating circumstances which the jury might take into consideration in fixing punishment."

The Commonwealth had its ruling. Encouraged, they obtained a trial date on the accessory to commit the murder of William Gilbert for May 7, 1925.

On that date lawyers for Lillian showed up in court without their client, asking for a continuance. Her attorneys now numbered three as J. B. Allensworth of Paducah, and Charles Wilson of Smithland had come aboard free of charge to assist Mr. Grassham. Lillian had returned to Paducah from Louisville three days before and was staying at the Settlement House. According to the affidavits of two Paducah doctors she was ill and would not be able to come to court.

The Commonwealth responded to the continuance motion by asking for an increased bond and a bench warrant for her arrest. Judge Bush refused the Commonwealth's request, and moved the trial date to August 20.

Late summer 1925. The little river town of Eddyville was seething in a haze of humidity. Screen doors slammed, dogs barked and people moved about in slow motion. The circus came and went, baseball was played on Sunday, and the saloons were shut down by prohibition. Bootleggers thrived. Young boys swam in the tepid stream, farmers came to town on Saturdays, and church revivals heated up.

The "Tex Walters case" had become like the penitentiary itself—part of the community. Almost two years had passed since the revolt, yet the trials were still going on. Babies not yet conceived at the time of the uprising were now walking. Some older citizens had passed away. Life had moved on. If the anger and outrage had subsided, the infatuation with the drama and Lillian Walters hung on. For this sleepy little burgh, it was a continuous hit. Even though the theater crowd was now thoroughly familiar with the plot, it remained good entertainment.

For Lillian Walters it was much different. She was worn down, both physically and emotionally. In addition to the grieving for Tex, she had endured two murder trials, and still faced more of the same. Much of that time had been spent in jail, and since her release she had worked hard as a waitress trying to support herself.

So, when she arrived in the familiar Lyon County court room on Thursday morning, August 20, 1925, her health—both mentally and physically—was very fragile.

Even though public interest still engendered an overflow crowd of spectators, the lawyers seemed to have lost some of their zest. Any new enthusiasm the Commonwealth may have acquired by the favorable appellate court ruling, seemed to have been melted in the stifling court room. Special prosecutor Denny Smith made a cameo appearance and then vanished.

A Lyon County jury panel was depleted on the first day of trial. In order to save time, Judge Bush had fifty men from Christian County subpoenaed to report in for jury duty the next day. Most of them arrived on the 7:20 train on Friday morning. By mid-morning a jury had been seated.

Due to the hot weather, conditions on the upper floor had become unbearable on Thursday. For the second day, Judge Bush had ordered that only persons connected with the trial and newspaper reporters would be permitted in the court room. A year before such an edict would have caused an uprising. Now, there were only shrugs and sporadic complaints as the curious were turned away at the door.

According to one newspaper, which could no longer mask its sympathy for the beleaguered widow, "Mrs. Walters remained calm and brave."

Throughout that Friday the Commonwealth put on its case through sixteen witnesses. It was basically a repeat performance, with the surviving wife of William Gilbert replacing Emma Cunningham as the torch bearer for the dead. Once again Jim Sparks, still languishing in jail, laid out the conspiracy in detail. By 3:45 in the afternoon, the prosecution—its evidence honed by constant use—announced closed.

In order that most of Lillian's character witnesses could catch the night train back to Paducah and avoid hotel expenses, Judge Bush ran the trial past 5 o'clock.

By the time the sweltering day came to an end, Lillian was totally exhausted. Accompanied by her faithful companion, Nannie Boyd, she made her way to the Lester Hotel just down the street. There, after a light supper, she retired early in anticipation of her testimony the next morning.

On Saturday morning—with the country folk in town—Judge Bush reversed his blockade , and once again allowed spectators into the court room. His action was just in time for the overflow gathering to catch the main event—Lillian's testimony.

Although she was as convincing as ever, there was not the emotion in her voice as before. Also, the fervor of her cross-examiners did not match the rising temperature seeping through the open windows. Time and the weather had worn down the combatants so they appeared as spent boxers clinching and dancing on wobbly legs, listening for the final bell.

By 10:00 a.m. the defense had completed its case.

Like a good soldier, Judge Bush saluted the mandate of the Court of Appeals, and charged the jury that the defendant did not have to know that the guns were going to be used to shoot prison guards, but only that such conduct could be reasonably anticipated. According to the news reports, Judge Bush took great pains in doing it right, as the instructions were "lengthy—every conceivable phase of the case was covered."

In the afternoon the oratory began. Both Commonwealth Attorney James Coleman and County Attorney Coleman Molloy, Sr. argued the case for the state. All three defense lawyers took their turn. Each of the barristers were up to the occasion. But according to the newspaper the next day Charles Grassham really out did himself, and camp followers reported that it was the best closing argument ever given in the Lyon County Circuit court. So powerful had been the arguments for the defense that they were covered almost word for word in the next day's papers. Little space was given to the prosecutors final speeches.

The colorful Grassham was no doubt trying to put the Commonwealth away once and for all so that his failing client could get on with her life.

He hit upon all the old points of defense.

Tex had assured her that the guns would not be used inside the prison. "Tex was a pistol-toting man. He wanted his gun after he got out. Some men are like that. I have some friends who are always armed, though why they should want to carry a gun about with them I cannot see. There are some men who are just naturally pistol-toting men, and Tex was one of them."

Judge Bush, perhaps out of general fatigue or because he began to have doubts himself, even let the defense lawyer rip into the prison administration for their laxity and neglect. "The Negro Hawkins, a murderer up for life, was allowed to walk out of the penitentiary, and down the road for a mile or more, and when he returned, carrying a bundle which he said contained shirts, for the laundry, the firearms reached their destination."

Then turning and looking tenderly at the pretty and diminutive defendant, he intoned softly, "She sits there now, broken and frail and weary, the victim of an unnatural vengeance. She is losing weight; her stay in the jail has weakened her lungs; she may not be here very long. She may go away before the leaves fall. You should not wish to crucify her because she loved, because she obeyed, but let her gather round her a few friends that are pure as gold. . . . Her offense is loyalty, her chief crime is loving too much."

Defense lawyer J. B. Ellensworth came forth and eloquently tied the bow for the defense. "Why should you censure this woman because she loved with a steadfast loyalty which only death could sever? A young and virtuous wife who feels that she possesses the love of her husband, is more beautifully arrayed than the lilies, and envies not the diadem of queens."

It was all the large crowd came to hear and more.

And then—around 4 p.m.—it was in the hands of the twelve men from Christian County.

One of the jurors became sick from indigestion after supper. Since there was not another train to Hopkinsville until the next day anyway, Judge Bush sent them to a local hotel for the night.

They reconvened after breakfast on Sunday morning, August 23. After a short time they returned to the court room with a verdict of not guilty.

Once again relieved and elated, Lillian fainted into the arms of her friend Nannie Boyd. She recovered in time to thank the departing jurors. Her grasp with Judge Bush lingered tightly for a long moment, as their eyes embraced. A weathered old judge who had seen plenty, and a reckless young woman deeply grateful for another chance at life.

It was over. The Commonwealth threw in the towel, and would dismiss the indictments against her for accessory to the the murder of V. B. Mattingly and the wounding of William Gillihan.

Church bells from the Baptist church down the street were peeling as Lillian and her entourage of friends made their way down

the long steps to the street. Worshipers on their way to Sunday morning service stopped and watched the crowd emptying out of the court
house. Local well wishers and court officials stepped up and shook her
hand. They included Sheriff Nath Murray, the amputee widower, who
over the past several months had forged a meaningful friendship with
his captive.

Wearied and depleted by the trial, Lillian rested at the Lester
Hotel until Tuesday morning. On August 25, 1925, the widow of Tex
Walters dressed up in her man-killing best and was driven to the
Eddyville depot by her friends. They drove by the castle gate through
which she had passed so many times to anxiously greet her lover. On
this day she gave it only a painful glance.

The car moved down the hill and out of town. Around a long
bend in the road and across the Depot Bridge they traveled. Her head
turned ever so slightly to peer out over the railing into the horse weeds
and Johnson grass below.

At the station she boarded the train for Louisville. From the
open window she waved an emotional farewell to her true and tested
friends. Streams of hissing steam escaped from the belly of the resting
locomotive. All eyes were tearful as the sharp whistle blew and the iron
horse began to crawl out of the station. In moments the caboose had
disappeared around the wooded bend and puffs of white smoke
escaped above the tree line. As the thrashing sounds of the pounding
engine disappeared in the August haze, Lillian Walters vanished into
history.

⌗ ⌗ ⌗

At the same time Lillian Walters was leaving town evidence was
being heard in the Lyon Circuit court in the trial of Cellond Knudson,
alias Jim Sparks. As part of the agreement for him to testify against
Tex's widow, the Commonwealth dismissed the accessory to commit
murder indictments. That left them only with the meager charge of
accessory to commit assault against the wounded guard William
Gillihan.

It was scraping the bottom of the barrel. To the
Commonwealth, gearing up for this trial must have been difficult after
their unsuccessful attempt to convict the main defendant.

With Lillian departed, there were relatively few people in the
court room.

Most of Monday was taken up picking a jury, and a panel of
twelve Lyon Countians was seated in mid-afternoon.

The Commonwealth plodded through the evidence one last

time, almost an exact copy of previous trials.

Sparks took the stand once again, this time in his own defense. He related that he, too, was dominated by Tex Walters—not out of love as Lillian professed, but by fear. The dangerous-looking dirk found near the body of Walters was introduced by the defense. The defendant identified it as being the one Tex carried on him in prison. The two men worked together in the shirt factory and Walters constantly talked to him about his plan to escape and the role Sparks was to play. According to the ex-con, Tex had threatened repeatedly to kill him if he did not assist him to escape.

At 3:30 on Tuesday afternoon the jury got the case.

It was not until 10:30 the next morning that the jurors reached a verdict.

They found the former inmate guilty of the lessor offense of attempting to aid a convict to escape, and incredibly gave him the minimum of one year.

After almost two years, the book was closed on the Tex Walters case. The October harvest of violence in 1923 had produced three dead guards and one wounded, as well as the killing of three inmates. Thousands of dollars in damage had been incurred, and a National Guard unit had been pinned down for four days. The state of Kentucky had been stood on its head while the entire nation watched. All to the grand penal sum of one year.

Forty-eight men had sat in judgment and had given their collective verdict. The culprit primarily responsible for the whole bloody affair lay dead and buried in an unmarked grave.

Chapter 13

After a long and interesting visit in the warden's office, Mitch Cunningham and his two companions were escorted on a tour of the prison. Warden Bill Seabold led the three visitors through the back gate and onto the prison yard.

Hampered slightly by his aging knees, Mitch climbed the ancient steps leading from the administration building to the familiar roadway which circles the hill.

Directly in front of them, as they stepped upon the pavement, is a grassy knoll. It is now vacant, but upon it the hulking dining hall of the Tex Walters siege had once dominated the prison yard.

They turned and began walking parallel with number four cell-house. Just to their left and on the same gentle slope, V. B. Mattingly bled and suffered while his fellow guards looked on helplessly.

Up the hill, not far from the former site of the old greenhouse, is a battery of telephones. On this day, each one was manned by an inmate caller, while others waited in line. Members of the general population have virtual unlimited access to making collect calls to their family and friends—part of a new age in prison living. The telephone company makes a killing, and the Department of Corrections receives a hefty pay check each month. It is the last visage of private contracting on the prison yard.

The hill within the castle has changed beyond recognition

since Mitch Cunningham had last seen it as a barefoot boy. Gone is the manicured campus look of closely cropped lawns, shade trees, blooming flowers and shrubs. It is now a grim, barren landscape.

All of the buildings which were standing in the quad at the time of Tex Walters have been razed. The last to go was the old chapel in 1990.

Much of the terrain is divided by high chain-link fencing which partitions the yard for various types of inmate movements.

The prison environs are no doubt much more secure, but also more sterile and depressing.

Hodge Cunningham's son, obviously enjoying the tour, moves on around the prison yard, talking and gesturing with Warden Seabold. He is totally oblivious to the younger generation of prisoners lounging and walking around him. One can no longer find chicken thieves or first time cold checkers within this community of criminals. A more efficient classification system has made sure they all have serious and lengthy criminal records worthy of maximum security. A few are decorated to excess with tattooing and some sport bandanas or pony tails. Yet, taken away from the booze, the drugs and unspeakable tragedies of some of their childhoods, they appear, for the most part, like young men anywhere.

They glance at the old man and his friends with fleeting curiosity. They've never heard of Tex Walters.

To their right is big, blocky, five cellhouse built by the WPA in the late '30s. It has worn down to an ugly gray, and looks much older than the other stone cellhouses. It is not God's gift to architecture.

Warden Seabold leads the group down the hill and onto the first floor of the concrete cellhouse which is the prison dining room. It is dinner time and the large hall roars with the sound of talking and the clatter of metal trays. No silent lines. No segregated eating. Convicts come and go at will. They are served cafeteria style from steam tables, and eat their meals at round stainless steel tables with stools attached—six to a pod.

To the left is a wall with a recently installed window which looks into the back storage room. Within that pantry, Patricia Ross was bludgeoned to death.

Inmate servers wear sanitary gloves, the title floor is bright and clean, the food plentiful. The handful of supervising guards walk casually through the eating throng, exchanging friendly and casual conversation with the convicts. No somber and scowling overseer staring down from a raised platform. No seething tension or angry faces peering from the windows.

But history has left its mark.

High above the floor along the ceiling, and running the width of the large room is the gun alley. It is a fully enclosed tunnel large enough for several guards. So adeptly blended into the general dining room decor, it could easily be overlooked by the casual visitor. It is given away however by intermittent narrow slits each one large enough to accommodate the muzzle of a gun. These dark and slender eyes peer down upon the spacious mess hall. The tunnel can only be reached through a doorway leading from the outside of the penitentiary walls.

The ghost of Tex Walters guided the architect's hand.

Leaving the din of dining convicts, the quartet moved back onto the yard. Atop the wall nearby is historic number six wall stand. From there an alert guard had quickly dropped the rifle to a charging Porter Lady, and opened the sally port gate for the race against Robert Benewitz. It had also been the stand from which Ollie Williamson had responded to the orders of Walter Stephens and peppered the oncoming mass of convicts with buckshot in the uprising of 1952. From this lofty perch Sam Hooks had saved the life of guard Henry Phelps. The old wooden pill box has now given way to a modern capsule of plexiglass and steel.

Past the slop dock they walked, where guard Pat Kilgore had seen an inmate attempting to ride to freedom latched on to the axle of the garbage truck.

Not far from their path, up on the hill, once stood the stately old brick hospital. The place where Tex Walters had recovered from his wounds sustained in his foiled escape attempt is now just an empty plot.

They passed the clothing house which had been the basement of the law library. On top of it now, since the riot of '86, is a pavilion with picnic tables.

The tour of the yard continued as the group neared the split-level school squeezed into the southeast corner of the yard. The pride and joy of warden Luther Thomas is of contemporary architecture completed in 1964. It is constructed from the brick of the school and Baptist church of Old Eddyville, both razed during the relocation.

"The village belongs to the castle. . . ."

The ample gymnasium on the main floor had witnessed top-flight basketball, and first-rate boxing tournaments. But the wooden floor has also run red with the blood of murder victims, bludgeoned or stabbed to death as they were caught off guard in their recreational pursuits.

The small knot of strollers now moved casually along the time-worn roadway which encircles the hill. It has been trodden by misery and woe on the shuffling feet of hapless and forlorn thousands.

Beside the school they stopped and gazed out upon a broad asphalt plain, roughly the size and shape of a football field. It had once been flanked to the east by the broom works and collar factory. For many years, when it was dirt and grass, the elongated tract served as the drill field and recreation area. When the private contracts left the yard, many inmates were left idle. Regular military type drill was instituted for those convicts without jobs. For the better part of an hour each day, this section of the prison would be alive with the wholesome sounds of a basic training outfit. Instructors barking out commands were often times convicts, who as military veterans, took great pride in their prison unit. These regimented exercises did not cease until around 1962.

Far more enjoyable had been the football and baseball games played upon this plateau. Over a period of many years, outside teams paid regular Sunday afternoon visits in the summer time to take on the prison nine.

It was a most peculiar place to play baseball.

The long laundry building was located right behind second base. It totally concealed the right fielder playing up on the crest of the hill near the water tank. He was completely in the dark as to what was transpiring at home plate—or anywhere else on the field for that matter. An inmate umpire was stationed on the flat roof of the laundry to run to the back and observe the flight of the ball hit over the building. He would then return to the front, and motion to the rest of the players and packed house whether the ball had been caught by the right fielder for an out, or had dropped in safely for a long hit.

To the good natured jeers and laughter of the home crowd, this umpire almost always cheated for the visitors.

Line drives which would have been doubles on any conventional field, careened off the wall of the laundry to the pitcher who would throw out the incredulous batter at first base.

It was—all things considered—a lot of fun.

On this day of Mitch Cunningham's visit, the land of chatter, cheering and line drives had long been converted into a long quiet stretch of bleak asphalt. Baseball had left the yard about the time the Dodgers left Brooklyn. Instead there was now only the "weight pile," under a metal roof with open sides, where inmates gathered to pump iron. This gathering place of muscle builders had proven over the years to be a hive of violence. Weight bars were used as deadly weapons in assaults against fellow inmates. The weighty disks, once placed in the bottom of laundry bags, could be swung about with lethal results. Just a few months before, one convict had been bench pressing when another inmate brought a bar crashing down upon, pulverizing the victim's head. The reason for the killing: reportedly saving face over a bad debt.

As they stood watching several prisoners work out in the shed, Warden Seabold explained how he had finally received permission and money from Frankfort to take the free weights off the yard, and replace them with stationary weight machines which would be moved inside to a mini-gym and under the constant supervision of a guard.

Mitch shook his head, not only fascinated by the story, but obviously mystified as to why it took so long to rectify the situation. This son of the prison guard who was ruthlessly murdered by convicts in 1923 had a hard time fathoming modern penology.

As they walked the yard, the ancient walls were almost out of sight. Only the stone coping and and occasional guard stand could be seen peeping just above the line of vision. That is the unique nature of the Eddyville penitentiary. With the yard primarily on a summit, the stone barrier snaking around the side of the hill almost disappears from view. When walking the hill, it has the effect of a prison without walls.

Adding to the illusion are the hovering hills which rise just behind the penitentiary. Known by the locals as "Pea Ridge," it is a range of three wooded mounds joined by a common spine. Through most of the life of Eddyville and the prison it was sparsely populated and forested thick with hard wood trees and undergrowth. It was a popular place to go when citizens wanted to peer down onto the prison yard to view some happening. Since the impoundment of Barkley Lake, some of old Eddyville has crawled up on the ridge, and the several houses located there not only have a good look at prison life, but a beautiful view of the lake as well. Two views, worlds apart. As in the words of Byron, "I stood in Venice on the Bridge of Sighs, A palace and a prison on each hand."

A ribbon of asphalt winds down from the hills past the back of the prison and on to the front. From the prison yard, both the road and the surrounding forest appear within arm's reach. This bucolic setting of rural freedom, so close at hand, can be torturously tantalizing to an inmate doing time.

Moving across the paved plateau, the warden pointed to the modern brick hospital nestled in the northeast corner of the quad. It is well equipped and staffed by fully qualified civilian nurses, along with inmate aides. There is even a fully-furnished operating room, though it is never used. Surgery is scheduled at outside hospitals. A prison physician oversees medical attention to all inmates.

Making the turn to head back toward the front, Mitch Cunningham hobbled up a steep set of steps with some difficulty. Just to the left are the remains of a concrete platform which juts out toward the former playing field. It was here that the unsuspecting guard, Owen Davenport, was seated watching a baseball game when viciously murdered by inmate Virgil Moore. As a matter of fact, if crosses were erected at each place where blood has been spilled, the prison yard would resemble a cemetery.

Directly in their path now was the newly constructed six cellhouse. It is a six sided, four story brick monster of a building with narrow slits for windows in each of the 189 cells. Its modern, state of the art, penal architecture looks grotesquely out of place in the castle—like some gigantic space ship which has landed on the prison yard.

Solid metal doors electronically opened as Warden Seabold led them into the belly of this palace of gleaming steel and glass. In the middle of the cavernous hall is the central control tower from which correctional officers operate all gates and doors. From this location he can also look out over the open bull pens and directly into the front of each of the cells rising in tiers to the lofty ceiling.

Immediately to the left on entering the cell block is the section housing those inmates under the death sentence. The visitors were led down the walk to a small meeting room where the warden explained the operation of death row, and answered questions. They talked about death and dying—of the 25 to 30 condemned men just outside the door. The numbers changed almost monthly with the whims of the courts. Some had been under the sentence of death for over ten years. All were there for murder. Death for rape and armed robbery—crimes for which seventeen of their predecessors died—is no longer authorized by law. Unlike most death houses throughout the south, the majority were white. These men, dressed in red jumpsuits and marked for death, lounge away the days, lift weights, write writs, dine in the dining hall at special times, and watch cable television. It has been over thirty years since the last man was electrocuted at the Kentucky State Penitentiary. Most of the convicts had not been born. The growing number of executions in other states, however, is like distant thunder—ominous and unsettling.

Out of six cellhouse, and once again on the loop, the tour group headed toward the front of the prison. To their left was a low wall and above it a steep embankment leading up to the crown of the hill. Recent excavation and newly-added grass have replaced the old brick chapel which was built in 1902.

For about ninety years, this attractive old church with stained glass windows supplied the most critical commodity for any inmate doing time. Hope.

Prison chaplains and visiting preachers encouraged the constant stream of desperate souls to hold on, persevere, and keep the faith.

*For He hath looked down from the height of
his sanctuary; from heaven did the Lord behold the
earth;*
   *To hear the groaning of the prisoner; to loose
those that are appointed to death;*

The ancient chapel walls had reverberated with stirring renditions of old, uplifting hymns sung by the beautiful voices of an all-black inmate choir.

There, in the cozy library, housed within this place of worship, Tex Walters and Daddy Warner had talked about the Salvation Army and the salvation of the soul.

Next stop for the touring foursome was three cellhouse—the "jail within the jail." It was entered from the yard through a caged entrance. Within this original stone cellhouse is the prison's segregation unit—enough cells for 156 of the castle's malcontents. Those imprisoned criminals at Eddyville who cannot function in the general population without causing trouble are locked up here around the clock. This temple of doom is the end of the line. The only way down from here is. . . well downstairs, to the basement and the electric chair.

It's the same cellhouse where Mitch Cunningham's father pulled his last shift. But then it was the housing unit for blacks, with conventional cells of steel lattice doors opened and shut by the "slam." Totally renovated in 1956, it bears no resemblance to what it was. The walks are closed off and controlled from one caged operations center located at the end. From there, officers work up and down the steep metal stairway connecting the top four floors. Cell doors are solid steel to cut down on inmate abuse of staff—most notably the throwing of human waste upon the keepers as they walk by. Meals are slid through a slit in the middle of the door. A prisoner assigned to this unit wears a yellow jumpsuit, and his cell is furnished only with a bed, toilet, and limited reading and writing material. No television. No radio. No tobacco. He is allowed out of his cubicle for a shower three times a week, one hour of exercise 5 days a week on the walk, and two hour visitation on Thursdays—by scheduled appointment only. Otherwise he remains in his cell continually. Sometimes for months. Sometimes for years.

It is not a nice place to visit, although a far cry from the old dungeon of Warden Curry's day where inmates were left in the dark with their hands shackled to the cold stone walls by iron rings. It's also a marked improvement over "the hole" which was in use in the recent past. It was a plain concrete cell without any furnishings, and a small hole in the middle for the relief of bodily functions. They were all cuffed by their hands to the top bar of the door, forcing them to stand most of the time. The diet was bread and water, with one full meal a week. After a few weeks, some convicts returned to the yard unrecognized by friends.

Those confined to this catacomb of criminals vary from ones serving only a short stint for a relatively minor institutional infraction, to those who pose a serious threat to life and limb of both staff and inmates. Some wile away the time calm and subdued in their cubicles of concrete and steel, while others are loud and belligerent, even border line mental cases. Although their ability to see out of their narrow abode is almost completely curtailed, they can sense the happenings up the walk and even seem to know—in an uncanny way—when a stranger comes into the cellhouse. Depending on the time of day, and season, it can be a den reverberating with shouts and profanities. At other times it may sleep in a tomb-like silence. Veteran and grizzled old prison keepers swear that the noise level rises with the full of the moon.

But here in this lowly pit of human wreckage, heroes are born. They arise not out of some sudden and dramatic occurrence, but over time.

Here, correctional officers perform the most difficult job in state government at the lowest pay. Daily, they toil to maintain order and safety in a cauldron of discord and violence. They are subject to verbal and physical abuse constantly. These men and women of meager pay must circumscribe their responses within strict guidelines and regulations which almost defy human endurance. Great physical effort is often required to subdue or even move a flailing and deranged prisoner without using excessive force as defined by law. There on the lonely vigil of the midnight hour they are regularly and suddenly tested and must possess the courage of a lion, the judgment of a sage, and the patience of a saint.

Crime bills are debated, politicians talk of getting tough, and the electorate wants more people sent to prison. All of it drifts down through the complicated system of laws and corrections until the awesome burden finally settles upon the shoulders of these gallant few.

Yet Bobby Bonilla of the New York Mets will make more in two at bats than they will in a year.

"Neither the lords nor the shogun," wrote a Japanese philosopher, "can be depended upon to save the country, and so our only hope lies in grassroots heroes."

There is yet another strain of gallantry which grows from this lowly existence. Wallowing in this mire of desolation, there are a surprising number of men who actually begin to turn their lives around. After years of debauchery and defiance some of the hardened criminals of three cellhouse began that long hard road—not back to where they were—but to where they have never been. Whether it is the love and support of a good woman, religious conversion, a loyal friend, or nothing more than the biological discipline of age—something begins to transform their behavior. At first they make it back into general population. Over a period of months and even years of good behavior, they are reclassified to lower security and began their move through the system. Lines appear on the faces, the eyes are softer, and the tension disappears from their voices. Eventually they are paroled or serve out. Many never come back.

On the streets today, there are law-abiding graduates of three cellhouse. If one goes there and sees and hears the sights and sounds of this house without hope, the meteoric rise from its depths is—if not miraculous—at least heroic in itself. It also reflects again not only upon the valor, but the value of the keepers of the key.

In the basement Mitch passed by the empty cells of the old death row. These cubicles are ready, if and when the executions resume. At the end of the walk he and his friends reverently moved inside the death chamber and stared in awe at the old oaken chair.

They then climbed up the iron steps to the main floor, and turned to make their exit.

Mitch had been in three cellhouse many times before, often slipping in to see his father working the midnight shift. In the summertime, the doors connecting the cellhouses were left open in order to provide some draft through the stifling prison. The little adventurer would squeeze through the bars of the rod door in the administration building and scamper through the cavernous halls to his father's duty station. There they would play checkers until it grew late and he would be sent home.

"After my father was killed I was a lonely little boy," the old man sadly remarked to his friends as they waited for the electronic doors to slide open to leave three cellhouse. Seventy years of living had not erased the pain.

Mitch Cunningham now retraced the steps that his father took on that distant October morning when Calvin Coolidge was president. From three cellhouse he passed into two cellhouse—except it is no longer a housing unit. Still smelling of new concrete and steel, the old cell block has been blasted out and replaced at various levels with a hall for inmate visitation, mini-gym, and offices and conference room for caseworkers. From two into one—also renovated and converted into the inmate canteen and recreation hall, meeting rooms, chapel, more offices, and the staff canteen. Only the outside walls of gray stone are unchanged and had been there to watch his father pass.

At last they reached the fateful portal which led from one cell-house into the administration building. The warden and his guests were deep in conversation as he pushed a button and the heavy door slid open. The tottering old man with the gray hair stepped through the opening, totally oblivious that it was the same space through which his father had fallen, shot through and through.

With the tour completed, the four men moved back through the two gates and down the hallway of the administration building. Like a courtly southern gentleman, the warden showed his guests out the front door and down the long flight of steps in front. As he did so, they walked out of the prison under the huge archway which graces the front entrance. High above their heads was the historic keystone.

Raised in its surface is a set of crossed keys. Also, still clearly legible after one hundred years are the names of the three original prison commissioners. Two are written sideways and are difficult to read. But emblazoned across the top, in larger letters than the others is the name of H. B. Lyon. Deservedly, the hometown boy—the Confederate hero of burning court houses—is given top billing.

Under this arch have shuffled thousands of forlorn and wretched men, in leg irons and chains, to their allotted fate—some to their deaths. Under this arch marched a diverse group—Kelly Moss, James Bell Yager, and Daddy Warner.

Through this entranceway—under the names of the illustrious commissioners—trusty Andrew Hawkins carried his dirty laundry to Harry Ferland.

Wrote Ann Radcliffe:

"Fate sits on these dark battlements and frowns,"
"And as the portal opens to receive me,
A voice in hollow murmurs through the courts
Tells of a nameless deed."

Also, solid soldiers of corrections routinely moved under the stone passageway. An endless line of keepers who patrolled the yard, sat the stands, ushered men to their deaths, and taught convicts how to read. Thousands of dutiful and distinguished sentinels passed this way, including Louis Curry, Lloyd Armstrong and Sam Hooks.

Across this gaping threshold Hodge Cunningham walked with a worried mind. His small child followed eight hours later with a pounding heart. Now the son retreated once again back through the same gateway—and, as on that awful morning so long ago—much,

much older.

At last they were free of the humming gates, and arches of stone, as the group moved out the front door into the sun. There on the top step nearly one hundred feet above the street level they inhale the rush of cold winter air. Squinting to the new found brightness they took in the fantastic view of Barkley Lake. Slowly, eighty-year-old Mitch Cunningham began to make his way down the broad sweep of steps. His companions cautiously moved along beside him.

There are thirty-six steps and two landings from the archway down to the prison grounds. Once at the bottom the group turned to view the large brass plaque attached to the stone facing of the stairway. It honors the seven employees killed in the line of duty at the Kentucky State Penitentiary by listing their names and the dates of their deaths. Also added to the memorial is the name of correctional officer Charles Fredrick Cash, murdered by an inmate at the West Kentucky Farm Center in 1986.

A camera was brought out and Mitch proudly stood by the name of his father. For once, the loquacious elderly man fell silent.

The broad white face of the castle grew dark as a cloud aimlessly bumped into the winter sun. It was a small covering, however, and only the prison was in shadow. The surrounding grounds and street remained in the sun. Then, just as quickly, the shade shifted from the brooding stone edifice to the perimeter, framing the massive structure in light.

> *. . . . dark in light, light in dark*
> *what it means I do not know.*

At the street Warden Seabold extended a warm farewell to Mitch Cunningham and his relatives. Mitch thanked the prison keeper profusely for the visit, and pumped his hand with genuine appreciation. The three walked across the street to the parking lot.

Out from this overlook on Barkley Lake the water runs deep over the old lock and dam which had been under construction while Mitch and his family lived in Eddyville. Contractors had offered dynamite to blast the Tex Walters gang out of their lair. The workers—two of which were relatives of Hodge—had complained about the bullets. Now, they had all gone the way of the dam.

The three got into their car and pulled away from 226 Water Street. Slowly the vehicle eased down the road which is bordered on the prison side by an ancient low wall, topped with a spiked wrought iron fence. Shielded by it, Sam Litchfield had brought down Robert Benewitz with a .358 caliber rifle in 1937 as the prisoner came bounding down the front steps.

The road down Penitentiary Hill had once ran through the business district of town. It now runs into a boat ramp at the foot of the decline. Off to the left, just before reaching the ramp, there is a ragged stone wall holding back a grassy knoll. An abandoned set of steps breaks through the revetment and leads to nowhere. On this site had stood the old court house. Here Lillian Walters was tried three times, swooned and captured the hearts of at least thirty-six men and one circuit judge. On these grounds Mitch Cunningham had celebrated his eleventh birthday sitting in his mother's lap and softly caressing the murder weapon which had shot his father dead.

On this day Mitch's driver turned at the top of the hill, and followed the road running beside the prison parallel with five cellhouse. Between the street and the prison wall runs an abandoned sidewalk. A set of steps leads up to an empty lot. It was here where Hodge Cunningham's house had stood. Here little Mitch received that dreadful summons on that October morning seventy years before. He then pointed to the place, and explained how he and his friends played baseball in the open lot behind his home, where five cellhouse now stands.

The car moved on toward the rear of the prison as Mitch related how he heard his parents talking late at night in the privacy of their bed room about his father's fears and concerns about the suspected Walters conspiracy.

Past the prison industries located behind the penitentiary, the road bends to the left and begins its long, winding rise. The car in which Mitch was riding picked up speed.

High upon the hill to the right is an old moss-covered cemetery, guarded by tall, ancient evergreens. Notable and illustrious stalwarts of the past are buried there. A historical plaque marks the grave of Matthew Lyon—congressman, Revolutionary War soldier, and friend of Thomas Jefferson. Near that grave is the regal and substantial tomb of H.B. Lyon—Confederate war hero, businessman, political wheeler and dealer—bane of court houses, builder of penitentiaries.

The automobile carrying Mitch and his friends finally headed up the hill. Down the long embankment to the left is the prison firing range. Across the neatly cropped meadow is the woods. There, enmeshed in the soil, under the entanglement of underbrush and trees are the chalky remains of Tex Walters.

> *"As for man, his days are as grass; as a flower of the field, so he flourisheth. For the wind passeth over it, and it is gone; and the place thereof shall know it no more."*

"I sure missed my Dad," Mitch repeats to sympathetic ears, "I was a lonesome little boy."

The road curved to the right and the Kentucky State Penitentiary disappeared.

Afterthoughts and Acknowledgements

▨▨▨

The readers might be interested to know the fate of Lillian Walters after she left Eddyville for the last time on that August morning over 70 years ago.

She remarried and has children and grandchildren. Lillian and her husband celebrated their 50th wedding anniversary before his death. The former wife of Tex Walters lived a successful life as a house-wife and also dabbled in some small businesses. At this writing, she is still alive and in excellent health at the age of 93. She was located by the author after a very prodigious and extensive search. As promised, her anonymity is being protected.

▨▨▨

It would be impossible to chronicle all of the dramatic events which have occurred at the Kentucky State Penitentiary over the last 100 years. This is a mere sampling. Interesting, even fascinating, events unfold daily at the prison. Consequently, it has been difficult to pick and choose as to what to include in this book. Hopefully, what has been cho-sen will give the reader an appreciation of the magnitude of the castle and the awesome responsibility of those people who work there.

The accounts in this book are as accurate as research will allow.

They are based upon various sources, to include newspaper accounts, interviews, and the author's own lifetime experience with the penitentiary and some of the events that have transpired there. One name in this book has been changed for personal reasons.

The author has many people to thank for their contributions to this work.

First of all, Warden Phil Parker and his secretary, Vicki Patton, have been of tremendous assistance to this effort. Other staff members and employees of the Kentucky State Penitentiary who have contributed are: Duke Pettit, Doris Kilgore, Barry Bannister, Rick Pershing, Jerry Merrick, Serita Holt, and Steve Bell.

Former employees at the Kentucky State Penitentiary have also submitted valuable information. These sources include Pat Kilgore, Leo Wiseman, Stony Parker, Captain Billy Adams, Robert "R. P." Parker, Hugh Fralick, James Stovall, Dallas Gray and former warden Bill Seabold.

Lifetime friends and collectors of Lyon County history have provided a constant stream of information, and the help of these friends is greatly appreciated. They include Julian and Georgette Beatty, Ambros Miller, James "Tater" Mattingly, Charles Talley and Grace Litchfield.

Bill Buchanan, author of *Execution Eve,* published by New Horizon Press, and son of former Warden Jess Buchanan, has been kind enough to review this book and serve as a consultant. Bill lived in the warden's quarters in the penitentiary for many years and his friendship and assistance with this book are deeply appreciated.

Tom Saunders, Property Valuation Administrator in New Castle, Indiana, has gone the extra mile in obtaining valuable information for this book. I wish to thank him for his work as well as his hospitality.

Other persons contributing to this effort in varying ways are: G. L. Ovey Jr., Lon Carter Barton, Kyle Ellison, Velda Phelps, Danny and Cathy Beavers, Henry Payne Ashley, George Weakes, George Grayson "Bubs" Harralson III, Matthew McGovern, Bob Bennett, Bobby Richardson, Betty Austin, Dr. Forrest Pogue, Mary Grace Thomas, Murrell Trimble, Joe Freeland, Virginia Alexander, Dr. William Turner, Kenneth Lyle, Ruby Mae Farmer, Elaine E. Lundberg, Daniel Duff, Vicki Scott, Ramona Engler, Janice Bannister, James C. "Curly" Thompson, Bill White, David and Debbie Charpentier, Dorothy Crady, Benny Pinnegar, Bobbie Beans, John Filiatreau, Wallace Duncan, Joretta Palmer and Kelly P'Pool.

Thanks also to the following people: Ed Bolander, at Western Kentucky University; Kerry Rice, at the Kent School of Social Work in

Louisville; Judge Norman Curry, of Columbus, Indiana; Judge Kurt L. Wilke, Ft. Dodge, Iowa; Jane Fleischaker, of the *Courier Journal*; the entire staff of the Lyon County *Herald Ledger*; and Sharon True, with Department of Corrections.

Thanks to my inmate friends down through the years, who have contributed so much to my knowledge of the penitentiary and its ways.

Lastly, but certainly not least, a special and affectionate thanks to cousin Mitch.